William Gunion Rutherford, George Herbert Nall

Easy exercises on the First Greek syntax of W. Gunion Rutherford

William Gunion Rutherford, George Herbert Nall

Easy exercises on the First Greek syntax of W. Gunion Rutherford

ISBN/EAN: 9783337198138

Printed in Europe, USA, Canada, Australia, Japan

Cover: Foto ©Paul-Georg Meister /pixelio.de

More available books at **www.hansebooks.com**

EASY EXERCISES
ON THE FIRST GREEK SYNTAX

EASY EXERCISES

ON THE

FIRST GREEK SYNTAX

OF THE REV.

W. GUNION RUTHERFORD, M.A., LL.D.
HEADMASTER OF WESTMINSTER

BY THE REV.
G. H. NALL, M.A.
ASSISTANT MASTER AT WESTMINSTER

London
MACMILLAN AND CO.
AND NEW YORK
1892

PREFACE

THE great success of Mr. Rutherford's *First Greek Syntax* has induced the Publishers to add to their Greek Course an Exercise Book prepared specially to accompany this *Syntax*.

The book is divided into chapters and sections corresponding precisely with the divisions in the *Syntax*. The Greek examples given in the *Syntax* are collected (with a few unimportant changes), either at the beginning of each chapter or at the beginning of each sub-division of a chapter; and then a series of exercises follows, based very closely upon these examples.

The plan of the book supposes that the pupil will first read carefully a certain portion of the *Syntax*, endeavouring to master the rules and to understand the examples which are there translated and explained. He will then turn to the Exercise Book and read over again the collected examples, translating them into English. When these have been mastered and the rules which they illustrate have been discussed, he will proceed to the exercises. The earlier exercises in each division follow closely the words and constructions of the Greek examples; the later ones are more varied. On the more difficult portions of the *Syntax, e.g.* the Conditional Sentences, a large number of very easy exercises are given. It is hoped that this will make the book useful for quite young boys as well as for more advanced pupils.

To Mr. Rutherford, who has carefully revised the whole book, and to Mr. T. E. Pickering of Shrewsbury School, and other friends who have given similar assistance, the editor gratefully acknowledges his obligations. But the most careful revision must fail to detect every error and omission, especially in the Vocabularies, and the editor will feel much indebted to any one who will assist to make the book more useful by sending him either lists of misprints and errors, or offering suggestions for improvement.

The book does not, however, pretend to be anything more than what its title states. The Exercises cover but a small portion of the field of Greek idiom: that portion which is dealt with in the *Syntax*, the professed object of which was to 'drive great main lines through Greek Syntax, sticking to Attic, and even in Attic passing over all that is rare and exceptional.'

18 Dean's Yard, Westminster,
March 1892.

CONTENTS

CHAPTER I.—THE ARTICLE

	PAGE
The article as a demonstrative	1
The article with substantives	1
The article defining substantives that are themselves further defined in one way or another	2
Absence of the article before a complement of the predicate	2
The article with pronouns and pronominal adjectives	3
Exercises	4

CHAPTER II.—THE PRONOUNS

Possessive pronouns	8
Reflexive pronouns	8
Relative pronouns	9
Exercises	10

CHAPTER III.—CONCORD OF SUBJECT AND PREDICATE

	PAGE
Examples	13
Exercises	14

CHAPTER IV.—THE CASES

The nominative and vocative cases	16
The accusative case	16
Exercises on nominative, vocative, and accusative	20
The true genitive case	23
The ablative genitive	28
Exercises on genitive	30
The true dative case	36
The dative as defining verbs, adjectives, and adverbs	36
Dative of interest	37
The dative as successor to the instrumental case	37
The dative of the instrument or agency	37
The dative of accompaniment	38
The dative of manner	38
The dative of measure	38
The dative as successor to the lost locative case	39
Exercises on dative	40

CHAPTER V.—THE VOICES OF THE VERB

	PAGE
The active voice	43
The middle voice	44
The passive voice	45
Exercises	46

CHAPTER VI.—THE TENSES OF THE VERB

Tenses of the indicative mood	50
The future and the aorist	50
Tenses formed from the present stem	50
Tenses formed from the perfect stem	51
Tenses of the subjunctive, the optative, the imperative, and the infinitive moods	51
Tenses of the participle	51
Exercises	52

CHAPTER VII.—THE MOODS OF THE VERB IN INDEPENDENT PROPOSITIONS

Affirmative propositions	54
Expressions of a wish	54
Exercises	56

CHAPTER VIII.—THE MOODS OF THE VERB IN DEPENDENT PROPOSITIONS

                                                            PAGE

A. Propositions introduced by ὅτι completing the sense of verbs of saying, learning, knowing, thinking . 58

    Exercises 60

B. Dependent interrogative propositions . . . 63

    Exercises 64

C. Causal propositions . . 67

    Exercises 68

D. Consecutive propositions 70

    Exercises 72

E. Final propositions 75

    Exercises 76

F. Propositions introduced by ὅπως completing the sense of verbs of striving and the like . . . 79

    Exercises 80

G. Propositions introduced by μή completing the sense of verbs denoting fear, caution, or danger . . 82

    Exercises 84

H. Conditional propositions 87

    Exercises 90

I. Relative propositions 102

    Exercises 106

K. Temporal propositions . 110

    Exercises 112

CONTENTS xi

CHAPTER IX.—THE NOMINAL FORMS OF THE VERB

PAGE

The infinitive 116
   The infinitive with the article 117
   The infinitive without the article as genitive after substantives and verbs 117
   The infinitive without the article as the subject of other verbs 117
   The infinitive used as object to complete the sense of a verb 118
   Verbs of promising, hoping, and expecting . . . 118
   Peculiar use of δοκεῖν 118
   Special use of μή 118
   Verbs expressing effort or desire to do or prevent . . 119
   κωλύω 119
   Verbs denoting ability, knowledge, habit, obligation, etc. . 119
   The infinitive expressing purpose 120
   The infinitive defining the meaning of adjectives . . 120
   The infinitive absolute 121
   In exclamations 121
   As an imperative 121
   Exercises 122
The participle 129
   Use of the negative 129
   The participle with the article 129
   The participle without the article 130

	PAGE
Absolute use of the participle	132
Genitive absolute	132
Accusative absolute	132
The participle limiting the meaning of certain verbs expressing very general notions	133
The participle completing the meaning of certain verbs	133
Exercises	134
The verbal adjectives	143
Exercises	144

CHAPTER X.—PARTICLES

The negative particles	147
Exercises	148
Interrogative adverbs	149
Exercises	150
Copulative and disjunctive conjunctions . .	152
Exercises	154
Adversative conjunctions	155
The causal conjunction γάρ	156
Illative conjunctions	157
Exercises	158
Miscellaneous Exercises	161
GREEK-ENGLISH VOCABULARY . . .	169
ENGLISH-GREEK VOCABULARY . . .	191

CHAPTER I.—THE ARTICLE

EXAMPLES

I.—THE ARTICLE AS A DEMONSTRATIVE. §§ 1-3

ὁ δὲ ταῦτα λέγει. οἱ δ' οὖν βοώντων. τὸ δ', οἶμαι, οὐχ οὕτως ἔχει. τοὺς μὲν ἔνδον ηὗρον, τοὺς δ' οὔ. ἔμπειρός εἰμι τῆς Αἰολίδος τὰ μὲν διὰ τὸ ἐκεῖθεν εἶναι, τὰ δὲ διὰ τὸ ἐστρατεῦσθαι ἐν αὐτῇ. ὄρος τῇ μὲν ῥᾴδιον ἀναβαίνειν, τῇ δὲ χαλεπώτατον.

II.—THE ARTICLE WITH SUBSTANTIVES. §§ 4-14

τῷ κανθάρῳ δώσω πιεῖν. αἴρεται εἰς τὸν ἀέρα. Κῦρος καταπηδήσας ἀπὸ τοῦ ἅρματος τὸν θώρακα ἐνέδυ καὶ ἀναβὰς ἐπὶ τὸν ἵππον τὰ παλτὰ εἰς τὰς χεῖρας ἔλαβεν. οὐδὲ κολάσαι ἔξεστί μοι τοὺς οἰκέτας. τὴν χεῖρα δός. ὁ κάνθαρος ζῷόν ἐστιν. ὁ ἄνθρωπος θνητός ἐστιν. οἱ γονῆς φιλοῦσι τὰ τέκνα. ἡ ἀρετὴ ἀεὶ ἐπαινετή ἐστιν. οὐδέποτ' ἄρα λυσιτελέστερον ἀδικία δικαιοσύνης (§ 8). ἡ Ἀττικὴ ἐν μέσῃ ἐστὶ τῆς Ἑλλάδος. ἐτύγχανον εἰς ἄστυ ἀνιὼν Φαληρόθεν. ἥλιος ἐδύετο. ἅμ' ἡμέρᾳ ἐπορεύοντο οἱ στρατιῶται.

ἅμ' ἕῳ πάντες συνῆλθον. νὺξ ἐπεγένετο τῷ ἔργῳ. ἡμέρα ὑπέφαινε. μέγεθος περὶ πεντεκαίδεκα σταδίους μάλιστά ἐστιν.

III. — THE ARTICLE DEFINING SUBSTANTIVES THAT ARE THEMSELVES FURTHER DEFINED IN ONE WAY OR ANOTHER. §§ 15-22

ὁ πρεσβύτερος ἀδελφός. ὁ ἀδελφὸς ὁ πρεσβύτερος. ἡ προκειμένη ἡμέρα. ἡ ἡμέρα ἡ προκειμένη. οἱ πάλαι Δωριῆς. οἱ Δωριῆς οἱ πάλαι. ἡ ἐπὶ τῷ ποταμῷ πόλις. ἡ πόλις ἡ ἐπὶ τῷ ποταμῷ. ὁ σὸς πατήρ. ὁ πατὴρ ὁ σός. ἡ τῶν Περσῶν ἀρχή. ἡ ἀρχὴ τῶν Περσῶν. ἡμῶν ἡ πόλις. ἡ πόλις ἡμῶν. ὁ ἐμαυτοῦ ἀδελφός. ἡ ἐμαυτοῦ καρδία. ὁ τούτου ἀδελφός. ὁ τοῦ γεωργοῦ ἵππος. ὁ ἵππος τοῦ γεωργοῦ. ἡ Φιλοκράτους οἰκία. ἐν ἀρχῇ τοῦ λόγου. ἐπὶ βλαβῇ τῆς πόλεως. ὁ Ἀλκιβιάδου τούτου νεώτερος ἀδελφός. οἱ ἀπὸ τῆς Σικελίας Πελοποννησίων ἑκκαίδεκα νῆες. Ἀλέξανδρος ὁ τοῦ Φιλίππου. τῇ ὑστεραίᾳ οὐκ ἐφάνησαν ἔτι οἱ πολέμιοι. τὴν μουσικὴν φιλοῦσιν οἱ σοφοί. ἐν μουσικῇ καὶ γυμναστικῇ πάντες οἱ Ἕλληνες ἐπαιδεύοντο. οἱ ἐπὶ τῶν πραγμάτων οὐκ ἀεὶ εὖ πράττουσι τὰ τῆς πόλεως.

IV.—ABSENCE OF THE ARTICLE BEFORE A COMPLEMENT OF THE PREDICATE. §§ 23-25

τὸ θαυμάζειν ἀρχή ἐστι τῆς σοφίας. Ἀλέξανδρος

έφασκεν είναι Διὸς υός. ὁ λιμὴν τὸ στόμα ἔχει εὐρύ. βέβαιον ἄξεις τὸν βίον δίκαιος ὤν. πολὺ ἔχει τὸ ἀργύριον. μεγίστην ἔχουσι τὴν δύναμιν. ἐν μέσῃ τῇ χώρᾳ κεῖται. ἐπ' ἐσχάτῳ τῷ λιμένι ἐφάνη τὸ τεῖχος. πρότεροι ἐπῆσαν οἱ Ἀθηναῖοι. πρῶτος ἀφίκετο ὁ Κόνων. σκοταῖοι ἐπορεύοντο οἱ Ἕλληνες. μεσημβρινοὶ ἦλθον οἱ ἄνδρες. ἄκων ὑπέστη ὁ Ξενοφῶν. ἄσμενοι ἐκοιμήθησαν οἱ ναῦται. μόνος ἐσώθη ὁ Ξενοφῶν.

V.—THE ARTICLE WITH PRONOUNS AND PRONOMINAL ADJECTIVES. §§ 26-31

οἱ τοιοῦτοι ἄνθρωποι ῥᾴδιοί εἰσιν ἐξαπατᾶν. ἡ ἄλλη πόλις οὐδὲν ᾔδει. ὁ ἕτερος στρατηγὸς ἀπέπλευσε. ἡ αὐτὴ φύσις παντοίους ποιεῖ τοὺς ἀνθρώπους. ὁ πᾶς ἀριθμὸς τοσοῦτος ἐγένετο. τὸ ὅλον στράτευμα εἰς πεντακισχιλίους ἦν. τοιοῦτος ἦν ὁ ἀγών. ὁ ἀγὼν ἐγένετο τοιόσδε. πᾶσαν ὑμῖν τὴν ἀλήθειαν ἐρῶ. ὅλη ἡ πόλις ἐταράχθη. αὐτὸς ὁ βασιλεὺς τοῦτ' ἔδρα. ἐκτῶντο τὴν τιμὴν ταύτην. τοῦτο τὸ ἔργον ἐπράχθη. οὗτος ὁ ἀνὴρ ἀεὶ ταῦτα λέγει. ὁ ἀνὴρ οὗτος ἀεὶ ταὐτὰ λέγει. ἀμφοῖν τοῖν ποδοῖν φεύγομεν. ἀμφότερα τὰ στρατόπεδα ἐπὶ τοῦ λόφου ἦν. καθ' ἑκάτερον τὸν ἔσπλουν ὥρμησαν ἐπὶ τοὺς πολεμίους. περὶ ἑκάστης τῆς τέχνης οὕτως ἔχει. ἑκάστη τέχνη τὸ αὑτῆς ἔργον ἐργάζεται.

EXERCISES

I.—§§ 1-3

1. Some shouted, but others were silent.   2. But this, said my friend, was not always so.   3. The hill was at one point difficult to climb, at another very easy.   4. Of the citizens some are good, but the others are bad.   5. In one way this is true, in another false.   6. Some of your friends I love, but others I do not.   7. Partly I believe you, but partly not.   8. But she, having come to the house, could not find her mother.   9. The dogs found a hare, but it escaped.   10. Here you will find many hares, but there very few.

II.—§§ 4-14

1. The sun is in the heaven and burns the earth.   2. He seized his javelins and leapt down from his chariot.   3. The soldier found his horse in the stable.   4. Parents, I suppose, will love their children.   5. Soldiers often hate their generals.   6. The beetle is a most beautiful creature.   7. Xenophon mounted his horse at daybreak.   8. Virtue is difficult to most men.   9. The ditch was twenty feet in breadth.   10. At daybreak the soldiers advanced in column towards the hills.

III.—§§ 15-22

1. The elder brother is not always wiser than the younger. 2. On the appointed day they left the city. 3. The city on the island is about eight furlongs in size. 4. Your brother's horse is very swift. 5. The ancient Persians did not destroy the Empire of the Athenians. 6. Your friends will not easily catch the fish in the river. 7. At the beginning of his speech he praised the boys. 8. The farmer's five horses from the city were seized by thieves. 9. Cyrus the son of Darius wished to slay his brother in battle. 10. Wise boys love both music and gymnastics.

IV.—§§ 23-25

1. Death is the most terrible of all things to men. 2. The ancient Persians had a very great Empire. 3. The city has a very broad wall. 4. The walls of the city were the work of a wise man. 5. But he said that he was the son of my friend. 6. Your horse has a very beautiful head. 7. My house lies in the middle of the city. 8. The soldiers set out at daybreak and at mid-day came to the camp. 9. The enemies' ships lie at the end of the harbour. 10. Socrates the philosopher was the wisest of the Greeks.

V.—§§ 26-31

1. Such men are the most difficult to conquer.

2. The self-same danger frightens some men, but not others. 3. The general himself will come to our city. 4. The other camp was thrown into confusion by the enemy. 5. The rest of the citizens sailed away at daybreak. 6. This maiden has very beautiful hands. 7. Those ships came into the harbour by each inlet. 8. The whole city is considered most beautiful. 9. He has given both the horses to his son. 10. The citizens do not do what is honourable in every city.

VI

1. Boys do not always admire the beauty of virtue. 2. Philip's son was a very great general. 3. This stag has very large and very beautiful horns. 4. Your slave has loosened his fetters and escaped from the house. 5. Self-restraint is difficult to most men. 6. Man is often worse than a wolf. 7. All the soldiers love that general. 8. Every man admires a beautiful woman. 9. Poor men do not love wealthy priests. 10. The wife of the king was the most beautiful woman in the country.

VII

1. He stationed his infantry in one place, his cavalry in another. 2. Philosophers do not always manage the affairs of a state well. 3. At daybreak he mounted his horse and went to the harbour. 4. Eagles have large wings and beautiful heads. 5. I love you but not your friends. 6. That soldier feared

the maiden more than death itself. 7. Virtue is always more profitable than vice. 8. You, my friends, are the judges of this matter. 9. The self-same danger is not terrible to all men. 10. He will not tell us the whole truth.

VIII

1. Injustice, said he, is more profitable to me than justice. 2. Such men, I think, are not the best generals. 3. Boys are not glad to go to bed. 4. I was the only man saved out of the whole of that army. 5. The self-same nature has made boys of all sorts. 6. The sum total of the king's army was very great. 7. Socrates died willingly, being a wise and just man. 8. This man's brother is my slave. 9. Our city is the most beautiful in Greece. 10. Hares love that island in the river.

IX

1. Philosophers wish to lead a tranquil life. 2. The Persian army was in confusion throughout. 3. Each boy shall do his own work. 4. All the citizens will acquire the same privilege. 5. The rest of the sailors did not tell the same (story). 6. The poor man asserted that he had money in plenty. 7. We shall reach the city in the dark. 8. Our sailors moved against the enemy gladly. 9. The boys shall go to bed in the dark. 10. Both armies marched from their camps at mid-day.

CHAPTER II.—THE PRONOUNS

EXAMPLES

I.—POSSESSIVE PRONOUNS. §§ 32-35

ὁ Κῦρος ἔλαβε τὰ παλτά. στυγῶ μὲν ἄστυ, τὸν δ' ἐμὸν δῆμον ποθῶ. ζητεῖς ποιῆσαι τἀργύριον πλεῖον τὸ σόν. πάρεστε εἰς τὸν ὑμέτερον νεών. αἰσχύνομαι δὲ τὰς ἐμαυτοῦ συμφοράς. ἄγε δή, κάτειπέ μοι σὺ τὸν σαυτοῦ τρόπον. τὸν ἐμὸν πατέρα ἐπαινεῖτε καὶ οὐ τὸν ὑμέτερον αὐτῶν. ἀποκτείνουσι τοὺς ἑαυτῶν παῖδας. στυγοῦσι τὸν ἑαυτῶν πατέρα. οὐ γὰρ ἀποκτενοῦμεν τὸν ἡμέτερον αὐτῶν βασιλέα. ἄσμενον ἀπέπεμψέ μου τὸν δεσπότην. ὁ πατήρ σου ἥκει. οἱ πρόγονοι αὐτῶν τοῦτ' ἔπραξαν. ἀλλ' οὐκ εἶδες τὸν ἐμὸν δεσπότην. οἱ ἐκείνων πρόγονοι τοὺς ἡμετέρους ἀπέκτειναν.

II.—REFLEXIVE PRONOUNS. §§ 36, 37

τύπτω ἐμαυτόν. γνῶθι σεαυτόν. ἀπέκτεινεν ἑαυτόν. τὰ ἄριστα βουλεύεσθε ὑμῖν αὐτοῖς. ἐδέδισαν μὴ οἱ Ἀθηναῖοι διαφθείρειαν σφᾶς. οὐκ ἂν ᾤετο ὁ

Κλέων τὸν Νικίαν οἱ ὑποχωρῆσαι. Δαρεῖος ἐβούλετο οἱ τὼ παῖδε παρεῖναι. ἐκέλευσε τοὺς οἰκέτας ἓ περιμένειν. ὁ τύραννος νομίζει τοὺς πολίτας ὑπηρετεῖν ἑαυτῷ.

III.—RELATIVE PRONOUNS. §§ 38-44

ἰδεῖν σε βούλομαι τὸν ὑὸν τὸν μόνον ὃν ἐγὼ φιλῶ μάλιστα. ὅπερ πάλαι ἐγώ, νῦν σὺ πράττεις. μακάριος ὅστις οὐσίαν καὶ νοῦν ἔχει. προδότης εἶ τῆς πατρίδος ὅστις τὰ τοιαῦτα δρᾷς. οὐκ ἔστιν οὐδεὶς ὅστις οὐ τοῦτον φιλεῖ. τίς ἔστιν ὅστις οὐ τοῦτον φιλεῖ; οἱ ἄνδρες οὓς εἶδες ἀπῆλθον. οὐ πιστεύσομεν ὑμῖν οἳ τὰ τοιαῦτα πράττετε. ἃ μὴ οἶδα οὐδὲ οἴομαι εἰδέναι. οἴμοι δὲ τῶν ἰχθύων ὧν κατήσθιον. τοῦτον τὸν οἶνον δέομαί σου πιεῖν μεθ' ὧν μάλιστα φιλεῖς. ὡς πολὺ μεθέστηχ' ὧν πρότερον εἶχεν τρόπων. οἴχεται ὃν ἦγες μάρτυρα. οὐδὲν ὧν βούλεσθε πράξετε. καὶ πεζὸς καὶ νῆες καὶ οὐδὲν ὅ τι οὐκ ἀπώλετο. οὐδενὸς ὅτου οὐ κατεγέλασεν. οὐδεὶς ὅστις οὐκ εὐτυχεῖν βούλεται. οὐδένα ὅντινα οὐκ ἀποκτεῖναι ἐβουλήθη.

EXERCISES

X.—§§ 32-35

1. He has made his money more. 2. He is ashamed of his own citizens. 3. You praise my virtue, friends, but not your own. 4. Parents do not hate their own children. 5. You have told me my character; come now, tell me your own. 6. Your father has given me all these books. 7. Soldiers love their own generals. 8. They think that the goddess loves her own grove. 9. We have killed our own friend. 10. My brother hates town and longs for his parish.

XI.—§§ 36, 37

1. He struck himself with his hand. 2. Such men love themselves more than their friends. 3. We shall take the best counsel for ourselves. 4. He thought that the maiden loved him. 5. Bad boys think that their masters hate them. 6. They feared that the enemy would pursue them. 7. The king wished his sons to give way to him. 8. The maiden bade her servants wait for her. 9. A wise man gives himself many presents. 10. The cowardly boys feared that the dog would bite them.

XII.—§§ 38-44

1. This is my native-land which I love very much. 2. My present servant does just what my former one used to do. 3. Happy are they who have money and friends. 4. Who is there who does not love himself more than his friends? 5. Woe is me for the wine which I have drunk. 6. The boy has changed from the manners we once admired. 7. He left his money to those whom he loved best. 8. He took with him all the soldiers he had (tr. the soldiers as many as he had). 9. I will give you such books as I promised to you. 10. There is no one whom the tyrant does not hate.

XIII

1. I have given your dog to the servant. 2. The slaves said that you had praised them. 3. Sensible men are not ashamed of their ancestors. 4. There was no one who did not trust you. 5. He is a traitor whoever tells such things to the enemy. 6. Horses and servants and everything (§ 44) were lost. 7. You act wisely in giving (§ 39) nothing to the poor man. 8. He chose wisdom rather than the things which many long for. 9. Poor men desire the good things which their neighbours have. 10. Sending to the Great King he asked that these cities should be given him.

XIV.

1. I pity the mother for having such a beautiful daughter. 2. He loves the dog with which he has caught so many hares. 3. No good citizen hates his own native land. 4. I will gladly tell everything to such a man. 5. He hates himself more than he hates other men. 6. You act strangely in not wishing to accept these presents from your friends. 7. He longed for more money in addition to what he had before. 8. The judge went to his house a wiser man. 9. We will enjoy the good things we possess and not long for more. 10. Every one loves such a man as that.

XV

1. The wise citizens chose liberty before all the good things which he promised to them. 2. He is ashamed at last of his own baseness. 3. This is the man we saw in the island. 4. I honour wisdom more than all the wealth I possess. 5. You have lost the best friend you ever had. 6. Is there any one you love more than me? 7. This is the man to whom I once trusted all my money. 8. He was defeated by the very soldiers whom he had often defeated before. 9. He cannot be my friend inasmuch as he has not acted honourably. 10. Noble men are never ashamed of their parents.

CHAPTER III.—CONCORD OF SUBJECT AND PREDICATE

EXAMPLES

§§ 46-56

οἱ ἄνδρες ἦλθον. ἡ πόλις μεγάλη ἐγένετο. τὰ πράγματ' οὐχὶ διὰ σὲ πάντα γίγνεται; ἐφανήτην οὖν δύο δράκοντ' ἐκ τοῦ νεώ. δύο μάρτυρε οὐκ ἀεὶ ταὐτὰ λέγουσιν. οὕτω δρᾶτον σὺ καὶ ὁ ἀδελφός. ἆρα συμφωνοῦμεν ἐγὼ καὶ ὑμεῖς; ἡ τύχη καὶ Φίλιππος ἦσαν τῶν ἔργων κύριοι. φθόνος καὶ ἔρως ἐναντία ἐστίν. σὺ Ἕλλην εἶ καὶ ἡμεῖς. οὔτε σὺ οὔτ' ἂν ἄλλος οὐδεὶς δύναιτ' ἀντειπεῖν. τῶν κακῶν ἡ στάσις καὶ ὁ πόλεμος αἴτιός ἐστιν. αἱ χορηγίαι ἱκανὸν εὐδαιμονίας σημεῖόν ἐστιν. αὕτη ὑμῖν ἔσται σωτηρία. Περσικὸν ξίφος ὃν ἀκινάκην καλοῦσι.

πονηρὸν ὁ συκοφάντης ἀεί. χρησιμώτερον νομίζει χρήματα ἢ ἀδελφούς. πολὺ γένος ἀνθρώπων τοῖς μὲν ἐκ τῆς γῆς φυομένοις εἰς τροφὴν οὐ χρῶνται, ἀπὸ δὲ βοσκημάτων γάλακτι καὶ τυρῷ καὶ κρέασι τρεφόμενοι ζῶσιν. ἓν σῶμα καὶ ψυχὴν ἔχω. ἓν σῶμα καὶ μίαν ψυχὴν ἔχομεν. οἱ λίθοι καὶ ἀκόντια καὶ τοξεύματα οὐκέτι ἐξικνοῦνται τῶν στρατιωτῶν. οἱ Πελοποννήσιοι καὶ Συρακόσιοι καὶ σύμμαχοι παρῆσαν. οἱ Πελοποννήσιοι καὶ οἱ Ἀθηναῖοι πολέμιοι ἦσαν. ἥ τε ἤπειρος καὶ αἱ νῆσοι ὑπὸ τοῖς Πέρσαις ἐγένοντο.

EXERCISES

XVI

1. The affairs of the city were no longer in my power. 2. Two priests came out of the temple of the goddess. 3. Both my brother and I agree about this matter. 4. Good fortune and you are the masters of our city. 5. Envy and strife are the cause of much misery. 6. We admire in boys that fear which is called modesty. 7. This will be the cause of much happiness to us all. 8. Neither you nor I could do what he has done. 9. Wars are the cause of much misery to a state. 10. That Persian sword and that helmet are the work of a famous artist.

XVII

1. I consider my friends a more useful possession than wealth. 2. The large force of the Persians appeared on the next day. 3. Those (events) happened in our fathers' times. 4. Some things are in our power, and others are not. 5. A man has only one body and one soul. 6. The Persians and Athenians were at one time enemies, at another time friends. 7. Our javelins and arrows did not reach the enemy. 8. Those islands are a worthless possession to our city. 9. Many a race of men use for food flesh and milk and cheese. 10. Many nations still use javelins and arrows.

XVIII

1. You and he have often seen my brother. 2. The same things please some men but not others. 3. The two witnesses did not say the same things to the judge. 4. Virtue and vice are opposite principles. 5. The bones of the hare are a worthless possession to you but not to your dog. 6. Every thief is an unprincipled creature. 7. All such deeds are noble in war. 8. The mainland and islands were in the enemy's possession. 9. Wars are the cause of many evils to a city. 10. Good fortune and I are now friends.

XIX

1. There are many beautiful trees in the island. 2. Both my brother and I love your friend. 3. Two sailors were speaking to the judge. 4. It is neither number nor strength which gains (def. article with pres. part. of ποιῶ) the victories in war. 5. The arms of the goddess were beautiful but terrible. 6. Milk and cheese and flesh are worthless for a horse. 7. The affairs of the state were not in the power of the king. 8. Such a witness is a most useful possession to you. 9. Soul and body are often enemies to one another. 10. That will be the salvation of the citizens.

CHAPTER IV.—THE CASES

EXAMPLES

I.—THE NOMINATIVE AND VOCATIVE CASES. § 57

οἱ Θρᾷκες ἴτε δεῦρο.   ὤμοι ἐγὼ δειλός.

II.—THE ACCUSATIVE CASE

1.—*The Accusative Case after Transitive Verbs*
§§ 58-65

τύπτει τὸν ἄνδρα. αἰδούμεθα τοὺς γονέας. ὁ στρατιώτης αἰσχυνεῖται τὸν στρατηγόν. οὐ φοβήσομαι τὸν θάνατον. ἐκπλήττονται τὴν τῶν πολεμίων δύναμιν. θαυμάζει τὸ τῆς πόλεως κάλλος. εὖ ποιῶμεν τοὺς φίλους. κακῶς ποιήσω τοὺς Πέρσας. ὁ διδάσκαλος εὖ λέγει τούτους τοὺς παῖδας. κακῶς ἔλεξε τὸν διδάσκαλον. ὁ φὼρ ἔλαθε τὸν οἰκέτην. ὁ στρατηγὸς φθάνει τοὺς πολεμίους. ὄμνυμι πάντας τοὺς θεούς. ἀπώμοσα τὸν Δία. οἱ πολέμιοι ἐπιωρκήκασι τοὺς θεούς. νὴ Δία. μὰ τὸν Διόνυσον. ναὶ μὰ τὸν Δία. διαβαίνουσι τὸν ποταμόν. μέτεισι τὸν παῖδα. παραπλέουσι τὸν λιμένα. περιθέουσι τὴν πόλιν. ὑπερβαίνουσι τὴν τάφρον. ὑφίσταται τὸ ἔργον. κατασιωπᾷ τοὺς ἐναντίους. ἐπισχύουσι τὴν πόλιν. ἐπαληθεύει τὴν αἰτίαν. ὁ διδάσκαλος κατηχεῖ τοὺς μαθητάς.

II.—*The Double Accusative.* §§ 66, 67

τοῦτο τοὺς πολίτας ἐρωτᾷ. τοὺς θεοὺς αἰτεῖτε ἀγαθά. τὴν εἰρήνην ὑμᾶς ἀναμιμνήσκομεν. τὸ πρᾶγμα ἐκρύπτομεν τὸν πατέρα. τὸ ἱμάτιόν σε ἐνδύσω. τοὺς νεανίας διδάσκει τὴν μουσικήν. συλῶσι τὰς βοῦς τοὺς βουκόλους. τοῦτο ἐρωτῶνται οἱ πολῖται. τὴν εἰρήνην ἀναμιμνήσκεσθε. οἱ νεανίαι τὴν μουσικὴν διδάσκονται. τὰς βοῦς ἐσυλήθησαν οἱ βούκολοι. ὁ παῖς ἐνέδυ τὸν χιτῶνα.

III.—*The Predicate Accusative.* §§ 68-70

πάντων δεσπότην ἑαυτὸν πεποίηκεν ὁ Φίλιππος. τοῦτον εὐεργέτην ἡγούμεθα. τὸν Κῦρον ἡγεμόνα ἐποιήσαντο. πρέσβεις εἵλοντο Κλεινίαν καὶ Λυσίαν. τὸν παῖδα ὠνόμοσα Φίλιππον. τοῦτο φανερὸν ποιήσομεν. τὰς ἁμαρτίας μεγάλας ἡγεῖτο. ἐλευθέρους κατέστησε τοὺς παῖδας.

πάντων δεσπότης ὁ Φίλιππος ἐγένετο. οὗτος εὐεργέτης ἐνομίζετο. πρέσβεις ᾑρέθησαν ὁ Κλεινίας καὶ ὁ Λυσίας.

IV.—*Cognate Accusative.* §§ 71-75

χοὰς χέουσιν. ἥδονται τὰς μεγίστας ἡδονάς. νίκην ἐνίκησαν καλλίστην. τὸν σὸν φόβον οὐ φοβήσεται. μέμψιν δικαίαν μέμφομαι. ναυμαχίαν ὁ Λυκοῦργος ἐνίκα. πυγμὴν ἠγωνίσατο. τὴν γνώμην ἐνίκησαν. ὑψηλὰ πηδῶσιν οἱ αἶγες. εὐαγγέλια θύουσιν. μέγα δύναται ὁ Φίλιππος. οἱ πολέμιοι ὀξὺ βλέπουσι. τοῦτο λυπούμεθα. πολλὰ οὐχ ὁμολογῶ σοι. οὐδὲν ὑμῖν χρῆται. τὰ τοιαῦτα οἱ Ἀθηναῖοι ἠτύχησαν. τὰ τοιαῦτα τοῖς Ἀθηναίοις ἠτυχήθη. Θησεὺς ἐπολέμησε πολλοὺς πολέμους. οἱ ὑπὸ Θησέως πολεμηθέντες πόλεμοι. τὰ σοὶ καὶ τὰ ἐμοὶ βεβιωμένα πολὺ διαφέρει. τύπτει τὸν ἄνδρα πληγήν. ἐὰν ἐμὲ ἀποκτείνητε, οὐκ ἐμὲ μείζω βλάψετε, ἢ ὑμᾶς αὐτούς. ταῦτα ἐγκωμιάζουσι τὴν δικαιοσύνην. τοῦτο οὐκ ἠνάγκασέ με. ταῦτα ἐνεκωμιάσθη ἡ δικαιοσύνη. πολλὰ καὶ δεινὰ ἠδικήθην. τοῦτο οὐκ ἠναγκάσθην.

V.—*The Defining Accusative: Adverbial Accusative*
§§ 76-82

τὰ σώματα κάμνουσιν. ἀλγεῖ τὴν κεφαλήν. ὑγιαίνει τὴν ψυχήν. διέφθαρται τὴν ψυχήν. §§ 76, 77.
ἐνταῦθα ἔμενεν ἡμέρας τρεῖς. ὅλην τὴν πόλιν πλανᾶται. τὴν πᾶσαν ἡμέραν ἐλαύνει. τριάκοντα ἔτη γεγονώς ἐστιν. ἀπέχει τὸ ἄστυ τρία στάδια. § 78.
τὰ μὲν παρελθόντα ὑμεῖς μὲν Κῦρον ηὐξήσατε, Κῦρος δὲ εὐκλεεῖς ὑμᾶς ἐποίησεν. τὸ Αἰτωλικὸν

πάθος διὰ τὴν ὕλην μέρος τι ἐγένετο. τὸ κατ' ἐμὲ οὐδὲν ἐλλείψει. § 79.
τί τοῦτο πράττεις; αὐτὰ ταῦτα νῦν ἥκω. πάντα τρόπον ἔφυγον τοὺς πολεμίους. τὴν ταχίστην ἐπορεύοντο. ἐν τῷ παραχρῆμα οὐκ ἔστιν ἀρχὴν ὀρθῶς βουλεύεσθαι. τὸ πάλαι ἦσαν βασιλῆς. τὸ πρῶτον ἐρήσομαι ταῦτα. § 80.
πᾶσαν ἀδικίαν ἄδικός ἐστιν. ὑγιεῖς τὴν ψυχὴν ἐσόμεθα. τοιοῦτος ἦν τὸ ἦθος. βελτίονές εἰσι τὴν γνώμην καὶ τὴν ἰδέαν. ἄπειροι τὸ πλῆθός εἰσιν οἱ Πέρσαι. ἀνὴρ ἀγαθὸς τὰ πολιτικά, δεινός τε τὰ πάντα. διὰ μέσης τῆς πόλεως ῥεῖ ποταμὸς Κύδνος ὄνομα, εὖρος δύο πλέθρων. Λυδός εἰμι τὸ γένος. §§ 81, 82.

EXERCISES

XX.—§§ 58-65

1. Good boys respect their parents. 2. The strangers were amazed at the beauty of the city. 3. The mother spoke well of her son's master. 4. By Zeus, it is hard to speak well of those who do ill to us! 5. The thief escaped the notice of the guards of the temple. 6. A wise general loves to forestall the enemy. 7. No, by Zeus; the soldiers shall not cross the river. 8. Our ship will sail past the harbour. 9. Your friend undertook a very difficult work. 10. The boys wished to run round the whole island.

XXI.—§§ 66, 67

1. The master asked the boys this (question). 2. The boys will be asked this (question) by the master. 3. You remind me of the battle in which you saved my life. 4 The slave concealed the matter from his master. 5. He was reminded of the cloak of which he had been robbed. 6. The pupils were taught music by the master. 7. The boys were putting on their cloaks. 8. It is not just to rob poor men of their pay. 9. The herdsmen were robbed of their cows by the thieves. 10. Who has taught our boys all this wickedness?

XXII.—§§ 68-70

1. The king made himself master of the whole country. 2. The citizens consider you a great benefactor of their city. 3. They were chosen ambassadors by the citizens. 4. He wished to name his son Alexander. 5. The slaves were set free by their master. 6. I consider such mistakes very serious. 7. This was made plain to me by my friends. 8. The king will become master of our city. 9. He was called this name only by his friends. 10. The boys cannot conceal anything from their master.

XXIII.—§§ 71-75

1. The priest poured drink-offerings to the goddess. 2. Stags have a very keen sight. 3. In many (points) I cannot agree with your brother. 4. The slave was struck a blow by his master. 5. They inflicted heavier injury on themselves than on the philosopher. 6. A wise man makes much use of his friends. 7. Our sailors always conquer in battles at sea. 8. The master struck the slave many blows. 9. A wise father will force his son to this. 10. Philosophers experience the greatest pleasures.

XXIV.—§§ 76-82

1. They suffer in mind more than in body. 2. The soldiers remained ten days in the city. 3. When thirty years old he was chosen general. 4. The

island is two furlongs distant from the mainland. 5. He shall not have a headache if I can help it (§ 79). 6. How will he use all that money? 7. A man clever at statecraft is not always noble and good. 8. No man is happy in all respects. 9. To some extent he persuaded the judges. 10. Why do you ask me such questions?

XXV

1. The thief felt shame before the judge. 2. The enemy's ships sailed past the harbour. 3. The mother taught her son music. 4. It is wise to conceal your misfortunes from your friends. 5. I can never consider you my friend. 6. Goats can leap higher than dogs. 7. In character he was gentle, in body beautiful. 8. The city is thirty furlongs distant from the sea. 9. They went to the harbour the quickest way. 10. In things past I find just fault with you.

XXVI

1. I shall never be afraid with that fear. 2. The enemy cannot escape the notice of our general. 3. It is not possible to silence this bad boy. 4. The enemy will rob the herdsmen of their cows. 5. Ten men were chosen ambassadors by the citizens. 6. Our sailors will gain a most glorious victory. 7. Justice was praised in these words by the philosopher. 8. Many men are corrupt in mind. 9. Partly you persuade me but partly not. 10. The girl is putting on her cloak.

III.—THE GENITIVE CASE

A. The True Genitive Case
§§ 84-124

EXAMPLES

1.—*The Local Use.* §§ 87-100

Θῆβαι Βοιωτίας. ἀφίκετο τῆς Ἀττικῆς εἰς Οἰνόην. μετὰ τὴν τῆς Αἰτωλίας συμφοράν. κατέκλησαν Πέρδικκαν Μακεδονίας. § 87.
ποῦ τῆς χώρας εὑρήσομεν τὸν παῖδα; ποῖ γῆς εἰμι; πολλαχόσε τῆς Ἀρκαδίας πέμπει ἀγγέλους. ἐνταῦθα τῆς ἠπείρου τὸ στρατόπεδον ἐποιήσαντο. τηλοῦ γὰρ οἰκῶ τῶν ἀγρῶν. § 88.
ἐνταῦθα τῆς πολιτείας μέγα δύναται. ἐκεῖ τοῦ λόγου ταῦτα ἔλεξε. § 89.
σὺ δ᾽ εἰς τοσοῦτον τῶν μανιῶν ἐλήλυθας. εἰς τοσοῦτον ἦλθον κινδύνου. § 90.
ὑπάγεθ᾽ ὑμεῖς τῆς ὁδοῦ. προϊόντες τῆς στρατείας. § 91.
ἐγείρεται τῆς νυκτός. ἑσπέρας δειπνεῖ. δέκα ἡμερῶν μαχεῖται. § 92.
ἐσθίει πολλάκις τῆς ἡμέρας. ὀψὲ τῆς ἡμέρας ἀφίκετο. τρὶς τῆς νυκτὸς ἠγείρετο. πόρρω ἤδη ἐστὶ τοῦ βίου, θανάτου δὲ ἐγγύς. πρῷ τῆς ἡλικίας ἐστί. §§ 93, 94.
Ἰθάκης βασιλεύει. ὁ Ξέρξης ἐβασίλευε τῶν Περσῶν. ἄρξαι σὲ δεῖ τῆς χώρας ἁπάσης. τοῦ

σώματος γὰρ οὐκ ἐᾷ τὸν κύριον κρατεῖν ὁ δαίμων. οὐ πάτριόν ἐστιν ἡγεῖσθαι τοὺς ἐπήλυδας τῶν αὐτοχθόνων. § 95.

πῶς ἔχεις τοῦ ἀγῶνος ; ἐγὼ δὲ τούτου τοῦ τρόπου πώς εἰμ' ἀεί. ἔπλεον ὡς εἶχε τάχους ἕκαστος. καλῶς παράπλου κεῖται ἡ Κόρκυρα. §§ 96, 97.

πρακτικὸς ἦν τῶν δικαίων. ἐξεργαστικοὶ ἦσαν τῶν τοιούτων πραγμάτων. § 98.

τυφλὸς ἦν τοῦ μέλλοντος. ἄξιος ἦν τιμῆς. ἄξιοί ἐσμεν κλοπῆς. ἐπιστήμονες ἐγένοντο τῆς θαλάττης. μακαρία ἡ χελώνη τοῦ δέρματος. ὀλίγωροί εἰσι τῆς εἰρήνης. § 99.

φεῦ τοῦ κάλλους. § 100.

II.—*After certain Verbs.* § 100

To congratulate, envy : accuse, acquit : remember, forget, care for : hit, miss : desire.

σοφίας φθονῆσαι μᾶλλον ἢ πλούτου καλόν. αὐτὸν εὐδαιμονιεῖ τῆς περιουσίας. αἱ χελῶναι μακαριοῦσί σε τοῦ δέρματός. ᾐτιάσατο Φίλιππον κλοπῆς. διώξομαί σε δειλίας. ἔφυγε φόνου. ἀπολύουσιν αὐτὸν προδοσίας. τῶν νόμων οὐ φροντίζουσι. ἐπιλανθάνεται τοῦ πατρός. ἄνθρωπος ὢν μέμνησο τῆς κοινῆς τύχης. κακῶς γὰρ ἐπεμελεῖσθ' ἡμῶν τότε. ἀνέμνησε τὸν ἄνθρωπον τοῦ κινδύνου. οὐ μέλει μοι τούτου. οὐ τοῦ δοκεῖν μοι τῆς δ' ἀληθείας μέλει. τῇ πόλει πολλάκις ἤδη μετεμέλησε τῶν κρίσεων. μακάριος ὅστις τυγχάνει γενναίου φίλου. γνώμης ἁμαρτάνει. ἐψεύσθησαν τῶν ἐλπίδων. οὐκ ἔσφαλται τῆς ἀληθείας. στοχαζώμεθα τῆς τῶν θεῶν διανοίας. ἐρᾷ τῆς εἰρήνης. ἐπιθύμει τῶν ἀρίστων. διὰ τί τῶν κερδῶν ἐφίει;

III.—*Partitive Genitive.* §§ 101-104

Note the order of the words.

τῶν πολιτῶν οἱ καλοί τε κἀγαθοί. οἱ γεραίτατοι τῶν Ἀχαρνέων. οἱ χρηστοὶ τῶν ἀνθρώπων. οἱ ἄλλοι τῶν ἀνθρώπων. ὀλίγοι τῶν πολιτῶν. οὐδεὶς τῶν ἀνθρώπων. ἀνὴρ τῶν ῥητόρων. τῶν δέκα στρατηγῶν Λέων καὶ Ἐρασανίδης. Σόλων τῶν ἑπτὰ σοφιστῶν ἐνομίζετο. ὁ ἥμισυς τοῦ χρόνου. ἡ ἡμίσεια τῆς γῆς. ἔτεμον τῆς γῆς τὴν πολλήν. τὴν πλείστην τῆς στρατιᾶς παρέταξε.

IV.—*After Substantives: Genitives of Material, Possession, Amount: Objective and Subjective Genitive.* §§ 106, 107

στέφανος χρυσοῦ. ποτήριον οἴνου. ἡ στήλη λίθου ἐστίν. ἡ τῶν Λοκρῶν γῆ. τὸ κράτος ἐστὶ τοῦ βασιλέως. ὀκτὼ σταδίων τεῖχος. τριάκοντα ταλάντων οὐσία. τριῶν ἡμερῶν σιτία.

ὁ τῶν πολεμίων φόβος (Objective or Subjective). τὸ τῶν πολιτῶν μῖσος. οἱ τῶν θεῶν ὅρκοι.

V.—*Similar Genitives after certain Adjectives.* § 108

ποταμὸς πλήρης ἰχθύων. πλούσιός ἐστιν οὐ χρυσίου ἀλλ' οὗ δεῖ τὸν εὐδαίμονα πλουτεῖν.

ἔμπειρός ἐστι κακῶν. μεστὴ παντοίων κακῶν ἡ πόλις.

ἡ πόλις ἁπάντων τῶν πολιτῶν κοινή ἐστιν. κίνησις τοῦ σώματος οἰκεία. ἱερὸν γάρ ἐστι τοῦ Πλούτου πάλαι. κίνδυνοι τῶν ἐφεστηκότων ἴδιοι. μέτοχοί ἐσμεν ἐκείνων τῶν ἐλπίδων.

VI.—*The Genitive after Verbs denoting Action which affects part only of the Object.* §§ 111-117

φέρει τῶν λίθων. ἐνεγκάτω τις ἔνδοθεν τῶν ἰχθύων. κατεάγη τῆς κεφαλῆς. πίνει τοῦ οἴνου. ἔτεμον τῆς γῆς. πέμπει τῶν στρατιωτῶν. ἤκουον τοῦ ἐμοῦ πατρός. ἀκούω τοῦ ῥήτορος λέγοντος. οὐκ ἀκροασόμεθα τῶν λόγων. ᾐσθόμην τῶν κακῶν. §§ 111, 114.

τοῦ βωμοῦ ἐλάβετο. πυρὸς οὐχ ἅπτομαι. οὗτοι ποθ᾽ ἅψει τῶν ἄκρων ἄνευ πόνου. ἐχόμεθα τοῦ δικαίου. νόμων ἔχεσθαι πάντα δεῖ τὸν σώφρονα. ἄρχει τῶν λόγων. ἄρχεται τοῦ λόγου. § 112.

μίαν ναῦν ἐπλήρωσαν τούτων. πλουτῶ φίλων. εὐπορεῖ χρημάτων. § 113.

ἔγευσε Φίλιππον τοῦ μέλιτος. ὁ Φίλιππος ἐγεύσατο τοῦ μέλιτος. ὀσφραινόμεθα οἴνου. · § 114.

μετέχομεν τοῦ ἔργου. μεταλάβωμεν τοῦ χρυσοῦ. μεταλαγχάνει τῶν χρημάτων. τῆς ἀρχῆς μετέδωκε τῷ υἱῷ. § 115.

μετέδωκέ τι τῆς ἀρχῆς τῷ υἱῷ. τὸ πέμπτον μέρος μετέλαβε τῶν ψήφων. § 116.

οἴνου κάκιστον ὄζει. τί γὰρ ἄλλ᾽ ἂν ἀπολαύσαιμι τοῦ μαθήματος ; § 117.

VII.—*The Genitive of Value.* §§ 118-120

πολλοῦ ἄξιός ἐστιν. δόξα χρημάτων οὐκ ὠνητή. τῶν πόνων πωλοῦσιν ἡμῖν πάντα τἀγάθ' οἱ θεοί. οὐκ ἂν ἀπεδόμην πολλοῦ τὰς ἐλπίδας. τὸν φόρον τοσούτου ἔταξεν. ὁ δοῦλος πέντε μνῶν τιμᾶται. τιμᾶταί μοι ὁ ἀνὴρ θανάτου. τίνος τιμήσειν αὐτῷ προσδοκᾷς τὸ δικαστήριον ; μισθοῦται ταλάντου τὸν ἀγρόν. οὐκ ἔχω πλοῖα τετιμημένα χρημάτων. § 119. δέκα μνῶν ἐργάζεται. πόσου διδάσκει ὁ Ἰσαῖος ; πέντε μνῶν διδάσκει. § 120.

VIII.—*Genitive after Compound Verbs.* §§ 121-123

πρόκειται τῆς γῆς ὄρη μεγάλα. τῶν ὑμετέρων δικαίων προΐστασθε. ὑπερεφάνησαν τοῦ λόφου. ὑμῶν ὑπεραλγῶ. ἐπέβησαν τοῦ τείχους. ἀποτρέπει με τούτου. κατὰ τοῖν κόραιν ὕπνου τι καταχεῖται γλυκύ. ὤνθρωπε, παῦσαι καταγελῶν μου. κατεφρόνησας τοῦ κινδύνου. καταψεύδονταί μου μεγάλα. § 121. καταγιγνώσκουσι ζημίαν Κλεινίου. κατέκριναν θάνατον Σωκράτους. ἐνίων κατεψηφίσαντο θάνατον. ὁ κριτὴς ζημίαν καταδικάζει τοῦ πολίτου. καταγιγνώσκομεν κλοπὴν ἐκείνου τοῦ φωρός. καταψηφιούμεθα δειλίαν τῶν στρατηγῶν. κατηγοροῦσι ἀδικίαν τοῦ θεοῦ. οὐδεὶς αὐτὸς αὑτοῦ κατηγόρησέ πώποτε. §§ 122, 123.

B. The Ablative Genitive

§§ 125-135

IX.—§§ 125-129

ὁ Κῦρος ἐγένετο Καμβύσου. τοιούτων ἐστὲ προγόνων. § 125.
ἡ νῆσος οὐ πολὺ διέχει τῆς ἠπείρου. ἡ πόλις πολὺ ἀπέχει τοῦ λιμένος. οὐδὲν διαφέρεις Χαιρεφῶντος τὴν φύσιν. ἀπέχου τῶν αἰσχρῶν ἡδονῶν. εἶτ' ἐγὼ σοῦ φείσομαι; ἐπαύσατο τοῦ πόνου. λήγουσιν ἔριδος. τοῦ σώματος χωρίζουσι τὴν ψυχήν. πολέμου καὶ κακῶν σε ἀπαλλάξω. τῶν δεσμῶν ἐλευθεροῖ τὸν ἄνδρα. ἔπαυσε Ξενοφῶντα τῆς ἀρχῆς. ἐκωλύσαμεν αὐτὸν τῆς ὁδοῦ. § 126.
Φιλίππῳ παρακεχωρήκαμεν τῆς ἐλευθερίας. ὑπείκω σοι τῶν λόγων. § 127.
διάφορός ἐστι τῶν ἄλλων πάντων. ἐλεύθερός ἐστιν αἰτίας. § 128.
ἐξέρχεται ἐκ τῆς πόλεως. ἐξέπλευσαν ἀπὸ τῆς νήσου. ἀποσπῶσι τὸν φῶρα ἀπὸ τοῦ νεώ. ἀποτρέπουσιν αὐτὸν ἀπὸ τοῦ ἐρωτήματος. ἀποτρέπει τοὺς πολίτας τοῦ ἐρωτήματος. § 129.

X.—*After Words denoting Deficiency, etc.; Comparison, etc.*

§§ 130-134

δεῖται γὰρ ὄρνις καὶ διακόνου τινός. ἀπορεῖς δὲ τοῦ σύ; ἀργυρίου σπανίζω. πάντων ἐκένωσαν τὴν ναῦν. ἀποστερεῖς τὸν πατέρα τῆς τυραννίδος. οὐ

δεῖ τείχους. πολλοῦ δεῖ οὕτως ἔχειν. ὀλίγου δεῖ τοῦτον ἐκφυγεῖν. τοὺς πολίτας ἐλάχιστα ἐδέησε διαφθεῖραι τὸ πῦρ. § 130.
ναῦς κενὴ ἀνδρῶν ἦν. ἡ νῆσος ψιλὴ δένδρων. γυμνός ἐστιν ὅπλων. ἄτιμοί εἰσι γερῶν. ἄμοιρός ἐστι τῆς ἀρετῆς. § 131.
ἐν ταῖς ἀνάγκαις χρημάτων κρείττων φίλος. μείζονα σὲ νομίζομεν εἶναι τοῦ ἀδελφοῦ. § 132.
ἄλλα ἐστι τῶν δικαίων. ἑτέρως πως ἐπράχθη τῶν εἰωθότων. ὕστεροι ἀφίκοντο οἱ Θεσπιῆς τῶν Πλαταιῶν. τῇ προτεραίᾳ τῆς μάχης παρῆσαν. τὸ τῶν πολεμίων πλῆθος πολλαπλάσιον ἦν ἡμῶν. § 133.
ἡδέως πλεονεκτοῦμεν τῶν ἐχθρῶν. πολλὰ ἐλαττοῦται Αἰσχίνου. ὁ Κῦρος ὑστέρησε τῆς μάχης. ἀπελείφθη προθυμίας. § 134.

EXERCISES

XXVII.—§§ 87-99

1. He came to Thebes in Boeotia. 2. Where in the city did you find your friend? 3. Late in the day they came to their camp. 4. Philip reigned over many nations. 5. Good men are in the habit of performing noble actions. 6. Good judges are worthy of the highest honour. 7. One of my servants is guilty of theft. 8. Our sailors are skilful in seamanship. 9. You seem to be careless about truth. 10. You have become a philosopher early in life.

XXVIII.—§ 100

1. I congratulate you on your good fortune. 2. They envied me for my wealth. 3. We shall prosecute the slave for theft. 4. Such men as these care not for the gods. 5. Let us not forget the evils of the poor. 6. Saying that, you err greatly in judgment. 7. The soldiers of Cyrus were deceived in their hopes. 8. Many men long for wealth and honour. 9. The judge acquitted the general of cowardice. 10. When he became rich he forgot his mother.

XXIX.—§§ 101-104

1. Many of the sailors were not willing to go. 2. The oldest and wisest of the citizens did not trust Philip. 3. The enemy ravaged half our land. 4. The general has drawn up most of his army four furlongs from the enemy. 5. Most of mankind love wealth rather than wisdom. 6. The orator persuaded few among the citizens. 7. The better-bred of the citizens are taught music and gymnastics. 8. Philip used to be thought one of the greatest of generals. 9. The fire destroyed half the city. 10. No man in the world is more hateful to me than you (are).

XXX.—§§ 106, 107

1. He gave a cup of wine to the soldier. 2. The citizens voted a crown of gold to the orator. 3. My father's house is in the middle of the city. 4. In the land of the Persians the whole authority belongs to the king. 5. The sailors have provisions for four days in the ship. 6. A wall of thirty furlongs surrounds the city. 7. The enemy have violated all their oaths to the gods. 8. The boy gave back the money owing to his fear of me. 9. The sailors laughed at my fear. 10. The praise of the citizens is most useful to an orator.

XXXI.—§ 108

1. This river is full of all sorts of fish. 2. You are rich both in gold and in wisdom. 3. An army is the common property of all the citizens. 4. This temple is sacred to the goddess Artemis. 5. We hope to be sharers in your wisdom. 6. Such a hope is peculiar to boys and young men. 7. The whole city was full of soldiers. 8. Your life has been rich in evils and misfortunes. 9. Troubles are the common lot of all mankind. 10. In Athens there was a famous temple sacred to the goddess Athena.

XXXII.—§§ 111-117

1. The general sent some of the cavalry against the enemy. 2. My friend seized my hand. 3. I will willingly touch neither fire nor love. 4. Let us cling to the virtue which we learnt as boys. 5. The orator now wishes to begin his speech. 6. The city of the Athenians abounded in beautiful temples. 7. The bad boy wished to have a taste of the wine. 8. The master perceived the servant stealing some of the honey. 9. Honourable men will have no share in such wickedness. 10. This city has a very bad smell of fish.

XXXIII.—§§ 118-120

1. Wisdom is not to be bought for money. 2. The farmer's dog is valued at twenty minae. 3. At what price does that famous philosopher teach your son? 4. He hired the boat for a mina a month. 5. Your Persian sword is worth a great deal. 6. We will not sell our virtue for money or reputation. 7. The court will fix death as his penalty (lit. fix the penalty against him at death). 8. Men can buy many good things at the price of labour. 9. The orator sold himself to Philip for a bribe. 10. A soldier works for his country at very small wages.

XXXIV.—§§ 121-123

1. High mountains lie before Attica. 2. The enemy appeared above the hill early in the day. 3. Mounting his horse he rode forth from the city. 4. It is not wise to laugh at bad men. 5. No man ever accuses himself of cowardice. 6. A wise general never despises his enemy. 7. The court found the philosopher guilty of impiety (lit. voted the crime of impiety against the philosopher). 8. My former friends told great falsehoods against me. 9. Our fathers condemned many to death for cowardice. 10. The judge passed sentence of death against the thief.

XXXV.—§§ 125-129

1. Two sons were born of Darius. 2. The city was fifty furlongs distant from the sea. 3. I will not spare men who have told such falsehoods against me. 4. We cannot free mankind from toil. 5. The son yielded the house to his father. 6. I will drag you from my house and drive you from the city. 7. We will not yield up our independence to the king. 8. It is impossible to separate the soul from the body. 9. Cease, my boys, from hatred and strife. 10. The soldiers wish to deprive the general of his command.

XXXVI.—§§ 130-134

1. All men need friends. 2. The thieves emptied my house of everything in one night. 3. I do not wish to rob you of your reputation, far from it indeed. 4. The whole of that country is bare of trees. 5. Boys honour reputation more than wisdom. 6. It is always pleasant to get the advantage over one's enemies. 7. Such men, I think, fall short of true wisdom. 8. The Greeks were braver than the Persians in the battle. 9. I think that my father is taller than you. 10. Most men think that wealth is better than virtue or wisdom.

XXXVII

1. Sensible people never do what you have done. 2. I came too late for dinner (§ 134). 3. Thrice a day they pray in this way to their god. 4. When far advanced in years my father lost all his money. 5. Your horse is eager to drink some water. 6. They were talking and drinking till late in the night. 7. I am a man of great importance in my own country. 8. He will never give his sons any of his money. 9. The old orator loved to cut down trees many years old (lit. of many years). 10. To what part of the world shall I go when banished from my native land?

XXXVIII.—RECAPITULATORY

1. Bad boys teach their friends impudence. 2. We always experience the greatest pleasure in your house. 3. You were asked that question by me before. 4. A good man will have no fear of death. 5. We cannot admire men corrupt in mind. 6. Bring one of the cloaks from indoors and put it on this old woman. 7. He went out of the house early in the morning and ran round the whole island. 8. It is wise not to ask one's friends for money. 9. The soldier swore by Zeus that he had never loved another maiden. 10. On the day after the battle they offered thank-offerings for the good news in all the temples of the city.

IV.—THE DATIVE CASE

A. The True Dative Case

§§ 136-171

EXAMPLES

1.—*The Dative as defining Verbs, Adjectives, and Adverbs*
§§ 137-147

δίδωσι μισθὸν τοῖς στρατιώταις. χρήματα διανέμω τοῖς πολίταις. τὴν μάχην ἀγγέλλει τῷ βασιλεῖ. καὶ γὰρ ἥκειν ὄρτυγι. ἀφομοιωσόμεθα τοῖς μαινομένοις. ὁ Κῦρος ἐπλησίαζε τῷ στρατοπέδῳ. ἴσοι τὰ ἑαυτοῦ κακὰ τοῖς ἐμοῖς. κενταύροις ἤκασαν αὐτούς. τὸν ἄνδρι ἐπλησίασε τῷ ἵππῳ. ἱμάτιον παραπλήσιον τῷ σῷ. τὸ αὐτὸν ἔπραξεν Ἀμεινίᾳ. ἐξ ἴσου ἐγενόμεθα ὑμῖν. δεῖ μοι τοῦ οἴνου. ἔμελέ σοι τοῦ ἔργου. τὸ μηδὲν ἀδικεῖν πᾶσιν ἀνθρώποις πρέπει. προσήκει μοι ταῦτα λέγειν. οὐδέν μοι προσήκει τῆς αἰτίας ταύτης. ὁ θεὸς τὴν ψυχὴν ἡμῖν ἐνέφυσε. τὰ ἔργα συμφωνεῖ τοῖς λόγοις. συναποθνῄσκει μετὰ τῆς γυναικός. αἰσχύνην περιάπτει τῇ πόλει. ἀντετάχθησαν τοῖς πολεμίοις. οἱ Θηβαῖοι ἐπολέμησαν τοῖς Πλαταιεῦσι. θεῷ μάχεσθαι δεινόν ἐστι καὶ τύχῃ. ἐδεδίκαστο ἄν μοι. τότε ἐσπεισάμεθα τοῖς βαρβάροις. πολέμιοι ἀεὶ ἦσαν τῇ πόλει. ἐπολέμησε πρὸς τοὺς Βυζαντίους. σπενδώμεθα πρὸς ἀλλήλους.

II.—*Dative of Interest.* §§ 149-156

ἦσαν Κροίσῳ δύο παῖδες. σοῦ μὲν κρατοῦντος δουλεία ὑπάρχει αὐτοῖς, κρατουμένου δὲ σοῦ ἐλευθερία. χρήματα πολλά μοι γίγνεται. αἴτιός εἰμί σοι τούτων. οὗτος ὁ οὐράνιος ἔρως πολλοῦ ἄξιός ἐστι καὶ πόλει καὶ ἰδιώταις. ἐβοήθησε τοῖς ἐχθροῖς. ἐπικουρήσω τοῖς νόμοις. ἀφείλετό μοι τὸν ἀγρόν. τάδε ὑμῖν μέμψεται. φασὶ τοὺς πολίτας φθονεῖν σφίσι. τί λοιδορεῖ ἡμῖν; οἱ γὰρ βλέποντες τοῖς τυφλοῖς ἡγούμεθα. ἀμυνοῦμεν τῇ πόλει. τέθνηχ᾽ ὑμῖν πάλαι. Ἐπίδαμνός ἐστι πόλις ἐν δεξιᾷ εἰσπλέοντι τὸν Ἰόνιον κόλπον. τοῦτό ἐστιν ἐμοὶ βουλομένῳ. θαυμάζω εἰ μὴ ἀσμένοις ὑμῖν ἀφῖγμαι. τούτῳ πάνυ μοι προσέχετε τὸν νοῦν. ἀπ᾽ ἐκείνου τυφλός εἰμί σοι. πῶς ἡμῖν ἔχεις;

B. The Dative as Successor to the Instrumental Case

I.—*The Dative of Instrument or Agency.* §§ 158-165

τοιαῦτα τοῖς Κορινθίοις ἐπράχθη. ταῦτά σοι εἴρηται. εἴ τί μοι τοιοῦτον εἴργαστο. ἡ ἀρετή σοι ἀσκητέα. μιμητέον ἐστὶν ἡμῖν τοὺς ἀγαθούς. ὠφελητέα σοι ἡ πόλις ἐστίν. οὔ σοι πείθομαι. ὑμῖν οὐ πεισόμεθα. Ἕλλησιν ὠργίσθη ὁ Δαρεῖος. Κορινθίοις ἤχθεσθε κἀκεῖνοί γέ σοι. Εὐριπίδῃ θυμούμεθα. ἅπαντες ἡδόμεθα τῷ ἀγῶνι. ἐλυπήθη τῷ πράγματι. ἔχαιρον τῇ σιωπῇ. ἠγανάκτει τῷ Κλεάρχῳ. ἐχαλέπηνα τῷ πράγματι. ἀποθνήσκουσι νόσῳ. φθόνῳ τοῦτο ἔδρασε. φόβῳ ἀπέδραμεν. εὐνοίᾳ τῇ σῇ ἐκεῖνα ἔλεξα. τούτοις γιγνώσκει ἀληθεῖς εἶναι τοὺς λόγους. τὰ μέλλοντα τεκμαίρομαι τοῖς γεγενημένοις. εὔνοια καιρῷ κρίνεται. πληγαῖς ἐκόλασε τὸν δοῦλον. ζημιοῦμεν τοὺς τοιούτους χρήμασιν, ἀτιμίᾳ, τοῖς ἐσχάτοις, θανάτῳ.

II.—*The Dative of Accompaniment.* §§ 166, 167

πολλῷ στρατῷ πορεύεται. ὀλίγοις ἱππεῦσι στρατεύεται ὁ στρατηγός. ἵπποις τοῖς δυνατωτάτοις καὶ ἀνδράσι πορευώμεθα. ναυτικῷ ὁρμᾶσθαι ἐθέλει. ναῦν εἷλον αὐτοῖς ἀνδράσιν. πολλοὶ ἤδη κατεκρημνίσθησαν αὐτοῖς τοῖς ἵπποις. ἐκείνῳ ἕπεται ὁ δεσπότης. τί τῷδε ἀκολουθοῦμέν ποτε, ὦ δέσποτα; τὸ φῶς ἅπασι κοινόν.

III.—*The Dative of Manner.* §§ 168, 169

τούτῳ τῷ τρόπῳ ἡ μάχη ἐγένετο. βίᾳ εἷλον τὸν δοῦλον. δόλῳ ἐνίκησαν τοὺς στρατιώτας. σχολῇ ἐκεῖνα πράξω. πολλῇ κραυγῇ εἰς χεῖρας ἦλθον οἱ βάρβαροι. οἱ Ἀθηναῖοι ἀτελεῖ τῇ νίκῃ ἀνέστησαν. πολλῷ θορύβῳ ἐπῇσαν.

IV.—*The Dative of Measure.* §§ 170, 171

πολλῷ κρεῖττόν ἐστιν ἐμφανὴς φίλος ἢ πλοῦτος ἀφανής. δυοῖν ἡμέραιν ὑστέρησαν τῆς μάχης. τοσούτῳ προεῖχε τῶν ἄλλων. κέρατι ὑπερεῖχον τῶν πολεμίων. τοσούτῳ ἥδιον ζῶ. τέχνῃ ἀνάγκης ἀσθενεστέρα μακρῷ. πολλῷ ἄριστος πάντων ἐστίν. μακρῷ εὐδαιμονέστατος ἡμῶν ἐστιν. δέκα ἔτεσι πρὸ τῆς ἐν Σαλαμῖνι ναυμαχίας ἀπέθανεν. τῇ κεφαλῇ μείζων ἐστὶ τοῦ ἀδελφοῦ.

C. The Dative as Successor to the lost Locative Case

§§ 172, 173

List of Locatives proper

χαμαί. οἴκοι. Πυθοῖ. Μεγαροῖ. Πλαταίασιν. Ἀθήνησιν.

Dative for Locative

ἡ Μαραθῶνι μάχη.

Time expressed by Dative without Preposition

(1) θέρει. χειμῶνι. ἦρι. ὥρᾳ θέρους, χειμῶνος, etc. (2) τῇ τρίτῃ ἡμέρᾳ, τῇ τρίτῃ νυκτί, τῷ τρίτῳ μηνί, τῷ τρίτῳ ἔτει, τῇ προτεραίᾳ (ἡμέρᾳ), τῇ ὑστεραίᾳ (ἡμέρᾳ). (3) Παναθηναίοις. Διονυσίοις. νουμηνίᾳ.

EXERCISES

XXXIX.—§§ 137-147

1. The rich men distributed food to the poor citizens. 2. Your friend is very like my brother. 3. Demosthenes lived about (κατά) the same time as Philip. 4. All men have need of food and clothing. 5. His words do not agree with his deeds. 6. The natives will not fight with our soldiers on the plain. 7. The brothers were disputing with one another about the maiden. 8. You have nothing to do (προσήκει) with our quarrel. 9. The cavalry drew near to the river. 10. You fasten shame on yourself and your city.

XL.—§§ 149-156

1. The general has many beautiful horses. 2. You are the cause of all these evils to the city. 3. A good man will be the champion of the poor and weak. 4. I cannot blame you, but I blame your parents. 5. The city lies on the right hand as one sails into the harbour. 6. Your good fortune is pleasing to me. 7. Give this book to your brother, please. 8. Poor men envy rich and prosperous priests. 9. The thieves have taken away all my silver from me. 10. By killing that man you did me a very great favour.

XLI.—§§ 158-165

1. We ought to help our parents. 2. Such words have never been said by us. 3. You ought to imitate the deeds of noble and good men. 4. The general did not obey the citizens. 5. We were all very grieved at the words of the messenger. 6. It is impossible to be angry with a beautiful maiden. 7. Friendship is tested by misfortune. 8. We see with our eyes and hear with our ears. 9. He is dying from violence not from disease. 10. It is necessary to judge your words by your deeds.

XLII.—§§ 166-169

1. The natives advanced down the hill with loud shouting. 2. The enemy defeated our cavalry by cunning. 3. Cyrus marched forth from Sardis with a large army. 4. That dog will follow the thief for the whole day. 5. It was by cunning not by force that he defeated me in boxing. 6. The ship was captured in the night time crew and all. 7. They fled away early in the day horses and all. 8. Such pleasures as these can be shared in by all. 9. The enemy captured our ships crews and all. 10. I shall scarcely do that for you, said my friend.

XLIII.—§§ 170, 171

1. To a young man good friends are far better than wealth. 2. Old men think wealth far better than friends. 3. The natives out-flanked the army of the Greeks by a wing. 4. He was a head taller than the rest of the soldiers. 5. You were an hour too late for dinner. 6. He is far the best of all the sailors that I know. 7. So much the more happily do philosophers live than other men. 8. Far better an open enemy than a worthless friend. 9. Falsehood is little better than theft. 10. Our five ships were three days too late for the battle.

XLIV.—§§ 172, 173

1. The Athenians defeated the Persians in the battle at Marathon. 2. At Plataea the Persians were again defeated by the army of the Greeks. 3. He died on the same day as his mother (§ 139). 4. The city was taken by the enemy in the tenth month. 5. In the winter season the farmer pursues the hares with dogs and arrows. 6. At the new moon they poured many drink-offerings to their god. 7. In winter time the nights are much longer than in the summer. 8. At the Dionysia many strangers used to come to the city. 9. On the day before the whole city was thrown into confusion. 10. On the day after the battle they set up a large trophy on the hill.

CHAPTER V.—THE VOICES OF THE VERB

EXAMPLES

I.—THE ACTIVE VOICE. §§ 175-184

ὁ πατὴρ φιλεῖ τοὺς παῖδας. ὁ Ξέρξης τὸν Ἄθων διώρυξε. Δημοσθένης Πύλον ἐξετείχισε. § 175. ἔχει γὰρ οὕτως, εἰσὶν οὐ πάντες κακοί. ἔχει κατὰ χώραν. οἱ πλούσιοι εὖ πράττουσι. τῷ γὰρ καλῶς πράττοντι πᾶσα γῆ πατρίς. ὁ Κῦρος ἤλασεν ἐπὶ τὸν ἀδελφόν. ὁ στρατηγὸς ἐλαύνει πρῲ τῆς ἡμέρας. οἱ βάρβαροι ἀπῇρον ἀπὸ Σαλαμῖνος. οἱ φιλόσοφοι διάγουσιν ἥδιστα. οἱ ἀγαθοὶ τελευτῶσιν ἑκόντες. οἱ κριταὶ προσέχουσι τῷ πράγματι. προσέχωμεν τὸν νοῦν τούτῳ τῷ λόγῳ. §§ 176-178. ὥρα γ᾽, ἔφη, βουλεύεσθαι ὅπως τις τοὺς ἄνδρας ἀπελᾷ ἀπὸ τοῦ λόφου. ἀπέθανεν ὑπὸ τοῦ Ἀλεξάνδρου. ὁ δεσπότης κακῶς ποιεῖ τὸν δοῦλον. ὁ δοῦλος κακῶς πάσχει ὑπὸ τοῦ δεσπότου. οἱ πολῖται εὖ λέγουσιν ἡμᾶς. εὖ ἀκούομεν ὑπὸ τῶν πολιτῶν. οἱ παῖδες ἐξέβαλον τὸν κύνα. ὁ κύων ἐξέπεσεν ὑπὸ τῶν παίδων. γυμνὸς θύραζ᾽ ἐξέπεσον. οἱ πολῖται τοὺς φυγάδας κατάξουσιν. οἱ φυγάδες ὑπὸ τῶν πολιτῶν κατίασιν.

Μειδίας ἐδίωξε φόνου τὸν ἀδελφόν. ὁ ἀδελφὸς ὑπὸ Μειδίου ἔφυγε φόνου. §§ 179-183.
οἰκτείρομεν τὸν παῖδα. ὁ παῖς ὑφ' ἡμῶν ἐλέου τυγχάνει. ὁ κριτὴς συγγιγνώσκει τῷ φωρί. ὁ φὼρ συγγνώμην ἔχει ὑπὸ τοῦ κριτοῦ. ἐπῃνέσατε τοὺς ναύτας. οἱ ναῦται ὑφ' ὑμῶν ἐπαίνου ἔτυχον. § 184.

II.—THE MIDDLE VOICE. §§ 185-196

ἐλούσαντο ἐν τῷ ποταμῷ. ἠλείψαντο οἱ νεανίαι. κείρονται ἐπὶ τῷ τάφῳ. αἱ γυναῖκες κόπτονται. αἱ γρᾶες ἐκόψαντο τὸν τεθνηκότα. ὁ δὲ τύπτει ἑαυτόν. πληγὰς ἐμαυτῷ ἐνέβαλον. ὁ στρατηγὸς αἰτιᾶται ἑαυτόν. § 188.
ἐφυλάττοντο τοὺς λῃστάς. ὠφελείαν τινὰ ἐπειρῶντο ἀπ' αὐτῶν εὑρίσκεσθαι. μάρτυρας ἐπορίσατο. σῖτον ᾑροῦντο. ἀλλὰ δίδωμί σοι, ἔφη ὁ Χειρίσοφος, ὁπότερον βούλει ἑλέσθαι. ὁ δὲ Ξενοφῶν αἱρεῖται πορεύεσθαι. γυναῖκα ἠγάγετο. πολὺν χρόνον ἠμύνοντο τοὺς πολεμίους. ἐγὼ τῇ βοῇ ταύτῃ σε τρέψομαι. ποιώμεθα τὸν πόλεμον. ἐποιήσαντο τὸν πλοῦν. § 189.
πολλὰς ναῦς παρέσχοντο. γνώμην ἀπεφήνατο. ἀπεκρύψαντο τὸ πρᾶγμα. ἤρξατο τοῦ λόγου. οἱ στρατιῶται τὰ ὅπλα ἐτίθεντο. § 190.
ἐδιδάξατο τοὺς ὑεῖς ἱππεύειν. § 191.

III.—THE PASSIVE VOICE. §§ 197-202

ὁ δεσπότης αἰτιᾶται τὸν δοῦλον. ὁ δοῦλος αἰτίαν ἔχει ὑπὸ τοῦ δεσπότου. εἱλόμην ἐκείνους. ἐκεῖνοι ὑπ' ἐμοῦ ᾑρέθησαν. § 198.
ἀναγωγὴν ποιούμεθα. ἡ ἀναγωγὴ γίγνεται. ταύτην τὴν πρόφασιν ποιεῖσθε. ἡ πρόφασις γίγνεται ὑφ' ὑμῶν αὕτη. § 199.
οὐκ ἀμελεῖ τῶν νοσούντων. οἱ ἠμελημένοι ἄνθρωποι ἀπέθανον. κατεγέλασας τοῦ Κλέωνος. κατεγελάσθης ὑπὸ Κλέωνος. πιστεύετε τοῖς πλουσίοις. πένης λέγων τἀληθὲς οὐ πιστεύεται. ἐπεβούλευσαν τῷ δήμῳ. ὁ δῆμος ἐπεβουλεύθη ὑπ' αὐτῶν. § 200.
ἐπέτρεψα ἰατρῷ τὸν νοσοῦντα. ἰατρὸς ἐπετράπη τὸν νοσοῦντα. τοῖς Βοιωτοῖς ἵππον προσέταξαν. οἱ Βοιωτοὶ ἵππον προσετάχθησαν. § 201.
βεβοήθηταί μοι τῷ τεθνεῶτι. ἐτετιμώρητο τῷ Λεωνίδῃ. παρεσκεύασται τῷ πλῷ. παρεσκεύαστο τῇ ναυμαχίᾳ. § 202.

EXERCISES

XLV.—§§ 175-178

1. The general will fortify the city within ten days. 2. The citizens built two walls from the city to the harbour. 3. All the boys did not keep on the spot. 4. Bad men do not always fare ill. 5. It is not right to live so disgracefully. 6. The citizens will not pay attention to that philosopher. 7. Cyrus mounted his horse and rode against the enemy. 8. The general will march from the city on the fourth day. 9. The soldiers marched early in the day towards the hills. 10. The Persians sailed away having fared ill in the sea-fight.

XLVI.—§§ 179-184

1. Cyrus was killed in battle by his brother's soldiers. 2. We have been treated ill by the king. 3. Most boys are spoken well of by their mothers. 4. The corn was thrown out of the ship by the sailors themselves. 5. The exiles were restored by the Persians. 6. The slave was prosecuted for theft by his master. 7. That poor man is pitied by many of the wealthy citizens. 8. Such boys are in bad repute with their masters. 9. This philosopher is praised by all his pupils. 10. The cowardly general will not be pardoned by the citizens.

XLVII.—§§ 185-189

1. The boys will bathe in the sea. 2. The soldiers anointed themselves before the battle. 3. All mourned for the brave hero. 4. The savages flogged themselves in honour of the goddess. 5. The master blamed himself more than the boys. 6. The sailors tried to find for themselves a safer harbour. 7. The farmer defended himself against the wolves for a short time. 8. The sailors turned themselves to piracy. 9. The priest came to the camp of the Greeks to ransom (fut. part. mid.) his daughter. 10. The soldiers set up a trophy for themselves in the middle of the plain.

XLVIII.—§§ 189-196

1. The orator began his speech late in the night. 2. The sailors of old days made their voyages in small ships. 3. The ambassadors took care to keep their business dark (§ 190). 4. When the soldiers came (participle) to the trench they grounded their arms. 5. The Persians had their sons taught to shoot, to ride and to speak the truth. 6. The philosopher did not wish to defend himself to the court. 7. That geometer is gaining for himself a great reputation. 8. That dog will not, I think, bite the boys. 9. When the thieves arrived (participle) at the house they began to encourage one another. 10. Wise men do not go to law with one another about such matters.

XLIX.—§§ 197-202

1. The general was blamed by all the citizens. 2. Themistocles was chosen general with nine others (tr. himself the tenth). 3. The master was forced to speak ill of the boy. 4. This excuse was often made by you. 5. The orator was laughed at by all the citizens. 6. Few boys neglected by their parents become noble and good men. 7. When the thief defended himself (participle) to the judge he was not believed. 8. The general was plotted against by some of the soldiers. 9. This money was entrusted to you by the exiles. 10. The citizens were ordered to supply corn for the soldiers.

L.—§§ 197-202

1. The men who were neglected by the physician lived a long time. 2. All, said he, is prepared for our voyage. 3. My aid has been given to those neglected by the physicians. 4. Vengeance has been exacted for those slain by the savages. 5. A good priest does not neglect the poor and sick. 6. The master was laughed at by the boys. 7. The sick and the poor were not neglected by the priest. 8. I entrusted much money to the slave. 9. This slave was entrusted with much money by his master. 10. The rich men are ordered to supply five ships for the king.

LI

1. They saw that the natives had dug canals through the plain. 2. The defendant will not easily procure witnesses. 3. The boy thought that he had been treated ill by his master. 4. It was not always so in our country. 5. The citizens loved to honour those who died nobly. 6. Many tortoises were bought by the boys from the old man. 7. The young man contrived to dance five times with the beautiful maiden. 8. We will rout the enemy, said he, with this cry. 9. The worthless servant was driven out of the house by his master. 10. The natives will not be on their guard against our soldiers to-night.

LII

1. They contrived to fortify the island in the river. 2. My father, when he heard the whole matter, was no longer angry. 3. He was forced by his wife to forget all his former friends. 4. The Persians set sail when the Greek ships appeared (gen. absol.) 5. The old men sat down in the market-place and talked with one another for a long time. 6. The worthless son was driven out of doors by his old father. 7. You always seem to oppose that orator. 8. We did not wish to prosecute the boy for theft. 9. I hope that sail will be made early in the day. 10. You are always contriving some cunning scheme.

CHAPTER VI.—THE TENSES OF THE VERB

EXAMPLES

I.—FUTURE AND AORIST. §§ 207-209

βασιλεύσει ἐν τοῖς τεθνεῶσι. ταῦτα πράξας ὁ Κῦρος βασιλεύσει. τῶνδ' ἀκούσας ἐγέλασεν. πολλάκις ἐθαύμασα τὴν σὴν ἀρετήν. οὔπω εἶδον τοιοῦτον ἄνδρα. μέλλουσι κάειν τὴν ναῦν. ἔμελλε προσβαλεῖν τῇ Ποτειδαίᾳ.

II.—PRESENT AND IMPERFECT. §§ 210-212

πείθει ἐμὲ ἀδικῆσαι. ἕκαστος ἔπειθεν αὐτὸν ὑποστῆναι τὴν ἀρχήν. ἔφευγον ἐκ τῆς πατρίδος. νικῶ τῇδε τῇ ἡμέρᾳ πάντας τοὺς ἐχθρούς. ἥκω ἱκέτης παρά σε. πάντες ᾤχοντο ἐκ τῆς οἰκίας. αἱ δὲ τριάκοντα νῆες ἀφικνοῦνται εἰς τὰ ἐπὶ Θρᾴκης καὶ καταλαμβάνουσι Ποτείδαιαν. οἱ Ἀθηναῖοι τοὺς πρώτους φύλακας οἷς ἐπέδραμον εὐθὺς διαφθείρουσι. τῇ δ' ὑστεραίᾳ οἱ μὲν πρυτάνεις τὴν βουλὴν ἐκάλουν, ὑμεῖς δ' εἰς τὴν ἐκκλησίαν ἐπορεύεσθε. πάλαι ταῦτά σοι λέγω.

III.—PERFECT, PLUPERFECT, AND FUTURE PERFECT.

§§ 213, 214

τέθνηκεν ὁ πατήρ. κέχηνεν ὁ παῖς. τότε δὴ τεθνήξει πάντων ὧν οἶδα ἄριστος. ἀκήκοα μὲν τοὔνομα, μνημονεύω δ' οὔ. κἂν τοῦτο νικῶμεν, πάνθ' ἡμῖν πέπρακται. ταῦτ' ἐγεγράφη πρὶν ἐκεῖνα ἐγένετο. φράζε καὶ πεπράξεται. ἢν δὲ μὴ γένηται, μάτην ἐμοὶ μὲν κεκλαύσεται, σὺ δὲ τεθνήξεις.

IV.—TENSES OF SUBJUNCTIVE, OPTATIVE, IMPERATIVE, AND INFINITIVE. §§ 215-217

ἔλεξεν ὅτι ἡ γυνὴ ἀποθνήσκοι. ἔφη τὸν παῖδα ἀποθνήσκειν. ἔλεξεν ὅτι ἡ γυνὴ ἀποθάνοι. ἔφη τὴν γυναῖκα ἀποθανεῖν. ἔλεξεν ὅτι ἡ γυνὴ ἀποθάνοιτο. ἔφη τὴν γυναῖκα ἀποθανεῖσθαι.

V.—TENSES OF THE PARTICIPLE. §§ 218-221

λύων τὸν ἵππον πληγὰς ἐνέβαλεν. λύσας τὸν κύνα τυπτήσει. λύσων τὸν βοῦν τύπτει.

ἐπίστασθε Κόνωνα μὲν ἄρχοντα Νικόφημον δὲ ποιοῦντα ὅ τι ἐκεῖνος προστάττοι.

εὖ γ' ἐποίησας ἀναμνήσας. τόδε μοι χάρισαι ἀποκρινάμενος.

οἱ δ' ἄνδρες καταπεφευγότες ἀθρόοι πρὸς μετέωρόν τι συνέβησαν. Ἱστιαῖος ἀπέδρα βασιλέα Δαρεῖον ἐξηπατηκώς.

EXERCISES

LIII

1. When he saw me he burst out laughing. 2. As he heard the news he began to take heart. 3. He intended to attack the enemy's camp as night came on. 4. Those men had been exiled from their native land. 5. I have never yet seen thirty ships in the harbour. 6. I have been saying this for a long time to you, but you do not seem to hear. 7. They tried to persuade me to undertake the command. 8. Alas! another of my old friends will have passed away. 9. The boy lay awake till late in the night; to-day he yawns and is silent. 10. Speak the word and all that you wish shall be done.

LIV

1. He said that he had often admired your virtue. 2. Before striking the dog he showed him the bones of the sheep. 3. You did well to try to persuade your father. 4. On hearing the master's voice he fled from the house. 5. You know that my son used to do whatever I ordered him (opt.) 6. The wolves descending from the hills in the night kill many of the sheep. 7. I have come to you poor, a suppliant, an exile from my city. 8. The Persians intend to burn our city; all that we love will have perished. 9. On seeing the slave he tried to persuade him to steal the money. 10. The boy felt shame before his father, now that he (was in the position of one who) had deceived him (§ 221).

LV.—RECAPITULATORY

1. Good parents teach their sons wisdom and self-restraint. 2. You seem to have been acquainted with every kind of misfortune. 3. You were not taught such wickedness by your brother. 4. Well, let them shout (§ 2)'; they cannot frighten brave men. 5. He is healthy in body but corrupt in mind. 6. Give me your hand, my friend: I admire you for your courage. 7. That hare was the boy's gift to his master. 8. They built themselves a small house at that spot in the island. 9. The farmer often pursued the same hare; but he did not catch it. 10. That temple is five furlongs distant from the city.

LVI.—RECAPITULATORY

1. For this very reason men fear to swear falsely by the gods. 2. Health is a more precious possession than wealth or prosperity. 3. Three times to-day the same beggar has asked me for money. 4. In his prosperity he did not forget his former friends. 5. The soldiers crossed the river in this way. 6. You are not a Greek by birth: your voice betrays you. 7. Injustice after all has not been more profitable to you than justice. 8. Life is pleasant to the young but a burden to the old. 9. The thieves robbed the herdsmen of half their cows. 10. No man in the world could (aor. opt. with ἄν) run round the whole island in one day.

CHAPTER VII.—THE MOODS OF THE VERB IN INDEPENDENT PROPOSITIONS

EXAMPLES

I.—AFFIRMATIVE PROPOSITIONS. §§ 223-225

ὁ νεανίας θεῖ. οὐκ ἴστε. ἀποφεύξονται οἱ πολέμιοι. ἀπέστη ἡ Μένδη. εἰ καλῶς ἔχει, χαίρω. § 223.

ἡδέως ἂν ἴδοιμι ἐκεῖνα. ἡδέως ἂν ἔγωγ' ἐροίμην Λεπτίνην, τίς αὕτη ἡ ἀτέλειά ἐστιν; οὐκ ἂν λέγοις ὅτι μαίνεται. βουλοίμην ἂν τοῦτο οὕτως γενέσθαι. § 224.

ἔφασκε πρὸς αὐτὸν ἂν τάδε. πολλάκις ἠκούσαμεν ἄν τι κακῶς βουλευσαμένους μέγα πρᾶγμα. § 225.

II.—EXPRESSIONS OF A WISH. §§ 226-233

φέρε νυν, ἐγὼ τῶν ἔνδοθεν καλέσω τινά. φέρε δή, τὰς μαρτυρίας ὑμῖν ἀναγνῶ. ἄγε νυν ἴωμεν εἰς τὴν πόλιν. ἄγε δὴ σκοπῶμεν τὴν αἰτίαν. μὴ μέλλωμεν τάδε πράττειν. § 226.

Deliberative Subjunctive. § 227

εἴπω ταῦτα; βούλει οὖν καλέσω τῶν ἔνδοθέν τινα; ποῦ δὴ βούλει καθιζόμενοι ἀναγνῶμεν; βούλεσθε τὸ ὅλον πρᾶγμα ἀφῶμεν καὶ μὴ ζητῶμεν; § 227.
τί τις φῇ εἶναι τοῦτο; πότερόν σέ τις, Αἰσχίνη, τῆς πόλεως ἐχθρὸν ἢ ἐμὸν εἶναι φῇ;

Commands and Prohibitions. § 229

εἰπέ μοι. τοὺς θεοὺς φοβοῦ. μὴ φοβηθῇς τοῦτο. μὴ κλέπτε. μὴ κλέψῃς τὸ ἀργύριον.

Wish referring to Future. § 230

πόλλ᾽ ἀγαθὰ γένοιτό σοι. οὕτω νικήσαιμί τ᾽ ἐγὼ καὶ νομιζοίμην σοφός. εἴθ᾽ ἀναλωθείη τἀργύριον. μήθ᾽ οἱ Θηβαῖοί ποτε παύσαιντο τοὺς ἑαυτοὺς ἀγαθόν τι ποιοῦντας ἀτιμάζοντες μήθ᾽ ὑμεῖς τοὺς εὐεργέτας τιμῶντες. εἰ γὰρ ἔλθοι.

Wish referring to Present or Past. §§ 231-233

εἴθε παρῆσθα. εἴθε ἀπέθανες. εἰ γὰρ μὴ ἀπέθανες. εἴθ᾽ ἐξεκόπη πρότερον τὸν ὀφθαλμὸν λίθῳ.
ὤφελες ἀποθανεῖν. εἴθ᾽ ὤφελες ζῆν. μὴ ὤφελες ἀποθανεῖν. εἰ γὰρ ὤφελον ἀπολέσθαι.

For "Questions" see Chapter X.

EXERCISES

LVII.—§§ 223-225

1. The islands revolted from the Athenians. 2. The wolves will escape to the mountains. 3. I should like to see your brother's dogs. 4. He would not say such things to his father. 5. I should like to hear that orator speaking. 6. I should wish to leave some money to the poor. 7. The young man would often ride in the early morning from the city. 8. The master would often strike the worthless slave. 9. My friends and I often used to bathe in the sea in the summer time. 10. Cyrus would often send gifts of all kinds to his friends.

LVIII.—§§ 226-228

1. Come now, let me ask you these questions. 2. Come, let us summon some of the witnesses. 3. Let us not delay to advance against the enemy. 4. Come, let me read to you the words of the poet. 5. Am I to tell you the whole truth? 6. Do you wish then that I should read the evidence to you? 7. Are we not to go from the house before night? 8. Am I not to inquire into this charge? 9. Is one to call you a fool or a philosopher? 10. Where pray are we to sit and listen to your wisdom?

LIX.—§ 229

1. Tell me the cause of this uproar. 2. Do not steal your master's money. 3. Boys, respect your parents. 4. Do not listen to the words of bad men. 5. Fear the gods and respect the king. 6. Do not say such dreadful things to me, my son. 7. Think not that a philosopher is always wise. 8. Come, call one of the servants from the house! 9. Never speak ill of your friends. 10. Come, speak well of the rich and prosperous, and abuse the poor and weak.

LX.—§§ 230-233

1. So may you conquer all your enemies. 2. Oh that my money had not thus been spent. 3. May we never cease dishonouring cowards and traitors. 4. Would that I had never been considered a wise man. 5. Sooner may my eye be knocked out with a stone. 6. Would that all traitors may thus perish. 7. Would that I had seen the glory of the goddess. 8. Oh that I had never believed the lies of the orator. 9. Oh that I could see the light of the sun. 10. Would that the thief had not stolen the birds which I love.

CHAPTER VIII.—THE MOODS OF THE VERB IN DEPENDENT PROPOSITIONS

EXAMPLES.

A. PROPOSITIONS INTRODUCED BY ὅτι COMPLETING THE SENSE OF VERBS OF SAYING, LEARNING, KNOWING, THINKING. §§ 235-245

Rule.—When principal verb is primary, same mood and tense as if an independent proposition : when principal verb historic, either (1) same mood and tense, or (2) same tense of optative.

ἀγγέλλει ὅτι ἥκουσιν οἱ ἄνδρες. ἀνέκραγεν ὅτι οἱ πολέμιοι προσέρχονται. εἶπεν ὅτι γράψοι τῷ φίλῳ. ἔλεγεν ὅτι μάχῃ ἡττημένοι εἶεν ὑπὸ τῶν πολεμίων. οὗτοι ἔλεγον ὅτι Κῦρος μὲν τέθνηκεν, Ἀριαῖος δὲ πεφευγὼς ἐν τῷ σταθμῷ εἴη. ὁ δὲ ἀπεκρίνατο ὅτι οὐκ ἴοι. ἔγραψεν ὅτι πέμψει τοὺς ἵππους. ἔγνωσαν ὅτι κενὸς ὁ φόβος εἴη. προϊδόντες ὅτι ἔσοιτο ὁ πόλεμος, ἐβούλοντο τὴν Πλάταιαν προκαταλαβεῖν. ἐπειρώμην αὐτῷ δεικνύναι, ὅτι οἴοιτο μὲν εἶναι σοφός, εἴη δ᾽ οὔ. φανερῶς εἶπεν ὅτι ἡ πόλις σφῶν τετείχισται. ἤκουσεν ὅτι ἡ μήτηρ τέθνηκεν. ἐπύθετο ὅτι οἱ Λακεδαιμόνιοι μέλλουσιν εἰς τὴν χώραν εἰσβαλεῖν. οὐκ ἠπίσταντο ὅτι οἱ πολῖται ἐνδώσοιεν.

ἦσαν ὅτι εἰσπλέουσιν οἱ πολέμιοι εἰς τὸν λιμένα.
ἔμαθεν ὅτι μεμάχηνται. γνοὺς δὲ ὁ βασιλεὺς ὅτι
ἔσοιτο περὶ τῆς καθόδου λόγος καὶ ὅτι οἱ Ἀθηναῖοι
ἐνδέξονται αὐτήν, ἐβουλεύσατο τάδε.
νομίζει ὅτι ἀνὴρ ἥκει. ὑπενοεῖτε ὅτι ταῦτα λέγοιεν
διὰ φθόνον. ἡγήσαντο ὅτι δεήσει διαβαίνειν τὸν
ποταμόν.

Anticipatory Construction. § 244

Κῦρος ᾔδει τὸν βασιλέα ὅτι μέσον ἔχοι τοῦ
Περσικοῦ στρατεύματος. καὶ γὰρ ἐμὲ οὐκ ἠγνόησαν
ὅτι ἦν ἐξ ἐκείνης αὐτῷ γεγονώς.
περὶ τῶν Θρᾳκῶν ἐπύθετο ὅτι πλησιάζουσιν.

EXERCISES

LXI

1. The cavalry announce that the enemy are coming. 2. I said that I would write to you first. 3. The messengers said that Cyrus was dead. 4. The judge made it plain that the slave had not stolen the money. 5. I wrote that I would not send him the book. 6. The citizens heard that the army was defeated. 7. The generals were informed that the Persians intended to land at Marathon. 8. We perceive now that we cannot trust you. 9. You did not know that we had seen your father. 10. He had been told that he would be prosecuted for theft.

LXII

1. He thought that his friends would come to his house. 2. They were told that the battle had taken place three days before. 3. I thought in my heart that you had said that out of envy. 4. The soldiers perceived that it would be necessary to cross the river. 5. The soldiers cried aloud that the enemy were fleeing. 6. He proclaimed that they would leave the camp early in the morning. 7. How did they know that you were my friend? 8. You will learn to-morrow that he is dead. 9. I never said that I would send you the dog. 10. The old orator does not know that he never speaks the truth.

LXIII

1. I know now that you are not my friend. 2. They saw that the enemy were not willing to descend into the plain. 3. I am not ignorant that you have often spoken ill of me. 4. They told me that you did not wish to be general. 5. I am told that the natives are drawing near with a very large army. 6. Cyrus saw that his brother kept the middle of the Persian army. 7. They learnt that the generals had suffered dreadful things at the hands of (ὑπό) the Persians. 8. The soldiers perceived that Xenophon was a brave man. 9. I thought that you had never spoken ill of me. 10. I knew that the sailors could not enter the harbour.

LXIV.—RECAPITULATORY

1. Gold is the most precious of metals to man. 2. Slaves and foreigners are deprived of privileges in every city. 3. Happy is the man who finds a noble wife (§ 100). 4. He differs greatly from his brother both in nature and in appearance. 5. Many of us are willing to accuse the gods of injustice. 6. From that day I have always trusted your father. 7. When old and infirm the king shared his authority with his son. 8. He promised to send some of the soldiers next day. 9. Death frees us from all our toils. 10. After this the thieves emptied the house of everything.

LXV.—RECAPITULATORY

1. He will not come to the house owing to his fear of you.　2. The soldiers are in want of food and water.　3. I would rather be a slave on earth than reign beneath the earth.　4. The judge replied that he could not condemn the man to death.　5. The citizens voted to deprive the general of his command.　6. The whole of this island is bare of trees.　7. My fear made all of you afraid.　8. The mother put the cloak on the maiden.　9. The savages despised our soldiers when they saw that they were few in number.　10. Our boys love to contend in boxing.

LXVI.—RECAPITULATORY

1. In former days sailors always trusted the stars.　2. It is not wise to contend with the gods.　3. All has happened just as I wished (§ 155).　4. You have been the cause of all this misery to your parents.　5. The fort used to lie on the left as one sailed into the harbour.　6. The enemy will never refuse to make a truce with us.　7. You cannot journey for the whole day without any food.　8. The poor citizens were put on an equal footing with the rich.　9. During my whole life I have tried to be pious towards the gods and just towards men.　10. I am not surprised that his visit did not please you (§ 155).

B. DEPENDENT INTERROGATIVE PROPOSITIONS.

§§ 246-252

Single: introduced by ὅστις, ὁποῖος, ὁπόσος, ὅπου, ὅποι, εἰ, etc.

Double: introduced by εἰ ... ἤ, πότερον ... ἤ, εἴτε ... εἴτε.

Rule.—When principal verb primary, same mood and tense as if a direct interrogative proposition: when principal verb historic either (1) same mood and tense, or (2) same tense of optative.
For Interrogative Particles see Chapter X.

ἐρωτᾷ ὅστις ἐστίν. ἤρετο ὁπόθεν ἦλθον. οὐκ οἶδεν ὅποι τράπηται. οὐκ ἦσαν ὅποι τράπωνται. ἤρετο πότερον αὐτὸς εἶσιν ἢ σύ. ἠρόμην ὅστις εἴη. οὐκ ᾔδη ὅποι τραποίμην. ἤρετο πότερον ἐγὼ ἴοιμι ἢ σύ. §§ 247, 248.
ἤρετο εἰ οὐκ αἰσχύνεται. ἐρωτῶσι πότερον δέδρακεν ἢ οὔ. σκόπει εἰ ἔτι οὕτως ἔχει ἢ οὔ. οὐκ ἦσαν πότερον πορευθῶσιν ἢ μή. ἐβουλεύετο εἴτε πέμποιέν τινας εἴτε πάντες ἴοιεν. ἐβουλεύετο ὁ φὼρ εἰ λέγοι τἀληθὴ ἢ μή. § 249.

Anticipatory Construction. § 250.

τοὺς νόμους σκοπῶμεν ὅ τι διδάσκουσιν. ἠπόρει περὶ τῆς ὁδοῦ ὅποι φέρει. § 250.

EXERCISES

LXVII.—*Single*

1. He asked me who I was. 2. He asked me which way to turn. 3. They did not know where the road led to. 4. They asked the boy if the road led to the harbour. 5. I will ask him where his father is. 6. They asked me if I was ashamed. 7. The soldiers did not know whither to march. 8. The thieves asked the servant where his master's house was. 9. The ladies asked the sailor how large his ship was. 10. They asked the orator if he believed his own words.

LXVIII.—*Single Negative*

1. They asked me if I was not a rich man. 2. He asked the slave if the road did not lead to the city. 3. I will ask him if he is not my friend's son. 4. He asked me if I was not ashamed. 5. He asked me whether I really believed the orator. 6. The thief asked the boy if that was not his father's house. 7. The ladies asked the boy if he was really a sailor. 8. They did not know whether they were not to trust the general. 9. He asked if he was not to tell his wife the truth. 10. The sailors asked if they were not to go into the city.

LXIX.—*Double*

1. He asked whether you or your father would go. 2. He asked whether I was rich or poor. 3. We asked the sailor whether the road led to the harbour or the city. 4. I shall ask him if his father is at home or in the market-place. 5. They asked me if this was my house or my brother's. 6. The ladies asked the sailor if his ship was large or small. 7. He asked whether they believed the words of the orator or of the king. 8. He asked the citizens whether they believed his words or the king's. 9. We do not know whether to bathe in the river or in the sea. 10. He did not know whether to tell his wife truth or falsehood.

LXX.—*Double Negative*

1. You ask me if I am a rich man or not. 2. I shall ask if the road leads to the city or not. 3. I asked him if he knew my friend or not. 4. He asked me if I had done it or not. 5. I will ask them if they are ashamed or not. 6. He did not know whether to tell me the truth or not. 7. The soldiers did not know whether to trust their general or not. 8. We did not know whether to bathe in the river or not. 9. He asked whether he was to believe the words of the sailor or not. 10. The soldiers do not know whether they are to march or not.

LXXI.—RECAPITULATORY

1. He asked why we were always disputing with one another. 2. Last year I bought a cloak very like yours. 3. I am at a loss how to find money for my son. 4. The boy thought himself as good as his master. 5. But his friends compared the boy to a sheep. 6. Nothing of the sort has ever been said by me. 7. The father asked his son where he obtained his money from. 8. He always tries to act like his elder brother. 9. You shared our hopes and our fears. 10. When he came into the house he immediately smelt the fire.

LXXII.—RECAPITULATORY

1. After that he always kept on the spot. 2. Life seems pleasant to a prosperous man. 3. The enemy restored the exiles to the city. 4. After many years the general was recalled from banishment by the citizens. 5. So the beggar was pitied by you but not helped. 6. The boy was laughed at by all his friends. 7. He pleaded as his excuse that he was hungry and had no money. 8. They were on their guard against the savages night and day. 9. The slaves were cast out of the ship by the sailors. 10. He often tried to borrow money from his friends.

C. CAUSAL PROPOSITIONS. §§ 253, 254

Introduced by ὅτι, ὡς, ὅτε, ἐπεί, ἐπειδή, *with Indicative*

ἐλοιδόρουν με ὅτι Σωκράτει συνῆν. μετεμέλοντο οἱ Ἀθηναῖοι ὅτι οὐ συνέβησαν τοῖς Λακεδαιμονίοις. ἐπειδὴ οἱ πολέμιοι οὐκ ἀνήγοντο εἰσέπλευσαν οἱ Ἀθηναῖοι εἰς τὸν λιμένα. ἐθαύμαζον ὅτι οὐχ οἷός τ' ἦ εὑρεῖν. § 253.

Sub-oblique, implying that the cause is assigned by some other person than the speaker,—Optative, with ὅτι, ὡς, *or* ἐπεί

τὸν Περικλέα ἐκάκιζον ὅτι στρατηγὸς ὢν οὐκ ἐπεξάγοι. οἶσθα αὐτὸν ἐπαινέσαντα τὸν Ἀγαμέμνονα ὡς βασιλεὺς εἴη ἀγαθός. § 254.

EXERCISES

LXXIII.—§ 253

1. They abused the general because he did not conquer the enemy. 2. The citizens repented because they had not made terms with the king. 3. Since they were in need of water they sailed into the harbour. 4. We were surprised that we could not find you. 5. Since the enemy did not stand out to sea we sailed away. 6. They repented because they found the hill very difficult to climb. 7. I am not surprised that you love some of my friends, but not others. 8. He abused the dog because the hare escaped. 9. The citizens are not wise because they hate kings. 10. The horse was afraid because the ditch was twenty feet in breadth.

LXXIV.—§§ 253, 254

1. They abused the orator because he wished to betray the city. 2. He called the cavalry cowards because they did not charge the barbarians. 3. I did not win the race because your brother's horse is very swift. 4. I am not surprised that your friends did not easily catch the fish in the river. 5. The master is wise because at the beginning of his speech he praised the boys. 6. Cyrus charged the centre of the

army because he wished to slay his brother. 7. He spoke ill of me because (as he said) I had not spoken well of him. 8. I like your horse because it has a very beautiful head. 9. I do not praise you because wise boys love both music and gymnastics. 10. I will give you the money because (as you say) you are my dead brother's friend.

LXXV.—§§ 253, 254

1. I will not call you a coward, because the self-same danger frightens some men but not others. 2. The citizens rejoiced because the king was intending (he said) to come to the city. 3. The stranger stayed there three months because the whole city was most beautiful. 4. I do not blame you, because boys do not always admire the beauty of wisdom. 5. I was glad that the man was acquitted on the charge of theft. 6. I am not surprised, because every man loves his own children. 7. Men do not always manage the affairs of a state well because they are philosophers. 8. I say no more because you now are the judges of the matter. 9. I will not come to your house, because I love you but not your friends. 10. He acted thus disgracefully because (he said) injustice was more profitable to him than justice.

D. CONSECUTIVE PROPOSITIONS. §§ 255-259

1. *Introduced by ὥστε = 'and so,' the form of the Proposition being the same as if it were independent.* § 255

οὐχ ἧκεν ὁ Τισσαφέρνης, ὥσθ' οἱ Ἕλληνες ἐφρόντιζον. οὗτοι δὲ πολῖται γιγνόμενοι μείζω ἔτι ἐποίησαν τὴν πόλιν, ὥστε ὕστερον ἀποικίας ἐξέπεμψαν. οὕτω σκαιὸς εἶ ὥστ' οὐ δύνασαι οὐδὲν λογίσασθαι. οἱ δ' εἰς τοσοῦτον ὕβρεως ἦλθον ὥστ' ἔπεισαν ὑμᾶς ἐλαύνειν αὐτὸν ἐξ Ἑλλάδος.

2. *Introduced by ὥστε with the Infinitive.* § 256

πάντα ποιοῦσιν ὥστε δίκην μὴ διδόναι. οἱ ἀκοντισταὶ βραχύτερα ἠκόντιζον ἢ ὥστε ἐξικνεῖσθαι τῶν σφενδονητῶν. τοιαῦτα ἔπασχεν ὥσθ' ἡμᾶς μηδεμίαν ἡμέραν ἀδακρύτους διαγαγεῖν.

3. *ὥστε replaced by οἷος or ὅσος after τοιοῦτος or τοσοῦτος expressed or implied in the principal Proposition.* § 257

τοιοῦτος ἦν οἷος μὴ βούλεσθαι ἀποκτείνειν πολλοὺς τῶν πολιτῶν. ἐλείπετο τῆς νυκτὸς ὅσον σκοταίους διελθεῖν τὸ πεδίον.

4. ὥστε = 'on condition that,' with Infinitive. § 258

πολλὰ ἂν χρήματα ἔδωκεν ὥστ' ἔχειν τὸν ἀγρόν. οὐκ ἐθέλει λαβεῖν τὸ ἀργύριον ὥστε σὲ εὖ λέγειν.

5. ἐφ' ᾧ or ἐφ' ᾧτε = 'on condition that,' with Infinitive or Future Indicative, especially if ἐπὶ τούτῳ precedes. § 258

ἀφίεμέν σε ἐπὶ τούτῳ ἐφ' ᾧτε μηκέτι φιλοσοφεῖν. σπονδὰς ἐποιήσαντο ἐφ' ᾧ κομιοῦνται τοὺς ἄνδρας.

EXERCISES

LXXVI.—§§ 255-257

1. The generals did not come back and so the soldiers became anxious. 2. He sent a thousand of the soldiers back to the city and so the enemy retreated. 3. The boy is so stupid that he cannot learn this. 4. I admire your courage and so I give you my hand. 5. He loved the maiden and so he gave her many presents. 6. The citizens were so foolish that they banished the philosopher. 7. They hated Socrates and so they said that he despised the gods. 8. They became so lost to reason that they wished to put to death all the generals. 9. You are a sensible man and so I believe you will make this money more. 10. He is really brave and so he does not praise his own courage.

LXXVII.—§§ 255-257

1. The boys did everything to escape punishment. 2. He suffered so much that he wished to kill himself. 3. He is not the sort of man to be silent about his own courage. 4. We were so mad that we killed our own best friend. 5. The wolves were so many that they came down into the plain. 6. I am not the sort of man to speak ill of my friends. 7. We are not the sort of men to wish to prosecute you. 8. You

are not the sort of man to wish to rob the poor of their money. 9. Enough of the day is left for them to cross the river. 10. Enough of the night was left for us to attack the enemy in the dark.

LXXVIII.—§ 258

1. I will give you a mina on condition that you leave the city. 2. The farmer would have given more money on condition that he kept that farm. 3. The servant was willing to take the money on condition that he should be silent about the matter. 4. We will let you go on condition that you steal no more. 5. The judge let the boy go on condition that his father should flog him. 6. We will not take the money on condition that we speak well of you. 7. I will send you the dog on condition that you give me the first of the hares you kill. 8. We made a truce on condition that the enemy should give back our men. 9. You shall rule over the rest of the Greeks on condition that you yourselves obey the Great King. 10. The boy will promise anything on condition you do not flog him now.

LXXIX

1. The orator spoke so fast that we could not understand his words. 2. The boys made so much noise that the master could not hear his own words. 3. The father works hard so that his children will be

rich and happy. 4. The man did not return at night, and so his wife grew anxious. 5. He promised to spare the citizens on condition that they sent the orators to him. 6. He is not the sort of man to ever blame himself. 7. The citizens became very numerous and so they sent out colonies. 8. I will not punish you on condition that you promise never to do this again. 9. Nothing will be said by me, so you can return home without fear. 10. Do not offer me money on condition that I hold my tongue about that.

LXXX.—RECAPITULATORY

1. Nothing of the kind has ever been said by me. 2. They said that the house was of stone. 3. Now that you are young and prosperous you are rich in friends. 4. The old man lived for many years at Megara. 5. On the day before the battle the enemy descended from the hills. 6. The soldiers halted and waited for the cavalry. 7. Let us devote ourselves to helping the poor. 8. Strike, said he, but hear me. 9. Young men often wish to die, but old men never. 10. The thief said that he was forced to steal the money.

E. FINAL PROPOSITIONS. §§ 260-265

1. *Introduced by* ἵνα, ὅπως, ὡς, ἵνα μή, ὅπως μή, ὡς μή, *with the Present or Aorist Subjunctive, or, if the principal verb is a past tense or historic present, by either Subjunctive or Optative.* §§ 260-262

τοὺς φίλους εὖ ποίει ἵνα αὐτὸς εὖ πράττῃς. ἐπίτηδές σε οὐκ ἤγειρον ἵνα ὡς ἥδιστα διάγῃς. Ἀριστεὺς ταῦτα συνεβούλευεν ὅπως ἐπὶ πλέον ὁ σῖτος ἀντίσχῃ. Κῦρος φίλων ᾤετο δεῖσθαι ὡς συνέργους ἔχοι. φίλος ἐβούλετο εἶναι τοῖς μέγιστα δυναμένοις, ἵνα ἀδικῶν μὴ διδοίη δίκην. διανοεῖται τὴν γέφυραν λῦσαι ὡς μὴ διαβῆτε.

2. *After Imperatives and the equivalents of the Imperative* ὡς ἄν *and* ὅπως ἄν *with Subjunctive.* § 263

πρόσεχε τὸν νοῦν, ὡς ἂν εἰδῇς ὅσα σοὶ γενήσεται ἀγαθά, ἢν παρ' ἡμῖν μένῃς. ἄξεις ἡμᾶς ὅπως ἂν εἰδῶμεν. ὡς ἂν μάθῃς, ἀντάκουσον.

3. *After Optatives expressing a wish,* ἵνα, ὅπως, ὡς *with the Optative, by attraction.* § 264

εἴθε ἥκοις ἵνα γνοίης.

EXERCISES

LXXXI.—§§ 260-262

1. A wise man serves his friends in order that he himself may prosper. 2. I will awake you that you may see the fire. 3. He did not awake us that we might not be frightened. 4. I read to the old man that he might spend the time as pleasantly as possible. 5. We all need friends that we may have helpmates. 6. They sailed away from the city in order to find a safer harbour. 7. They threw the slaves overboard that they might not be found by our sailors. 8. They ate many strange animals that the food might hold out for longer. 9. He gave many presents to the maiden that she might love him. 10. They advanced at midnight in order that the barbarians might not follow them.

LXXXII.—§§ 263, 264

1. Listen, that you may become a wiser boy. 2. Go, that I may no longer see your wickedness. 3. Go, lest I slay you with my own hand. 4. Come tomorrow that I may show you my horses. 5. You will take a guide that you may not miss the road. 6. You will do this, that I may speak well of you to your father. 7. Oh that I might go to Athens to

see the beauty of its temples. 8. Oh that we could conquer the enemy that they might no longer ravage our land. 9. Would that my money were not spent that I might give you what you long for. 10. Oh that I were a man that I might do what pleased me.

LXXXIII

1. The young man works now in order that he may not be poor in his old age. 2. The sailor made a voyage to Asia in order to make his money more. 3. You praise my virtue that I may praise yours. 4. He flogged the boy to make him better. 5. Listen, that you may know the wisdom of the orator. 6. They returned to the camp lest the enemy should see them. 7. Oh that I had more money, that I might buy such a horse. 8. You will take the book that you may give it to your mother. 9. The traitor left the camp at night to announce this to the enemy. 10. Slay me, lest I tell you the truth.

LXXXIV

1. Your father will be present to prosecute my son for murder. 2. Let us do good to our friends that they may not speak ill of us. 3. He rode to the city at full speed to announce that the enemy were at hand. 4. Let us praise what is honourable that all men may speak well of us. 5. The soldiers will

gladly march for the whole night that they may be able to ravage the enemy's country. 6. You said that in order to deceive us. 7. Let us tell him what is false that he may miss his way. 8. Your brothers gave him a swift horse that he might escape from the city. 9. Listen that you may be a wise man for the future. 10. Oh that I had been present to save you from that danger.

LXXXV

1. The soldiers set out at daybreak in order to reach the camp at mid-day. 2. They fortified the city that they might be able to hold out against the attacks of the enemy. 3. Boys are taught self-restraint that they may become good and noble citizens. 4. The poor man asserted that he had money in plenty in order that his friends might admire him. 5. The boys shall for the future go to bed in the dark that they may not lie awake and talk to one another. 6. Wait, that I may give you the books I promised. 7. Oh that I were young again that I might lead a wiser life. 8. The poet praises the rich and powerful in order that they may give him gifts. 9. Stags have very keen sight in order that they may escape their many enemies. 10. He fled at night from the city in order that he might not be put to death by his enemies.

EASY EXERCISES IN GREEK SYNTAX 79

F. PROPOSITIONS INTRODUCED BY ὅπως COMPLETING
THE SENSE OF VERBS OF STRIVING AND THE LIKE.
§§ 266-269

1. ὅπως *or* ὅπως μή *with Future Indicative* (*or* ὅτῳ τρόπῳ, ὅπῃ, ὅποι, *etc., when their sense is more appropriate*). §§ 266, 267

φρόντιζ' ὅπως μηδὲν ἀνάξιον τῆς τιμῆς ταύτης πράξεις. ἔπραττον ὅπως τις βοήθεια ἥξει. σκόπει ὅπως μὴ ψευδῆ λέξεις. ὥσπερ τὸν ποιμένα δεῖ ἐπιμελεῖσθαι ὅπως σᾶ τε ἔσται τὰ πρόβατα καὶ τὰ ἐπιτήδεια ἕξει, οὕτω καὶ τὸν στρατηγὸν ἐπιμελεῖσθαι δεῖ ὅπως σῷοί τε οἱ στρατιῶται ἔσονται καὶ τὰ ἐπιτήδεια ἕξουσιν.

2. *The Future Optative may replace the Fut. Indic. when the principal verb is a past tense or historic present.* § 268

ἐπεμελεῖτο ὅπως μὴ ἄσιτοί ποτε ἔσοιντο. ἐμηχανώμεθα ὅπως μηδεὶς γνώσοιτο. ἐσκόπει ὅπως ταῦτα γενήσοιτο.

3. ὅπως *or* ὅπως μή *with Future Indicative introducing an emphatic warning or exhortation, without any principal Proposition expressed.* § 269

ὅπως οὖν ἔσεσθε ἄνδρες ἄξιοι τῆς ἐλευθερίας. ὅπως τοίνυν περὶ τοῦ πολέμου μηδὲν ἐρεῖς.

EXERCISES

LXXXVI

1. Let us take thought to do nothing unworthy of good men. 2. They exerted themselves to send help to the city. 3. See that you do what you promised me. 4. Take care, my son, to be friendly only with the rich and prosperous. 5. He took care that the poor young man should not see his daughter. 6. The herdsmen watched that the thieves should not carry off the cows. 7. The shepherds take care that wolves shall not kill the sheep at night. 8. The master takes care that the pupils have good food. 9. They prepared to make their city stronger than ever. 10. Prudent men take care to openly do nothing unworthy.

LXXXVII

1. Those parents were not careful that their children should never be without food. 2. A good general will be careful that his soldiers are safe. 3. I will see that you get your provisions. 4. The good priest exerted himself to get help for the poor. 5. He answered that he would take care that all was right. 6. Take care lest you are seen by the master. 7. Take care lest the wolves attack the sheep to-night. 8. Oh, indeed, show yourselves men worthy of your ancestors. 9. Now, pray, say nothing about the

matters which I told you. 10. Now, pray, do not say anything about this to your son.

LXXXVIII

1. They are exerting themselves to save their native land. 2. Take care not to tell everything to such a man. 3. The citizens were careful not to speak ill of the king. 4. See that you tell the judge the whole truth. 5. A prudent man will take care to enjoy the good things that he possesses. 6. The sailors were preparing to attack the enemy's ships. 7. Now, pray, do not speak ill of your own brother. 8. The slave took care to conceal the matter from his master. 9. Now, pray, do not ask me all these questions. 10. My parents took thought to have me taught music.

LXXXIX.—RECAPITULATORY

1. He said that nothing of the sort had ever been done by him. 2. They slept at night on the ground. 3. You overcame us by cunning and by force. 4. Are you angry with me or not? 5. You will not be able to reach the city on foot in three days. 6. I will not listen to such words. 7. The dog followed his master all day. 8. They are trying to deceive their own father. 9. Am I to spare you when I remember your evil deeds? 10. He said that to frighten you.

G. PROPOSITIONS INTRODUCED BY μη, COMPLETING THE SENSE OF VERBS DENOTING FEAR, CAUTION, OR DANGER. §§ 270-274

I fear lest (or that) . . . . φοβοῦμαι μή . . .
I fear lest (or that) . . . not . . . φοβοῦμαι μὴ οὐ . .

1. *Fear referring to the future: the same construction as Final Propositions, viz.—if the principal verb is primary, Subjunctive; if the principal verb is historic, Subjunctive or, sometimes, Optative.* § 271

δεδίασι μὴ οἱ πολέμιοι ἐπεκπλεύσωσιν. ἐδέδισαν μὴ οἱ πολέμιοι ἐπεκπλεύσωσιν (or ἐπεκπλεύσειαν). οὐδεὶς κίνδυνος ἐδόκει εἶναι μή τις ἐπίσποιτο.

Future Indicative sometimes, when the idea of futurity is to be emphasised. § 271

ὁρᾶν χρὴ μὴ οὐδ᾽ ἕξομεν μεθ᾽ ὅτου τῶν βαρβάρων κρατήσομεν.

2. *Fear referring to present or past,—Indicative.* § 272

νῦν φοβούμεθα μὴ ἀμφοτέρων ἅμα ἡμαρτήκαμεν. δέδοικα μὴ πληγῶν δέει. φοβοῦμαι μὴ διὰ φθόνον ἔδρασεν.

3. μὴ and Subjunctive (without any principal proposition) to convey anxiety or suspicion. § 273

μὴ ἀγροικότερον ᾖ τὸ ἀληθὲς εἰπεῖν. ἀλλὰ μὴ οὐ τοῦτ' ᾖ χαλεπόν.

4. Anticipatory Construction. § 274

ὑποπτεύομεν καὶ ὑμᾶς μὴ οὐ κοινοὶ ἀποβῆτε. ἐπεμελεῖτο τῶν ἀνδρῶν ὅπως πιστοὶ ἔσοιντο. περὶ τῶν φυλάκων φοβούμεθα μὴ οὐ ἀνταμύνωνται.

EXERCISES

XC.—*Future.* § 271

1. They fear lest the enemy should depart in the night.   2. They feared lest the enemy's ships should sail into the harbour.   3. There is no risk of any one reporting this to the enemy.   4. There was no risk of the enemy's ships sailing out against them.   5. I am afraid that you will miss both things at once.   6. I was afraid that you would think me very rude.   7. I am afraid that the boy will need a flogging.   8. They were afraid that the soldiers would not be faithful.   9. The general was afraid that he would not be able to conquer the enemy.   10. There was no risk of the sentries running away through fear.

XCI.—*Present and Past.* § 272

1. The general feared that the enemy had departed to the hills.   2. They feared lest more ships had sailed into the harbour in the night.   3. There is no risk that any one has reported this to the enemy.   4. He was afraid that he had missed the road to the city.   5. I am afraid that you think my boy very rude.   6. The general was afraid that the soldiers were not faithful.   7. I am afraid that the slave needs a

flogging. 8. I was afraid that you had said that from envy. 9. We fear that you have not told us the worst. 10. I am afraid that he often speaks ill of his friends.

XCII

1. The general is not afraid that his soldiers will run away from the barbarians. 2. I am not afraid that my dog will not be able to catch the hare. 3. I fear that you concealed the truth from your father. 4. The master feared that he would never be able to teach that boy music. 5. I fear that you will never consider me your benefactor. 6. The boy feared that he would never be able to make this clear to his father. 7. I am afraid that I have very keen sight. 8. I fear that you struck your brother a blow. 9. I fear that you were not forced to this. 10. I am afraid that you have not come the quickest way.

XCIII

1. I am afraid that it is impossible to teach some men wisdom. 2. The herdsmen were afraid that they would be robbed of their cows. 3. He was afraid that he would never be elected general by the citizens. 4. There is no risk of my ever feeling that fear of yours (§ 72, 1). 5. I am afraid that in many points I do not agree with you. 6. The

mother feared that her son would have a headache. 7. I am afraid that the ship is now twenty furlongs from land. 8. For this very reason I am afraid that you deserve a flogging. 9. I fear the philosopher is not good at statecraft. 10. I feared that you were not a Greek by birth.

XCIV.—RECAPITULATORY

1. The dog was killed by the farmer because it pursued the sheep. 2. Such men will always be held in bad repute among their neighbours. 3. The citizens defended themselves for two years against the enemy. 4. He asked me whether my horse was swifter than his. 5. Do not tell me that you were not found guilty of theft: I went to the city myself to see the trial. 6. I am afraid that you speak the truth: the boy is very foolish. 7. I know not whether what you say is false or not: but I hope that it is not true. 8. Let us never be persuaded by such men to do what is not honourable. 9. I am afraid that my slave will not come with the dog till mid-day. 10. They hoped to escape: but the judge condemned them all to death.

H. CONDITIONAL PROPOSITIONS. §§ 275-289
TABLE
ORATIO RECTA
I.—Present and Past Conditions
A. *PARTICULAR SUPPOSITIONS*
(1) *Nothing implied as to the fulfilment of the Condition*

Present. εἰ ταῦτα λέγει ἁμαρτάνει, if he says this he is wrong.

Past { εἰ ταῦτα ἔλεγεν ἡμάρτανεν, if he said this (at the time) he was wrong.
εἰ ταῦτα ἔλεξεν ἥμαρτεν, if he said this he was wrong.

(2) *Implied that the Condition is not fulfilled*

Present. εἰ ταῦτα ἔλεγεν ἡμάρτανεν ἄν, if he said this (now) he would be wrong.

Past { εἰ ταῦτα ἔλεγεν ἡμάρτανεν ἄν, if he had said this he would have been wrong.
εἰ ταῦτα ἔλεξεν ἥμαρτεν ἄν, if he had said this he would have been wrong.

But ἄν is omitted with ἔδει, χρῆν, προσῆκεν, ἐξῆν, οἷόν τ' ἦν, and verbals in -τέον with ἦν.

B. *GENERAL SUPPOSITIONS*

Present. ἐὰν ταῦτα λέγῃ ἁμαρτάνει, if ever (= whenever) he says this he is wrong.

Past. εἰ ταῦτα λέγοι ἡμάρτανεν, if ever (= whenever) he said this he used to be wrong.

II.—Future Conditions

Vivid { ἐὰν ταῦτα λέξῃ ἁμαρτήσεται, if he says this he will be wrong.
εἰ ταῦτα λέξει ἁμαρτήσεται, if he *will* say (i.e. insists on saying) this he will be wrong.

Less Vivid. εἰ ταῦτα λέξειε ἁμάρτοι ἄν, if he were to say this he would be wrong.

ORATIO OBLIQUA

IN PAST TIME

I. A. (1). *Present.* ἔλεξεν ὅτι εἰ ταῦτα λέγει ἁμαρτάνει.
ἔλεξεν ὅτι εἰ ταῦτα λέγοι ἁμαρτάνοι.
Past. ἔλεξεν ὅτι εἰ ταῦτα ἔλεγεν ἡμάρτανεν.
ἔλεξεν ὅτι εἰ ταῦτα ἔλεξεν ἥμαρτεν.
(2). *Present.* ἔλεξεν ὅτι εἰ ταῦτα ἔλεγεν ἡμάρτανεν ἄν.
Past. ἔλεξεν ὅτι εἰ ταῦτα ἔλεγεν ἡμάρτανεν ἄν.
ἔλεξεν ὅτι εἰ ταῦτα ἔλεξεν ἥμαρτεν ἄν.
B. *Present.* ἔλεξεν ὅτι ἐὰν ταῦτα λέγῃ ἁμαρτάνει.
ἔλεξεν ὅτι εἰ ταῦτα λέγοι ἁμαρτάνοι.
Past. ἔλεξεν ὅτι εἰ ταῦτα λέγοι ἡμάρτανεν.
II. *Vivid.* ἔλεξεν ὅτι ἐὰν ταῦτα λέξῃ ἁμαρτήσεται.
ἔλεξεν ὅτι εἰ ταῦτα λέξειε ἁμαρτήσοιτο.
ἔλεξεν ὅτι εἰ ταῦτα λέξει ἁμαρτήσεται.
ἔλεξεν ὅτι εἰ ταῦτα λέξοι ἁμαρτήσοιτο.
Less Vivid. ἔλεξεν ὅτι εἰ ταῦτα λέξειε ἁμάρτοι ἄν.

If the infinitive is used instead of a ὅτι clause the protasis is as above, the apodosis in the infinitive, the tense of the infinitive being the same as the tense which would be required if the sentence was direct, not indirect.

EXAMPLES

I

I. A. (1). εἰ θεοὶ εἰσίν, ἔστι καὶ ἔργα θεῶν. ἀλλ' εἰ δοκεῖ σοί, πλέωμεν. κάκιστ' ἀπολοίμην, Ξανθίαν εἰ μὴ φιλῶ. εἰ ἔδοξεν αὐτοῖς πράττωμεν. εἰ μὴ τοῦτον ἐφίλουν ἀπολοίμην. § 280.

I. A. (2). ταῦτα οὐκ ἂν ἐδύναντο ποιεῖν εἰ μὴ διαίτῃ μετρίᾳ ἐχρῶντο. οὐκ ἂν νήσων ἐκράτει ὁ Ἀγαμέμνων, εἰ μή τι καὶ ναυτικὸν εἶχεν. καὶ ἴσως ἂν ἀπωλόμην εἰ ἐπεχείρησα τὰ πολιτικά. εἰ ἦσαν ἄνδρες ἀγαθοὶ φανερωτέραν ἐξῆν αὐτοῖς τὴν ἀρετὴν δεικνύναι. χρῆν δὲ σέ, εἴπερ ἦσθα χρηστός, μηνυτὴν γενέσθαι. §§ 281, 282.

I. B. γελᾷ δ' ὁ μῶρος κἄν τι μὴ γελοῖον ᾖ. ἅπας λόγος ἐὰν ἀπῇ τὰ πράγματα μάταιόν τι φαίνεται καὶ κενόν. οὐκ ἔπινεν εἰ μὴ διψῴη. εἴ τις ἀντείποι εὐθὺς ἐτεθνήκει. § 283.

II

II. ἐὰν ζητῇς καλῶς, εὑρήσεις. ἔσομαι πλούσιος ἢν θεὸς θέλῃ. ἐὰν μὴ ἐκ προνοίας ἀποκτείνῃ τίς τινα, φευγέτω.

εἰ Ἕκτορα ἀποκτενεῖς, αὐτὸς ἀποθανεῖ. εἰ δὲ φοβησόμεθα τοὺς κινδύνους, εἰς πολλὰς ταραχὰς καταστήσομεν ὑμᾶς. εἰ μὴ φράσεις ἀπολῶ σε κακῶς.

εἰ θησαυρῷ τις ἐντύχοι, πλουσιώτερος ἂν εἴη, οἰκονομικώτερος δ' οὔ. εἰ βούλοιο ἰατρὸς γενέσθαι, τί ἂν ποιοίης; §§ 284-286.

III

ἐὰν or εἴ πως = 'in case,' 'in hope that.' § 288

ἔπεμψαν πρέσβεις εἴ πως αὐτοὺς πείσειαν. ἐπιβουλεύουσιν ἐξελθεῖν ἢν δύνωνται βιάσασθαι. § 288.

IV

Concessive. § 289

γελᾷ δ' ὁ μῶρος κἄν τι μὴ γελοῖον ᾖ. μὴ θορυβήσητε μηδ' ἐὰν δόξω τι ὑμῖν μέγα λέγειν.

EXERCISES

Present and Past Conditions

XCV

1. We cannot do this if we have not ships.   2. We could not have done this if we had not had ships.   3. You would not do this (now), if you were not brave.   4. If you said that, you were wrong.   5. If you say that, you are wrong.   6. If he used to say that, he was wrong.   7. If he had been brave, he would not have done that.   8. He laughs if that man speaks.   9. We laughed if ever that man spoke.   10. They would have laughed if that man had spoken.

XCVI

1. If the boy said that, he was wrong.   2. If the master says that, he is wrong.   3. He is not good if he says such things.   4. If he were saying such things he would not be good.   5. If he had said that, he would not have been wrong.   6. If he had not said that, he would have been wrong.   7. If any one said such things he used to be put to death.   8. If any one says such things he is put to death.   9. If he had said such things he would have been put to death.   10. If he were good he would not say such things.

Future Conditions

XCVII

1. We shall not be able to do this if we have not ships. 2. We should be able to do this if we were to have ships. 3. You will be able to do that, if you are brave. 4. You would be able to do that, if you were to be brave. 5. If you say that, you will be wrong. 6. If you were to say that, you would be wrong. 7. He will laugh if the orator speaks. 8. He would laugh if the orator were to speak. 9. We should laugh if you were to speak. 10. You will laugh if we speak.

XCVIII

1. If the boy says that, he will be wrong. 2. If the master said that, he would be wrong. 3. If the boy says that, the master will laugh. 4. If the master were to say that, the boy would laugh. 5. If the boy says such things he will not be good. 6. If we were to say such things you would laugh. 7. If any one says such things he will be put to death. 8. If any one were to say such things he would be put to death. 9. If you said that to the king you would be put to death. 10. If you say such things to the king you will be put to death.

Present and Past Conditions

XCIX

1. We should not have been able to do this if we had not been brave men. 2. We cannot rule over the islands if we have not ships. 3. I should not be laughing if it were not ridiculous. 4. He would not have drunk if he had not been thirsty. 5. If your friend says this he is wrong. 6. If you drank that you were very thirsty. 7. If he has killed the man he did it without premeditation. 8. I should have been rich if God had pleased. 9. If I were your brother I should wish to be a physician. 10. If it seems good to you let us leave the city to-day.

C

1. If ever you say that, you are wrong. 2. You cannot conquer the islands if you have no ships. 3. Boys eat even if they are not hungry. 4. He used to laugh if that man began to speak. 5. The master was wrong if he used to tell you that. 6. If they had been honest men they ought to have told the whole truth. 7. If he had been an honest man it would have been possible for him to give back the money. 8. If you had wished, you would have had a

chance of becoming a physician. 9. If any soldier refused to obey the general he was at once put to death. 10. Women weep even if there be no need for tears.

Future Conditions

CI

1. If you seek happiness you will not find it. 2. I should be rich if God were to wish it. 3. If you wish to be a physician what will you do? 4. If you were to kill a man you would yourself be slain. 5. If a man finds a treasure he will be richer but not more thrifty. 6. If you were to seek well you would find. 7. You would be able to do that, if you were brave men. 8. You will not be able to rule over the islands if you have no ships. 9. A fool will laugh even if a thing is not ridiculous. 10. A horse will not drink if it is not thirsty.

CII

1. If you were to kill a man without premeditation you would be banished. 2. If God pleases we shall become rich. 3. Those men would drink even if they were not thirsty. 4. If they are honest men they will give back the money. 5. If you were to wish it you could become a physician. 6. If the soldier refuses to obey the general he will at once be put to death. 7. If you do this men will think you foolish.

8. If you tell lies you will be flogged. 9. If you become an informer all men will despise you. 10. If you fear the risk do not go into the battle.

CIII.—§§ 288, 289

1. I will send ambassadors in the hope of persuading them. 2. I sent my friend in the hope of persuading you. 3. I gave him many gifts in the hope of pleasing him. 4. They wished to leave the city in case they could find a safe ship. 5. Do not laugh even if I say something foolish. 6. We shall not interrupt even if you do not persuade us. 7. He sent many gifts to the maiden in the hope of pleasing her mother. 8. I will give you the book in the hope that you will read it. 9. They formed the plan of killing the king in case they could escape the notice of the guards. 10. You will not find happiness although you seek it everywhere.

CIV

1. If you go to the city you will not find your friend. 2. If you really had a pain in your head you would not do that. 3. If you did this both you and your friends would fare well. 4. If I had really seen the enemy I should have told you. 5. Obey your parents if you wish to prosper. 6. If this is really

so it is time for us to go. 7. If you have the money give it to me. 8. If philosophers were kings the state would not prosper. 9. If you had loved me you would not have said that. 10. If philosophers were to be kings the state would not prosper.

CV

1. If you love me, love my dog also. 2. If he had told me that, I should not have believed him. 3. If you steal that money you will be punished. 4. If he told me that, I should not believe him. 5. If he had taken the dog he would have been prosecuted for theft. 6. If you do this you will injure the state. 7. If I had told him the truth he would not have believed me. 8. I should not be surprised if you were found guilty of murder. 9. If I had been tried for murder I should have killed myself. 10. If Cyrus had any money he would give it to the soldiers.

CVI

1. If we had done that we should not have fared ill. 2. If the wisest men had always managed the affairs of the state the citizens would not have been so bad. 3. If ever he saw a poor man he used to give him money. 4. If you·do this both you and your friends will prosper greatly. 5. If you *will* do this I cannot hinder you: but it is not honourable. 6. If you cannot do all this you must do what

you can. 7. If you do not obey the judge you will be punished for your insolence. 8. If I asked my father for money I should never get it. 9. If you had not talked so much you would not have had a headache. 10. If he were to be convicted of theft he would pay the severest penalty.

CVII

1. If you become a friend of Cyrus he will never abandon you. 2. He would have been put to death by the king if his mother had not begged him off. 3. If Cyrus had been the elder of the two sons he would have become king. 4. If Cyrus is able he will make himself king. 5. If the Persians had not plundered the camp the Greeks would not have been without food. 6. If the Persians wished they could destroy the army of the Greeks. 7. If Cyrus slew his brother he would become king himself. 8. If ever Cyrus loved a man he used to give him many presents. 9. If he sees soldiers marching well he always praises them. 10. If you come to Asia I will make you a friend to Cyrus.

CVIII

1. If you are silent about that I shall be chosen general. 2. If you advance against their lines the enemy will flee. 3. If you had stolen my dog you would have been prosecuted for theft. 4. If you were wise you would not go to the city. 5. If he

had not seen you he would not have told me that. 6. If the citizens were worthy of death they would be punished. 7. If he had spoken the truth I should have given him the money. 8. If this had not been so I should not have gone away. 9. If you were to be found guilty of murder the citizens would put you to death. 10. If you were wise you should manage my affairs.

CIX

1. If the philosopher had been really wise the citizens would not have put him to death. 2. If I have the money to-morrow, I will give it to you. 3. If he did that he would greatly injure his friends. 4. If he had really been wise he would have managed his own affairs better. 5. If philosophers were to manage the affairs of the state the citizens would not prosper. 6. If you had been prosecuted for theft you would have been found guilty. 7. If you cannot do all this you will be punished. 8. If you *will* ask me such questions I shall not answer. 9. If he had not died I should not have been poor. 10. If you do not know that to-morrow, the master will flog you.

CX

1. If your brothers had given him a swifter horse he would have escaped to the hills. 2. If he were prosecuted for murder he would not be found guilty.

3. If there is any necessity I myself will send a messenger. 4. If he were to wash himself once a day he would become more beautiful. 5. If the king knew that, he would not lay waste our land. 6. His brother would have escaped if the ship had not been destroyed crew and all. 7. If such acts as these are praiseworthy why do you not do them? 8. If those men had been savages they would not have acted more disgracefully. 9. The judge would not praise the defendant if he were wise. 10. If the soldiers ravage the greater part of our land their king will praise them.

CXI

1. If the dog had not killed the sheep I should not have beaten it. 2. If my dog were to pursue sheep I should kill it. 3. If a man kills another he is tried for murder. 4. If you were a true philosopher you would not be afraid to die. 5. Do not speak so fast if you wish us to obey you. 6. If your friends were wiser they would be faring better. 7. If I had seen the horse before, I should never have wished to possess it. 8. If his wife was present he always used to drink water. 9. If you really saw a wolf you would run away. 10. If he had not been a fool he would never have believed that woman.

ORATIO OBLIQUA

CXII

1. He said that we could not do that if we had not ships. 2. He said that if I had been brave I should not have done that. 3. I said that I would not laugh if he spoke. 4. I told the boy that if he said that, he was wrong. 5. They told us that if we spoke ill of the king we should be put to death. 6. I told him that if he had been good he would not have said such things. 7. They said that they would not have been able to do that if they had not had ships. 8. He told me that I could do it if I were brave. 9. The general told the soldiers that if they were brave they would be able to conquer the enemy. 10. He said that he would not have laughed if he had seen me.

CXIII

1. He said that horses never drink unless they are thirsty. 2. He told his friends that he would give them a share of the money if he ever got it. 3. He said that if God had pleased, he would have become rich. 4. He said that he would send his son to me in the hope of persuading me. 5. They said that they would have killed the king if they had escaped the notice of the guards. 6. He told me that if I had really loved him I should not have done that. 7. He said that if he were caught he should kill himself.

8. They said that if we had done this we should not have fared so ill. 9. The slave said that even if he had stolen the money he would not have been punished. 10. He said that if his father had not died he would not have been so poor.

CXIV

1. He said that even if we killed a man we should not be prosecuted in such a city. 2. He told us that if we were wise we should not go to the king. 3. I told him that if he had seen me he would have been afraid to do that. 4. He answered that if this was really so he would go away at once. 5. He said that if ever he had money he used to give it to his wife. 6. The general said that if his own son had done that he would have put him to death. 7. He told us that if he had had any money he would have given it to us. 8. I answered that if the king had not been wise the state would not have been so prosperous. 9. He says that if a man speaks ill of his friends he is always abused by them himself. 10. He said that even if we did not believe him we ought at least to believe the words of all our friends.

CXV

1. I believed that if the enemy had not ravaged the country they would have acted more wisely. 2. He said that if we were wise we should not trust that man any longer. 3. He said that if I had been wiser

I should have admired the beauty of the islands. 4. He said that had he been able he would have gladly managed our affairs. 5. We told her that if she were wise she would admire her husband's wisdom. 6. He answered that if we came to the city he would not be able to see us. 7. I thought that you had come to the harbour in the hope of seeing the sailor. 8. Do you think that if Socrates were alive now men would listen to him? 9. He told us that if our father had bidden us do this it was wise to obey him. 10. I answered that if he really wished to know the truth I would tell it him.

CXVI

1. If you *will* drink such wine you will be ill to-morrow. 2. He believed that his brother would have escaped if he had given money to the judge. 3. I think that he will speak the truth if you ask him yourself. 4. You said that you would come whenever we wished. 5. I told him that if he would avoid the company of the bad, he would be a better and a happier boy. 6. If you *will* associate with worthless friends, you will be in bad repute with honourable men. 7. They said that they would have gone to the island if they had not feared the sea. 8. I will not punish you if you will tell me the whole truth. 9. He said that he should not be afraid even if he missed his way. 10. If you *will* give all your money to your friends you will be a beggar in your old age.

I. RELATIVE PROPOSITIONS. §§ 290-300

CLASS I

(1) *Dependent only in Form: same form as if independent*
§ 290

ὃ οὐ γενήσεται. ὃ οὐκ ἂν ἐγένετο. ὃ μὴ γένοιτο.

(2) *Indicating Cause: same form as if independent.* § 291

πῶς οὖν καλὸς ἔσται, ὃς ἠθέλησε τοιαῦτα λέγειν. θαυμαστὸν ποιεῖς ὅστις ἡμῖν οὐδὲν δίδως.

(3) *Indicating Consequence; generally ὅστις: same form as if independent.* § 292

τίς οὕτως μαίνεται ὅστις οὐ βούλεταί σοι φίλος ειναι; ἐβουλήθη τοιοῦτον μνημεῖον καταλιπεῖν ὃ μὴ τῆς ἀνθρωπίνης φύσεως ἐστίν.[1] οὐκ ἔστιν οὔτε ζωγράφος, οὔτ' ἀνδριαντοποιὸς ὅστις τοιοῦτον ἂν κάλλος πλάσειεν οἷον ἡ ἀλήθεια ἔχει.

(4) *Indicating Purpose: always Future Indicative; negatived by μή.* § 293

ἔδοξε τῷ δήμῳ τριάκοντα ἄνδρας ἑλέσθαι οἳ τοὺς πατρίους νόμους συγγράψουσιν. οὐ γὰρ ἔστι μοι χρήματα ὁπόθεν ἐκτίσω. παῖδές μοι οὐκέτι εἰσὶν οἵ με θεραπεύσουσιν.

[1] μή not οὐ when a notion of purpose is to be imparted.

CLASS II.—CONDITIONAL RELATIVE PROPOSITIONS

§§ 295-300

I.—Present and Past Relative Conditions

A. *PARTICULAR SUPPOSITIONS.* §§ 295, 296

(1) *Nothing implied as to fulfilment of condition*

Present {ὅ τι βούλεται, δίδωμι or δώσω.
[εἴ τι βούλεται, δίδωμι or δώσω.]

Past {ὅ τι ἐβούλετο ἔδωκα.
[εἴ τι ἐβούλετο ἔδωκα.]

(2) *Condition not fulfilled*

Present {ὅ τι ἐβούλετο ἐδίδουν ἄν.
[εἴ τι ἐβούλετο ἐδίδουν ἄν.]

Past {ὅ τι ἐβούλετο ἔδωκα ἄν.
[εἴ τι ἐβούλετο ἔδωκα ἄν.]

B. *GENERAL SUPPOSITIONS.* § 297

Present {ὅ τι ἂν βούληται δίδωμι.
[ἐάν τι βούληται, δίδωμι.]

Past {ὅ τι βούλοιτο, ἐδίδουν.
[εἴ τι βούλοιτο, ἐδίδουν.]

II.—Future Relative Conditions. §§ 298, 299

Vivid { ὅ τι ἂν βουληθῇ δώσω.
[ἐάν τι βουληθῇ δώσω.]

Less Vivid { ὅ τι βούλοιτο, δοίην ἄν.
[εἴ τι βούλοιτο, δοίην ἄν.]

Examples of Conditional Relative Propositions

I. A. (1). ἃ νομίζει, ταῦτα λέγει. ἃ ἐνόμισαν, ταῦτα ἔλεξαν. ἃ μὴ οἶδα οὐκ οἴομαι εἰδέναι.

I. A. (2). οὐ γὰρ ἂν ἐπεχειροῦμεν πράττειν ἃ μὴ ἠπιστάμεθα. ἃ μὴ ἐβουλήθη δοῦναι, οὐκ ἂν ἔδωκεν. ὅ τι μὴ ἐγένετο οὐκ ἂν εἶπον.

I. B. ἃ ἂν νομίζῃ, ταῦτα λέγει. ἃ νομίζοι ταῦτα ἔλεγεν. οὓς ἴδοι εὐτάκτως ἰόντας, πάντας ἐπῄνει. συμμαχεῖν τούτοις ἐθέλουσιν ἅπαντες οὓς ἂν ὁρῶσι παρεσκευασμένους. ἐπορευόμεθα διὰ τῆς χώρας, ἣν μὲν ἐθέλοιμεν πορθοῦντες, ἣν δ᾽ ἐθέλοιμεν κατακάοντες.

II. ἃ ἂν νομίζῃ λέξει. νέος δ᾽ ἀπόλλυται ὅντιν᾽ ἂν φιλῇ θεός. ἃ νομίζοι λέξειεν ἄν. ὀκνοίην γὰρ ἂν εἰς τὰ πλοῖα ἐμβαίνειν ἃ ἡμῖν δοίη.

Attraction. § 300

ἔρδοι τις ἣν ἕκαστος εἰδείη τέχνην. ἐὰν πάντες οἳ ἂν δύνωνται ταῦτα ποιῶσι, καλῶς ἕξει. εἰ πάντες οἳ δύναιντο ταῦτα ποιοῖεν, καλῶς ἂν ἔχοι. συνεγιγνώσκετε γὰρ ἄν μοι εἰ ἐν ἐκείνῃ τῇ φωνῇ ἔλεγον ἐν ᾗπερ ἐτεθράμμην.

EXERCISES [1]

CLASS I

CXVII.—§§ 290-293

1. They said they would slay all the citizens, but that God forbid. 2. But this would not have been said if I had been present. 3. I cannot praise you who have acted thus. 4. He acts strangely in not giving money to his wife. 5. No one is so mad as to wish to be your friend 6. There is no painter who can represent the glory of the sun. 7. What sculptor is there who could mould the beauty of a goddess? 8. He wishes to leave behind him such a memorial as no man will be able to destroy. 9. Ten generals were appointed to lead the army against the Persians. 10. I have no friends to take my money and then abuse me.

CXVIII.—§§ 290-293

1. Miltiades had no money with which to pay (the fine). 2. The old man had no longer children to look after him. 3. I am not a tyrant to wish to rob you of your liberty. 4. He will be a fool who tries to teach you prudence. 5. There was no painter who could represent the beauty of my wife. 6. A good man leaves behind him a memorial which no one can

[1] See also Exercises on Chapter II. §§ 38-44.

destroy. 7. He says that he will make me ridiculous, but this shall not be done. 8. Oh that I had children to look after me in my old age! (§ 300). 9. He had no money to give to the poor man. 10. But you would not have done this if you had not been cowards and traitors.

CLASS II.—CONDITIONAL. PRESENT AND PAST

CXIX.—§§ 295-297

1. Foolish men say whatever they think. 2. We do not undertake to do things which we do not understand. 3. A wise man would not have said exactly what he thought. 4. Socrates did not think that he knew what he did not know. 5. I should not have reported to you what had not happened. 6. All wish to be the friends of those whom they see rich and prosperous. 7. The enemy went through the city slaying any whom they wished. 8. The pirates tried to capture any ships they saw. 9. A good general praises all whom he sees fighting bravely. 10. The wise master praised all boys whom he saw trying to learn.

CONDITIONAL. FUTURE

CXX.—§§ 298-300

1. He will not give us what he does not wish to give. 2. He will not report to us what does not

happen. 3. We will not undertake to do things that we do not understand. 4. The citizens will praise a general whom they see always prepared. 5. I should shrink from believing anything your friend says. 6. All would wish to be the friends of those whom they see rich and prosperous. 7. A good master would praise any servants whom he might see acting well. 8. Oh, if every man would say exactly what he really believes! 9. It would not be well if all men were to do what they think best. 10. If only every man would work at the trade which he knew!

CXXI

1. They sent the bravest of the officers to carry the news to the citizens. 2. I have no money to pay what my son has borrowed from you. 3. Formerly I used to go wherever I pleased. 4. He used to give his wife whatever she asked for. 5. I should like to see the dog which my brother gave you. 6. Can one call you a philosopher, you who talk so wisely but act so foolishly? 7. Do not listen to men who praise vice. 8. Oh that I could see the friends whom I love! 9. I should never have said what I did not believe to be true. 10. They would not have associated with men whom they knew to be bad.

CXXII

1. I should not have asked for what could not be bought with money. 2. The friends whom I trusted deceived and robbed me. 3. Such a boy would quickly spend any money that one gave him. 4. He acted strangely in wishing to die for his friend. 5. He desired to make a speech which should not be laughed at by his friends. 6. I should not have given money to a man who was not really poor. 7. Thieves would not steal things which were not valuable. 8. All will speak well of one who is rich and prosperous. 9. If only all men would do what they know to be right! 10. I should have pardoned you if you had told me all that you had done.

CXXIII

1. I will give you some wine which is more precious than gold. 2. Sensible men would not have done what you did. 3. You act wisely in giving no money to your son. 4. We should gladly flog a boy who told such lies. 5. If only every man would talk about what he understands! 6. We cannot trust men who have deceived us before. 7. He made a speech which no one could understand. 8. He has gained a reputation which he does not deserve. 9. We never forget friends whom we have benefited. 10. It would be well if you were to say exactly what you think.

K. TEMPORAL PROPOSITIONS. §§ 301-306

CLASS I.—§ 301

(1) ὅτε, ἡνίκα, ὁπότε, ἐπειδή, with *Indicative or Optative*
(2) ὅταν, ἡνίκ' ἄν, ὁπόταν, ἐπειδάν, with *Subjunctive*

[The types are the same as for Conditional and Conditional Relative Sentences.]

Note.—ἐπειδάν always requires the *Aorist* Subjunctive.

Types

I. A. (1). ὅτε ταῦτα λέγει ἁμαρτάνει.
        ὅτε ταῦτα ἔλεξεν ἥμαρτεν.
I. A. (2). ὅτε ταῦτα ἔλεξεν ἥμαρτεν ἄν.
I. B.   ὅταν ταῦτα λέγῃ ἁμαρτάνει.
        ὁπότε ταῦτα λέγοι ἡμάρτανεν.
II.   ὅταν ταῦτα λέξῃ ἁμαρτήσεται.
        ὁπότε ταῦτα λέξειε ἁμάρτοι ἄν.

EXAMPLES

ἐπειδὴ αἱ θύραι ἀνοιχθεῖεν εἰσῇμεν. χρὴ ὅταν τιθῆσθε τοὺς νόμους σκοπεῖν, ἐπειδὰν δὲ θῆσθε φυλάττειν. ταῦτ', ἐπειδὰν περὶ τοῦ γένους εἴπω, ἐρῶ. τίνα οἴεσθε αὐτὴν ψυχὴν ἕξειν ὅταν ἐμὲ ἴδῃ τῶν πατρῴων ἀπεστερημένον ;

CLASS II.—ἕως and μέχρι οὗ = " until," with Indicative, referring to a definite point in past time: in all other cases they follow the types of conditional relative propositions. §§ 302, 303.

τὴν νύχθ' ὅλην ἐγρηγόρεσαν ἕως διέλαμψεν ἡμέρα. ἐλεύθεροι ἦσαν μέχρι οὗ αὐτοὶ αὐτοὺς κατεδούλωσαν. μέχρι δ' οὗ ἂν ἐγὼ ἥκω, αἱ σπονδαὶ μενόντων. ἡδέως ἂν τούτῳ ἔτι διελεγόμην ἕως αὐτῷ πάντα ἀπέφηνα. περιεμένομεν ἑκάστοτε ἕως ἀνοιχθείη τὸ δεσμωτήριον. ἕως ἂν ταῦτα διαπράξωνται, φυλακὴν κατάλιπε.

CLASS III.—πρὶν = " until," " before," follows the types of ἕως = "until," if the principal proposition is negative or interrogative: the Infinitive is required if the principal proposition is affirmative. §§ 304, 305.

Note.—πρὶν ἂν requires the *Aorist* Subjunctive.

οὐκ ἤθελε φεύγειν πρὶν ἡ γυνὴ ἔπεισεν. ἐχρῆν μὴ πρότερον συμβουλεύειν πρὶν ἡμᾶς ἐδίδαξαν. ἐγώ σ' οὐκέτι ἀφήσω πρὶν ἄν μοι ἃ ὑπέσχησαι ἀποδείξῃς. ποιητὴς οὐ πρότερον οἷός τ' ἐστὶ ποιεῖν πρὶν ἂν ἔνθεος γένηται. τίς ἂν τοῦτο ποιοίη πρὶν ὀργισθείη; οὐκ ἀφίεσαν πρὶν παραθεῖεν αὐτοῖς ἄριστον. ἔπειθον μὴ ποιεῖσθαι μάχην πρὶν οἱ Θηβαῖοι παραγένοιντο. κατηγορεῖς γὰρ πρὶν μαθεῖν τὸ πρᾶγμά μου. ταῦτ' ἐπιλέλησται πρὶν μαθεῖν. πρίν σε ἐκπιεῖν τὸν οἶνον ἔβλεψεν ὁ δεσπότης. ἡμεῖς τοίνυν Μεσσήνην εἵλομεν πρὶν Πέρσας λαβεῖν τὴν βασιλείαν.

EXERCISES

CXXIV.—§ 301

1. When you said that, the doors were already open. 2. When you ask me about my birth I will gladly tell you. 3. What will he say when he sees me prosecuted for theft? 4. Whenever I could I gave you money. 5. Whenever he saw his son acting nobly he used to praise him. 6. That would never have been said when I was present. 7. I should not have praised them when they had acted thus. 8. I shall consider myself mad when I wish to be your friend. 9. I should consider you a sculptor when you could model a man. 10. Whenever a man becomes poor his friends desert him.

CXXV.—§ 301

1. Miltiades had not the money when he was ordered to pay (the fine). 2. You will be a burden to your children when you are old and weak. 3. I thought myself a fool when I tried to teach you prudence. 4. When a tyrant dies no one is really grieved. 5. When the citizens have made laws it is right to keep them. 6. I should have thought you ridiculous when you said that. 7. You will have many friends when you are rich and prosperous. 8. The savages

would have slain me when they saw me. 9. He will give you the present when he sees you. 10. The citizens used to praise a general when they found him always prepared.

CXXVI.—§§ 302, 303

1. The truce was kept until the dead were all buried. 2. I was talking with him until the day broke. 3. We waited until the prison was opened. 4. The citizens were free until Philip enslaved them. 5. He left a guard behind until all the money was paid. 6. He asked them many questions until they told him the whole truth. 7. They flogged the slave until he betrayed his master. 8. The robbers plundered the country until they were all captured. 9. The battle lasted till all the enemy's ships were captured or destroyed. 10. The boy worked till his head ached.

CXXVII.—§§ 302, 303

1. The boys always waited until the doors were opened. 2. Each time I used to talk with him until the day broke. 3. The truce will be kept until the ambassadors return. 4. He ordered the soldiers to remain there till the Thebans came. 5. You will remember our advice until you forget it. 6. The general will not be happy till he has conquered the enemy in battle. 7. The robbers will ill-treat me

until I promise them two talents. 8. God has made us free until we enslave ourselves. 9. I should have trusted him until he robbed me also. 10. The boy will not be happy until he gets this.

CXXVIII.—§§ 304, 305

1. I will not condemn you before you tell me the whole truth. 2. The general did not wish to fight till the soldiers persuaded him. 3. I should not give advice until you told me all. 4. The robbers did not let me go till I had given them all my money. 5. I did not speak ill of you till I was put in a rage. 6. That poet could not compose poems till he had eaten and drunk. 7. Who would believe you till he had talked with others? 8. Who would give you advice before you told him the facts? 9. What judge would condemn you before you had defended yourself? 10. The master did not flog the boy till he had been told all the circumstances.

CXXIX.—§§ 304, 305

1. He wished to run away before his friends persuaded him. 2. Foolish men wish to give advice before they know all the circumstances. 3. They let me go before I had explained all. 4. He flogged the slave before he had been told the circumstances. 5. He ordered the soldiers to collect provisions before the enemy came. 6. Boys forget a thing before they

learn it. 7. Some poets compose before they feel any inspiration. 8. You gave me this advice before you knew the whole truth. 9. We used to come to the prison before the doors were opened. 10. He worked for five hours before he ate lunch.

CXXX.—RECAPITULATORY

1. They sailed away before the enemy appeared. 2. If you had not fled away at full speed you would have been killed by the dogs. 3. He says that whenever he goes to the river he sees you trying to catch fish. 4. He left the city two days before you appeared. 5. I lent you the money on the understanding that you would repay it before you left Athens. 6. Before you accuse others of folly think if you are really wise yourself. 7. If this horse had had a smaller head it would have been worth much more money. 8. Would that the ship had never sailed away or that I had been on it! 9. He said that he would not allow me to go until I had promised to return next day. 10. I am surprised that you did not suspect the man was a thief.

CHAPTER IX.—THE NOMINAL FORMS OF THE VERB

I.—THE INFINITIVE. §§ 308-344

1. §§ 308-313

ὁ παῖς οἴεται τὸν διδάσκαλον ὀργίζεσθαι. οἱ στρατιῶται ἔλεγον Ξενοφῶντα ἄνδρα ἀγαθὸν γενέσθαι. οὐδὲν ἐπράχθη διὰ τὸ ἐκεῖνον μὴ παρεῖναι.

Ἀλέξανδρος ἔφασκεν εἶναι Διὸς υἱός. ἐκ τοῦ πρότερος λέγειν ὁ διώκων ἰσχύει. οὐκ ἐπὶ τῷ δοῦλοι ἀλλ' ἐπὶ τῷ ὁμοῖοι τοῖς λειπομένοις εἶναι ἐκπέμπονται οἱ ἄποικοι.

δεῖ ἐπιμελεῖσθαι τοῦ ἀγαθὸν ἄνδρα γίγνεσθαι. κακὸν πρᾶγμ' ἐστὶ γενέσθαι δοῦλον.

Κύρου ἐδέοντο ὡς προθυμοτάτου γενέσθαι. ἐδέοντό μου προστάτην γενέσθαι. ἐκείνῳ συνέβη γενέσθαι πλούσιον. ἅπασιν συνέβη γενέσθαι λαμπροῖς.

Ξενίᾳ ἥκειν παρήγγειλε λαβόντα τοὺς ἄνδρας. οὐ σχολή μοι κάμνοντα ἰατρεύεσθαι.

2. *The Infinitive with the Article.* §§ 314, 315

νέοις τὸ σιγᾶν κρεῖττόν ἐστι τοῦ λαλεῖν. οὐ πλεονεξίας ἕνεκα ταῦτ' ἔπραξε Φίλιππος ἀλλὰ τῷ δικαιότερα ἀξιοῦν τοὺς Θηβαίους ἢ ὑμᾶς. οὐδὲν θαυμαστὸν τὸ ὁμιλεῖν τοῖς πονηροῖς τοὺς πονηρούς. τὸν τοῦ πράττειν χρόνον εἰς τὸ παρασκευάζεσθαι ἀναλίσκομεν.
Μίνως τὸ ληστικὸν καθῄρει τοῦ τὰς προσόδους μᾶλλον ἰέναι αὐτῷ. τοῦ μὴ διαφεύγειν τὸν λαγὼν ἐκ τῶν δικτύων σκοποὺς καθίσταμεν.

3. *The Infinitive without the Article as Genitive after Substantives and Verbs.* §§ 316-318

οὐ βουλεύεσθαι ἔτι ὥρα ἀλλὰ βεβουλεῦσθαι. ἐν ἐλπίδι ἦν τὴν πόλιν ἑλεῖν. διάνοιαν εἶχε πρὸς Σικελίαν πλεῖν. νῦν ἄρά με ἅπασα ἀνάγκη ἐστὶν ἀποθανεῖν; λέγειν χρὴ ταχὺ πάνυ.
Οἴκοι μένειν δεῖ τὸν καλῶς εὐδαίμονα. πολλοῦ δεῖ οὕτως ἔχειν.
πολλοῦ δέω ὑπὲρ ἐμαυτοῦ ἀπολογεῖσθαι. τοσούτου δέω καταφρονεῖν τῆς παιδείας τῆς ὑπὸ τῶν προγόνων καταλειφθείσης.

4. *The Infinitive without the Article as the Subject of other Verbs.* §§ 319, 320

ἀναγκαῖόν ἐστι φέρειν τὰ τῆς τύχης. προσήκει μοι τοῦτο ποιεῖν. συνέβη μοι ἐκ τῆς πατρίδος φεύγειν. πᾶσιν ἔξεστι λαλεῖν. οὐ πρέπει μοι τοιαῦτα ποιεῖν. ἡμᾶς πρέπει βουλεύεσθαι. ἔξεστι πάντας λέγειν.

5. *The Infinitive used as Object to complete the Sense of a Verb.* §§ 321-325

λέγει τὸν ἄνδρα ἀποθνῄσκειν. οἴομαι τὸν βασιλέα τεθνηκέναι. ᾤετο ἂν ἐλθεῖν. οἴεσθε γὰρ τὸν πατέρα οὐκ ἂν φυλάττειν, καὶ τὴν τιμὴν λαμβάνειν τῶν ξύλων; ἆρ' ἄν με οἴεσθε τοσάδε ἔτη διαγενέσθαι εἰ ἔπραττον τὰ δημόσια; οἱ Πέρσαι οἴονται τοὺς ἀχαρίστους καὶ περὶ θεοὺς ἂν ἀμελῶς ἔχειν. πολλούς φασι γιγνώσκοντας τὰ βέλτιστα οὐκ ἐθέλειν πράττειν. νῦν δ' οὐκέτι σε ζῆν οἴεται. νόμιζε μηδὲν εἶναι τῶν ἀνθρωπίνων βέβαιον. εἴ τις νομίζει τι μὴ ἱκανῶς εἰρῆσθαι, ἀναστὰς ὑπομνησάτω. πῶς ἂν οἴει ἐκβῆναι τὸ πρᾶγμα; οὐκ ἂν ἡγεῖτο τοὺς ἄνδρας φυγεῖν.

6. *Verbs of Promising, Hoping, and Expecting.* § 326

τοῦτο γὰρ προσδοκῶ ἀπολεῖν με. τίς ἄν ποτ' ἤλπισ' ἀκοῦσαι; ὑπέσχετο οὐκ ἂν ἐλθεῖν.

Peculiar use of δοκεῖν. § 327

τὸ πρᾶγμα γιγνώσκειν δοκῶ. ποῖ ἰέναι δοκεῖς; οὐκ ἂν δοκῶ εὖ πρᾶξαι ἐκεῖσε ἀποδημήσας.

7. *Special use of μή.* §§ 328-330

(1) ἀπεκρίνατο μηδενὸς ἥττων εἶναι. ὁμολογοῦμεν μὴ παρὰ φύσιν εἶναι τὰ τοιαῦτα. ὑπισχνοῦντο μηδὲν χαλεπὸν αὐτοὺς πείσεσθαι.

(2) ὄμνυσιν οὐ δρᾶσαι. ὄμνυσι μὴ δρᾶσαι.
(3) ἠρνοῦντο μὴ πεπτωκέναι. ἔξαρνός ἐστι μή μ'
ἰδεῖν πώποτε. οὐκ ἠρνοῦντο μὴ οὐ πεπτωκέναι.
ἔξαρνός ἐστι μή μ' ἰδεῖν μὴ οὐ πώποτε ; ἐγώ τοι οὐκ
ἀμφισβητῶ μὴ οὐχὶ σὲ εἶναι σοφώτερον ἢ ἐμέ.

8. *After Verbs expressing Effort or Desire to do or prevent.* §§ 331-333

βούλεταί σ' ἰδεῖν. ἐδεήθην ὑμῶν ἰέναι. ἐδεήθην ὑμῶν μὴ θορυβεῖν. ἐπείσατε τὸν ἄνδρα μάχεσθαι. ἡ γυνὴ φεύγειν ἔπεισε τὸν ἄνδρα. οὐκ ἔπεισα τοὺς πολίτας πολεμεῖν. οὐκ ἔπεισε τοὺς πολίτας μὴ πολεμεῖν.
ἀντεῖπον οἱ ἰατροὶ τῷ ἀσθενοῦντι μὴ χρῆσθαι ἐλαίῳ. ὁ χειμὼν εἶργε τὰ φυτὰ μὴ βλαστάνειν.
οὐκ ἀντεῖπον οἱ ἰατροὶ τῷ ἀσθενοῦντι μὴ οὐ χρῆσθαι ἐλαίῳ. οὐδείς πώποτε ἀντεῖπε μὴ οὐ καλῶς ἔχειν τοὺς νόμους. ὁ χειμὼν οὐκ εἶργε τὰ φυτὰ μὴ οὐ βλαστάνειν. τί ἐμποδὼν μὴ οὐχὶ ὑβριζομένους ἡμᾶς ἀποθανεῖν ;

κωλύω, *an exception.* § 334

κωλύουσιν ἡμᾶς μὴ πορεύεσθαι. οὐδέν σε κωλύει σεαυτὸν ἐμβάλλειν εἰς τὸ βάραθρον. σὺ τὴν ἐμὴν γυναῖκα κωλύσεις μ' ἄγειν εἰς Σπάρτην ;

9. *After Verbs denoting Ability, Knowledge, Habit, Obligation, etc.* § 335

ὁρᾷς ὅτι οὐκ ἔχει εἰπεῖν. κιθαρίζειν οὐκ ἐπίσταται.

πεφύκασιν ἅπαντες ἁμαρτάνειν. ἱππεύειν ἔμαθες. εἴσεται μὴ λέγειν τοιαῦτα. ποιήσω δακεῖν τὴν καρδίαν ἵν' εἰδῇ μὴ πατεῖν τὰ τῶν θεῶν ψηφίσματα. τοῖς φίλοις ὀφείλομεν τοὺς φίλους ἀγαθὸν μέν τι δρᾶν, κακὸν δὲ μηδέν.

10. *The Infinitive expressing Purpose, after certain verbs denoting 'to choose,' 'to give,' 'to take.'* § 336.

τοὺς ἱππέας παρείχοντο Πελοποννησίοις συστρατεύειν. ὃς γὰρ ἂν ὑμᾶς λάθῃ, τοῦτον ἀφίετε τοῖς θεοῖς κολάζειν. Δημοσθένη εἵλοντο ἄρχειν. τὸν παῖδα ἔλαβον ἐκθεῖναι. ἐπέτρεπε τὴν πόλιν διαρπάζειν. στρατηγεῖν ᾑρέθη. ἐμετρήθη ὑμῖν ὁ βίος εὐδαιμονῆσαι.

11. *The Infinitive (Active only) defining the meaning of Adjectives.* §§ 337-339

δεινός ἐστι λέγειν. ἀνὴρ ἱκανὸς βοηθεῖν. τἆλλα εὑρήσεις ὑπουργεῖν ὄντας ἡμᾶς οὐ κακούς. τοιοῦτος ἦν οἷος μὴ βούλεσθαι ἀποκτείνειν πολλοὺς τῶν πολιτῶν (see § 257). ἐλείπετο τῆς νυκτὸς ὅσον σκοταίους διελθεῖν τὸ πεδίον (*id.*)
ταῦτα χαλεπώτατά ἐστιν εὑρεῖν. ὁ ποταμὸς ῥᾴδιος ἦν διαβαίνειν. ἄξιός ἐστιν ἐπαίνου τυχεῖν. φοβερὸς γάρ ἐστι προσπολεμῆσαι. γυνὴ γάρ ἐστιν εὐπρεπὴς ἰδεῖν. ἐκεῖνο γὰρ ἐμοὶ μὲν ἀναγκαιότατον προειπεῖν ἡγοῦμαι, ὑμῖν δὲ χρησιμώτατον ἀκοῦσαι.

12. *The Infinitive Absolute.* §§ 340-342

ἢ οὖν ζωγραφικὸς Θεόδωρος; οὐχ ὅσον γ' ἔμ' εἰδέναι. τοῦτό που ὡς τὸ ὅλον εἰπεῖν ψεῦδος, ἔνι δὲ καὶ ἀληθῆ. εἰσέρχονται μαθηταὶ πολλοί, ἐμοὶ δοκεῖν. ἄνευ γὰρ ἀρχόντων οὐδὲν ἂν οὔτε καλὸν οὔτε ἀγαθὸν γένοιτο, ὡς μὲν συνελόντι εἰπεῖν, οὐδαμοῦ. καὶ οἱ Λακεδαιμόνιοι βαλλόμενοι ἀμφοτέρωθεν ἐν τῷ αὐτῷ συμπτώματι γίγνονται, ὡς μικρὸν μεγάλῳ εἰκάσαι, τῷ ἐν Θερμοπύλαις.

τὸ τὰς ἰδίας εὐεργεσίας ὑπομιμνήσκειν καὶ λέγειν μικροῦ δεῖν ὅμοιόν ἐστι τῷ ὀνειδίζειν. οἱ ἁρμόττοντες θώρακες ὀλίγου δεῖν οὐ φορήματι ἀλλὰ προσθήματι εἴξασιν.

ἀνάγκη ἔχειν ἀψεύδειαν καὶ τὸ ἑκόντας εἶναι μηδαμῇ προσδέχεσθαι τὸ ψεῦδος. τὸ ἐπ' ἐκείνοις εἶναι ἀπολώλατε. ἀπόχρη μοι τὸ νῦν εἶναι ταῦτ' εἰρηκέναι. ταῦτα πράξομεν ἡμεῖς οἱ νεώτατοι, τὸ νῦν εἶναι.

13. *In Exclamations.* § 343

τῆς μωρίας· τὸ Δία νομίζειν τηλικουτονί. τὸ δὲ μηδὲ κυνῆν ἔχοντα ἐλθεῖν. τὸ ἐμὲ παθεῖν τάδε.

14. *As an Imperative.* § 344

The Subject is in the Nominative.

ἀκούετε λεῴ· κατὰ τὰ πάτρια τοὺς χοὰς πίνειν ὑπὸ τῆς σάλπιγγος. σὺ δέ, Κλεαρίδα, τὰς πύλας ἀνοίξας ἐπεκθεῖν καὶ ἐπείγεσθαι ὡς τάχιστα συμμῖξαι.

EXERCISES

CXXXI.—§§ 308-313

1. The slave thought that his master was angry. 2. The boy thought that he was wiser than his master. 3. The soldiers said that they feared the enemy's cavalry. 4. The general said that the soldiers feared the noise of the barbarians. 5. Nothing is being done owing to the judge not being present. 6. One ought to make an effort to become good and noble. 7. It is a bad business to become blind when young. 8. He begged her to become his wife. 9. Alexander had the good luck to become a famous general whilst a young man. 10. I have no leisure to talk with you (when I am) working.

CXXXII.—§§ 314, 315

1. To be happy is better than to become rich. 2. The philosopher called speech silver but silence gold. 3. It is strange that my boys associate with yours. 4. Let us not spend in preparation the time for action. 5. He became rich by spending nothing on himself or his friends. 6. They build many ships in order to destroy the pirate navy. 7. The farmer took a bow that the hare might not escape his dog. 8. They destroyed all the ships that no one might escape from the island. 9. He loved you because you flattered him more than I did. 10. You persuaded the king because you made most just demands.

CXXXIII.—§§ 316-318

1. He had thoughts of making a voyage to Asia. 2. I am in hopes of persuading the maiden. 3. It is now time for me to tell you all that I know. 4. You must take the city soon if you wish to take it. 5. We must wait here till the ship is about to set sail. 6. I am far from thinking myself wiser than you. 7. We are far from despising the courage of the enemy. 8. It is absolutely necessary that you should defend yourself before the judge (dat.) 9. We were in hopes that you would become our champion. 10. It is time to beg the soldiers to be brave men.

CXXXIV.—§§ 319, 320

1. It is necessary to bear our misfortunes in silence. 2. It is right for you to listen to the words of your father. 3. It befell me to become the richest man in Greece. 4. In my house all may do whatever they wish. 5. It is not befitting that boys should talk much about such matters. 6. Oh that it were possible to banish such worthless men from the city! 7. It is not right to despise a constitution inherited from our ancestors. 8. It is in your power to become rich whenever you wish. 9. It is not befitting for a boy to speak ill of his father. 10. It is right to endeavour to become wiser and more prudent.

CXXXV.—§§ 321-325

1. They think that the king will die within a few days. 2. They said that they would come to the city next day. 3. The thief thought that the dog would not have been on the watch. 4. I should not have thought that he would live so many years. 5. The Persians think that they will easily conquer the Greeks. 6. He thought that the boy would refuse to speak the truth. 7. If any one thinks that I have not done what is just, let him say so. 8. I thought that all the soldiers would not run away. 9. Believe that I am no longer your friend. 10. He said that he should not have lived for so many years if he had been in public life.

CXXXVI.—§§ 326, 327

1. He promised to capture the enemy's camp. 2. I expect that he will be dead to-morrow. 3. Who would ever have expected to see you in this place? 4. I could never have hoped to live for so many years. 5. He promised that he would not speak unless I wished it. 6. I think I understand what you wish me to do. 7. To whom does your father mean to leave his money? 8. I do not think that I should live for many years in that city. 9. She does not think that she would have run away if she had been a soldier. 10. Most men think that they would become rich if the gods pleased.

CXXXVII.—§§ 328-330

1. The general replied that he was as brave as anybody. 2. They now agree that such acts are not worthy of philosophers. 3. The master promised that the slave should not be flogged. 4. The thief swore that he did not steal the cloak. 5. The soldier denied that he had spoken ill of the general. 6. He does not deny that he never saw me before. 7. I do not dispute that he is more prudent than I. 8. Can you deny that you promised me the book? 9. Did your brother deny that he had ever seen me? 10. Do I dispute that you are both wealthier and wiser than I?

CXXXVIII.—§§ 331-334

1. Alexander wished to be the son of a god. 2. The wife persuaded her husband to fight. 3. He besought the judge not to banish him from the city. 4. My doctor has forbidden me to drink any wine. 5. Nobody prevents you leaving the ship. 6. The mother persuaded the boy not to have his hair cut. 7. The master ordered the boys not to make a noise. 8. Winter prevents us bathing in the sea. 9. What saves us from being defeated and slain? 10. It is not kings and rich men that make a city prosperous and powerful.

CXXXIX.—§§ 334, 335

1. My boys are learning to ride and to shoot. 2. I will make you understand the baseness of the king. 3. That doctor would make a sick man die in a few days. 4. These boys do not know how to read the words of the Greek poet. 5. We owe it to ourselves not to speak ill of our friends. 6. Women are not able (πεφυκέναι) to do all the things that men do. 7. The bad boy makes his mother's heart ache. 8. Your son prevented my boy speaking the truth. 9. I shall never prevent you throwing yourself into the fire if you wish to do so. 10. Will nothing prevent you making your daughter unhappy?

CXL.—§ 336

1. He was chosen to command (the army) when thirty-five years old. 2. Let us leave bad men for the gods to punish. 3. The sailor chose a large ship to make the voyage to Asia. 4. I lent him my dog to chase the hares on the plain. 5. They sent ten thousand men to take the field with the Athenians. 6. The king gave the child to the slave to expose it on the mountains. 7. Only young men think that life is given to them to be happy in. 8. Philip gave up the town to the soldiers to sack. 9. This life has been given us to prepare ourselves for another life. 10. He sent the slave to invite me to lunch.

CXLI.—§§ 337-339

1. Wise men are not always good at speaking. 2. Of all things happiness is the most difficult to find. 3. Let us make friends of those able to help us. 4. The man who said that deserves to be praised. 5. My words, said the philosopher, are most profitable for you to hear. 6. A woman comely to the eye is more powerful than a king. 7. The most difficult things to discover are not always the most precious. 8. Let us endeavour to be good at serving our friends. 9. The message of the king is most hateful to the citizens to hear. 10. The orator thought that that was most necessary to proclaim.

CXLII.—§§ 340-344

1. Your friend is a fool in my opinion. 2. I have told you the whole cause as far as I know. 3. Between ourselves he is not as wise as he thinks. 4. Without officers, in a word, nothing can be done in war. 5. In short he was the one man at Athens whom all the citizens trusted. 6. The barbarians, as they fled to the river, were almost all slain by our men. 7. We shall not forget the words of our master, for the present at least. 8. What folly! to trust men who have deceived you so often before! 9. And do you, mounting your horse, ride to the camp with all speed. 10. To think that we ever believed in the existence of the gods!

CXLIII.—RECAPITULATORY

1. At the Dionysia many strangers were present in the city. 2. All men try to judge the future by the past. 3. Oh that death were the end of all things! 4. I am surprised that you did not prevent your son from suffering all this. 5. If only we had not been deceived by your words! 6. They told us that whoever was caught would be put to death. 7. You will never be able to prevent men doing what is not right. 8. Soldiers must obey their officers if they are to conquer in battle. 9. Every one thinks that he can manage his own affairs well. 10. What makes one man happy would make another most miserable.

CXLIV.—RECAPITULATORY

1. Some men love virtue, and others wisdom; but you seem to despise both. 2. Man is only happy when he thinks that he is happy. 3. Never call other men foolish till you know that you yourself are wise. 4. I am surprised that you did not leave your cloak for the slave to bring. 5. If it had been in my power I would gladly have given you the money. 6. He blamed himself justly for having betrayed his best friends. 7. Do you know (§ 386) that you are far weaker than your brother? 8. In this large city your house was very difficult to find. 9. A good priest will not neglect the sick and poor. 10. When dying he freed all his slaves and gave each some money.

II.—THE PARTICIPLE. §§ 345-376

1. The Use of the Negative. §§ 346, 347

οὐκ ἔστι μὴ νικῶσι σωτηρία. ψηφίσασθε τὸν πόλεμον μὴ φοβηθέντες τὸ αὐτίκα δεινόν. χρόνον πολὺν ἀντεῖχον οὐκ ἐνδιδόντες ἀλλήλοις. γνωσόμεθα οὐ τολμῶντες ἀμύνεσθαι.

2. The Participle with the Article. §§ 348-352

(1) *Referring to definite persons or things.* § 348

ὁ Μιλτιάδης ὁ Μαραθῶνι μαχεσάμενος τοῖς Πέρσαις. οἱ γραψάμενοι τὸν Σωκράτη. τοὺς στρατηγοὺς τοὺς οὐκ ἀνελομένους τοὺς ἐκ ναυμαχίας ἐβούλεσθε κρίνειν. ὁ φεύγων παρέσται αὐτίκα. οἶδα ὅτι ἀνήκεστα κακὰ ἐποίησαν τοὺς οὐ μέλλοντας οὐδὲν τοιοῦτον δρᾶν.

(2) *Referring to classes of persons or things.* § 349

ὁ ἀδικηθεὶς ῥᾳδίως βοήθειαν εὑρίσκεται. ὁ μὴ δαρεὶς ἄνθρωπος οὐ παιδεύεται. οἱ πολιτευόμενοι οὐκ ἀεὶ σοφοί.

(3) *Idiomatic use of Future Participle.* § 351

οὐκ ἔστιν ὁ τολμήσων περὶ σπονδῶν λέγειν. ἀποθανεῖται δι' ἔνδειαν τοῦ θεραπεύσοντος. νόμον τὸν ταῦτα κωλύσοντα τέθεινται. εἴθε οἱ ὁπλῖται οἱ τὴν νύκτα πορευσόμενοι παρεῖεν.

(4) *Article sometimes omitted.* § 352

τίς ἂν πόλις ὑπὸ μὴ πειθομένων ἁλοίη; πλέομεν ἐπὶ πολλὰς ναῦς κεκτημένους.

3. *The Participle without the Article.* §§ 353-359

(1) *Temporal.* § 354

ταῦτ' εἰπὼν ἀπῆλθεν. ἀπήντησα Φιλίππῳ ἀπιόντι. τίς ἂν εἴη τοιοῦτος ἰατρὸς ὅστις τῷ νοσοῦντι μεταξὺ ἀσθενοῦντι συμβουλεύοι μηδέν; οἱ βάρβαροι καὶ φεύγοντες ἅμα ἐτίτρωσκον. τὰ χρήματα καὶ κτωμένους εὐφραίνει τοὺς ἀνθρώπους καὶ κεκτημένους ἥδιον ποιεῖ ζῆν. ἐπιγενομένη ἡ νόσος ἐνταῦθα δὴ πάνυ ἐπίεσε τοὺς Ἀθηναίους.

(2) *Causal.* § 355

τούτου τοῦ κέρδους ἀπειχόμην αἰσχρὸν νομίζων. τοῦτ' ἔδρασα βουλόμενος σῴζειν τοὺς ἄνδρας. ὁ Κῦρος ἅτε παῖς ὢν ἥδετο τῇ στολῇ. μάλα χαλεπῶς ἐπορεύοντο οἱ Λακεδαιμόνιοι οἷα δὴ ἐν νυκτὶ καὶ ἐν φόβῳ ἀπιόντες. τὸν Περικλέα ἐν αἰτίᾳ εἶχον ὡς πείσαντα σφᾶς πολεμεῖν καὶ δι' ἐκεῖνον ταῖς συμφοραῖς περιπεπτωκότες. λέγω δὲ τοῦδ' ἕνεκα, βουλόμενος δόξαι σοὶ ὅπερ ἐμοί.

(3) *Final.* § 356

(a) *The Future Participle with* ὡς

Ἀρταξέρξης συλλαμβάνει Κῦρον ὡς ἀποκτενῶν. παρεσκευάζοντο ὡς τῷ τειχίσματι προσβαλοῦντες.

(b) The Future Participle without ὡς after Verbs of Motion

συνήλθομεν ὀψόμενοι τὸν ἀγῶνα. ἔπεμψε τὸν δοῦλον ἐροῦντα ὅτι ἀσθενεῖ. τὸν στρατηγὸν ἐθαύμαζον καὶ εἰς πόλεμον σφᾶς ἄγοντα τρωθησομένους ἢ ἀποθανουμένους. τῷ Γυλίππῳ εὐθὺς ὡς ἀπαντησόμενοι ἐξῆλθον.

(4) *Conditional.* § 357

οἴει σὺ Ἄλκηστιν ὑπὲρ Ἀδμήτου ἀποθανεῖν ἂν μὴ οἰομένην ἀθάνατον μνήμην ἀρετῆς πέρι ἑαυτῆς ἔσεσθαι; πληγὰς γὰρ ἔξω μὴ μαθὼν ταῦτα. τοιαῦτ' ἂν σωφρονῶν ἔχοις. δυνηθεὶς ἂν Ποτίδαιαν ἔχειν εἰ ἐβουλήθη, Ὀλυνθίοις παρέδωκεν.

(5) *Concessive.* § 358

ὀλίγα δυνάμενοι προορᾶν περὶ τοῦ μέλλοντος πολλὰ ἐπιχειροῦμεν πράττειν. ταῦτα συμβουλεύω σοι καίπερ νεώτερος ὤν. πολὺν χρόνον ἀντεῖχον καίπερ οὐκ ὄντες ἀντίπαλοι. οἰκτείρω αὐτὸν καίπερ ὄντα δυσμενῆ. φεύγουσι καὶ πολλοὶ ὄντες. φοβεῖται μὴ ἡ ψυχή, ὅμως καὶ θειότερον ὂν τοῦ σώματος, προαπολλύηται.

(6) *Other relations.* § 359

οἱ Θηβαῖοι Μεγαρεῦσιν ὁμόροις οὖσιν ἠπείλουν. τὸν πηλὸν ἐπὶ τοῦ νώτου ἔφερον ἐγκεκυφότες καὶ τὼ χεῖρε εἰς τοὐπίσω συμπλέκοντες. Πρόξενον ἐκέλευσε λαβόντα ὅτι πλείστους παραγενέσθαι. ἐγὼ δεῦρό σοι ἔσπευδον σπονδὰς φέρων. τὸν Πλοῦτον ἥκει ἄγων. ἀδίκοις κάκιστα σύμπαντα ἀρξάμενα ἀπὸ τῆς ὑγιείας.

4. *Absolute Use of the Participle.* §§ 360-367

(a) *The Genitive Absolute.* §§ 361-365

ταῦτ' ἐπράχθη Κόνωνος στρατηγοῦντος. ἀπελογήσατο ὅτι οὐχ ὡς τοῖς Ἕλλησι πολεμησόντων σφῶν εἴποι. Ἀθηναίων δὲ τὸ αὐτὸ τοῦτο παθόντων, διπλασίαν ἂν 'οἶμαι τὴν δύναμιν εἰκάζεσθαι. ἐπιλέλησμαι ἅτε χρόνου παρελθόντος πολλοῦ. οἴμοι τί δράσω παραφρονοῦντος τοῦ πατρός;
πολλοὶ οὕτω πρός τινας ἔχουσιν ὥστε εὐτυχούντων λυπεῖσθαι. εἶπον ἐρομένου ὅτι Μάκρωνές εἰσιν. οὐχ οἷόν τε μὴ καλῶς ἀποδεικνύντος καλῶς μιμεῖσθαι. ἐξαγγελθέντος εὑρίσκουσι τοῦτον ἠσθέντα.
σαφῶς δηλωθέντος ὅτι ἐν ταῖς ναυσὶ τῶν Ἑλλήνων τὰ πράγματα ἐγένετο.

(b) *Accusative Absolute.* §§ 366, 367

σιγᾷς, ἀποκρίνασθαι δέον; ἐξόν σοι πλουτεῖν πένης διατελεῖς ὤν. καὶ ἐνθένδε πάλιν προσταχθέν μοι ὑπὸ τοῦ δήμου Μένωνα ἄγειν εἰς Ἑλλήσποντον ᾠχόμην.
ηὔχετο πρὸς τοὺς θεοὺς τἀγαθὰ διδόναι ὡς τοὺς θεοὺς κάλλιστ' εἰδότας ὁποῖα ἀγαθά ἐστιν. τοὺς υἱεῖς οἱ πατέρες ἀπὸ τῶν πονηρῶν ἀνθρώπων εἴργουσιν ὡς τὴν τῶν πονηρῶν ὁμιλίαν κατάλυσιν οὖσαν τῆς ἀρετῆς.

5. The Participle limiting the meaning of certain Verbs expressing very general notions. §§ 369, 370

ᾤχετο ἀπίων. ἔτυχον τότε καθεύδοντες. ἔτυχε καταδαρθών. οἱ Ἕλληνες διετέλουν χρώμενοι τοῖς τῶν πολεμίων τοξεύμασιν. διαγίγνεται κολακεύων τοὺς πλουσίους. βουλοίμην ἂν λαβεῖν Κῦρον ἀπελθών. οἱ Ἕλληνες φθάνουσιν ἐπὶ τῷ ἄκρῳ γενόμενοι τοὺς πολεμίους. ἡ ψυχὴ φαίνεται ἀθάνατος οὖσα. ἠρώτων εἴ τι σφᾶς ἀγαθὸν δεδρακότες εἰσίν. ἦσάν τινες καὶ γενόμενοι τῷ Νικίᾳ λόγοι. ἐάν τις ἡμᾶς εὖ ποιῶν ὑπάρχῃ, οὐχ ἡττησόμεθα εὖ ποιοῦντες. ἀνανδρία γὰρ τὸ μὴ δύνασθαι καρτερεῖν λυπούμενον. τὴν γυναῖκα ἔπαυσας κλάουσαν.

6. The Participle completing the meaning of certain Verbs. §§ 371-376

ἐπέδειξα τοῦτον δωροδοκήσαντα. ἐποίησας αὐτὸν διαλεγόμενον. ἐξελέγξει σε ἐπιορκοῦντα. ἐφωράσαμεν τὸν δοῦλον κλέπτοντα.
οἶδα αὐτὸν τεθνηκότα. ἀκούω σοῦ ᾄδοντος. ἐπύθοντο τῆς Πύλου κατειλημμένης. ᾐσθόμην τὸν ἄνδρα προσιόντα. εἴδομεν ἀναχωροῦντας τοὺς πολεμίους. μέμνησο θνητὸς ὤν. ἔγνων ἡττημένος. διαβεβλημένος οὐ μανθάνεις;
σύνοιδα ἐμαυτῷ ἀδικῶν (or ἀδικοῦντι). συνῄδειν ἑαυτῷ ἡμαρτηκώς (or ἡμαρτηκότι).
πᾶς ἀνὴρ κἂν δοῦλος ᾖ τις ἥδεται τὸ φῶς ὁρῶν. μή μοι ἄχθεσθε λέγοντι τἀληθῆ. χρημάτων οὐκ αἰσχύνει ἐπιμελούμενος ὅπως σοι ἔσται ὡς πλεῖστα;

EXERCISES

CXLV.—§§ 348-352

1. The soldiers who died at Thermopylae were brave men. 2. The cities which fought with the Persians saved Greece. 3. The prosecutors of Socrates were not distinguished men. 4. There is no hope for men who do not conquer. 5. The defendant wished to say nothing to the judge. 6. A boy who has not been flogged is not educated. 7. Any one who wishes can wrong a poor man. 8. The man who saved your city is present, citizens. 9. Public men are not always worthless creatures. 10. They slew men who were not likely to betray the city.

CXLVI.—§§ 348-352

1. There is no one who will dare to speak about peace. 2. There was no one who would dare to impeach the judge. 3. We will pass a law to prevent such acts in the city. 4. There was no one who would dare to slay the tyrant. 5. The old man has no children to nurse him. 6. The army which was to conquer the enemy set out from the city. 7. The pirates destroyed the ships which were bringing corn to the city. 8. We are making war upon a people possessing many ships. 9. Would that the ship were

here which is to carry us to the island. 10. A man who has not been wronged by the tyrant will not sympathise with me.

CXLVII.—§ 354

1. When they had heard the orator they straightway departed to their homes. 2. We met the philosopher as he was going away from the marketplace. 3. The Persian cavalry shot arrows even as they were fleeing. 4. The old man abused doctors even in the course of his illness. 5. I met the doctor immediately he had left the house. 6. Even as he was saying this he was wounded by a stone. 7. Riches do not make men more happy when they have acquired them. 8. The cavalry, advancing in numbers, then and there entirely crushed the enemy's infantry. 9. The general left the city and hastened to the camp. 10. The bad man abused the gods even when dying.

CXLVIII.—§ 355

1. This he said because he wished to persuade the citizens. 2. They blamed the judge because he did not abstain from this sort of profit. 3. They spoke ill of the general because he tried to persuade them not to go to war. 4. They were very much disheartened because they had involved themselves in

misfortunes. 5. I blame you for this reason, because I consider such profit disreputable. 6. The soldiers marched at night simply because they wished to escape the notice of the barbarians. 7. They fled because they did not dare to defend themselves. 8. I spoke thus much because I wished them to have the same views as I. 9. I gave money to the judge because I wished to save my friend. 10. He was delighted with the horse because it was swift.

CXLIX.—§ 356

1. The Persians seized the generals, intending to put them to death. 2. They prepared ten ships, intending to make an attack upon the island. 3. Cyrus collected an army with the object of marching against his brother. 4. I will send the slave to say that I cannot go. 5. The citizens flocked together to see the general. 6. He went out at night in the hope of meeting the thief. 7. They attacked the fort hoping to capture the king. 8. They flocked together on the walls hoping to see the struggle. 9. They made ready, intending to start early in the morning. 10. He sent a messenger to say that many soldiers were ill.

CL.—§ 357

1. He would have had this if he had been sensible. 2. She would not have died then if she had not wished. 3. What woman would die for her husband even if

he wished to live? 4. The memory of a woman will be everlasting if she dies for her husband. 5. The general might take the city if he wished. 6. Though he might have kept the city he handed it over to the king. 7. Though she might have lived for many years she wished to die for her husband. 8. We are lost if we shrink from defending ourselves (§ 346). 9. Do not vote for the war if you shrink from the immediate risk (§ 346). 10. Who would die for another man if he were sensible?

CLI.—§ 358

1. Though you are the older I give you this advice. 2. Though I cannot foresee the future I trust the gods. 3. They determined to fight though they were not equal in strength. 4. They held out for a long time though few in number. 5. We did not attack the fort though we were many in number. 6. You cannot foresee the future although you are very wise. 7. They think that the soul will perish although it is divine. 8. You will die within a few days although you are very young. 9. I will not betray you although you are my foes. 10. We would not run away though we were doomed to die.

CLII.—§ 359

1. The Athenians threatened the islanders their neighbours. 2. He ordered the general to come with

as many cavalry as possible. 3. He is here with his horse and his dogs. 4. He hastened home carrying the old man on his back. 5. The boys were standing clasping their hands behind. 6. Stooping down they took up much mud in their hands. 7. All, and you among the first, were hastening to praise him. 8. Young men have everything that is pleasant, beginning with health. 9. At last he began to praise the acts of the tyrant. 10. Justice in the long run is more profitable than injustice.

CLIII.—§§ 361-365

1. They conquered the Persians when Miltiades was general. 2. This was done after a long interval had elapsed. 3. I speak this in the belief that you will suffer this same fate. 4. If your power were double I should advise you to fight. 5. He cannot leave the city whilst his wife is absent. 6. They have forgotten us though but a short time has elapsed. 7. If the gods grant it we shall escape these evils. 8. The soldiers will fare ill if you are general. 9. If you had offered no defence the penalty would have been less. 10. If my ships were double as large I would make a voyage to the islands.

CLIV.—§§ 361-365

1. It was not possible to be disheartened when the news was brought. 2. But we, as they advanced, all

kept silent. 3. We ought ourselves to rejoice if men are happy. 4. If matters are so, why need we longer fear? 5. We said, when he asked us, that we were sailors from Athens. 6. It is not possible to teach unless one has learnt. 7. It is not possible to learn unless he teaches well. 8. As matters were well they found him delighted. 9. Whilst they were fighting a third army suddenly appeared. 10. We praise Themistocles because it was clearly shown that the ships saved Greece.

CLV.—§§ 366, 367

1. They are deliberating when they ought to be marching. 2. They are silent when they ought to answer. 3. He continued poor when he might have been rich. 4. He remained in the house when he was ordered to go to the market-place. 5. Though ordered to take the boy home he remained in the market-place. 6. I am ordered to find the book, though it is impossible to do so. 7. He prayed to Zeus, believing that the gods hear men's prayers. 8. They banish unprincipled men in the belief that their company corrupts the good. 9. Fly from bad men, believing that their company is a solvent of virtue. 10. They fled to the camp since it was impossible to resist any longer.

CLVI.—§§ 369, 370

1. The old man had just fallen asleep.   2. The sailor is always flattering the maiden.   3. He has sailed away to the island.   4. The other generals were present at the time.   5. They escaped to the camp without the enemy seeing it.   6. They continued to use the arrows of the Persians.   7. We should like to be on the top before the barbarians.   8. You will not be behindhand in flattering the king.   9. Let us stop the boy crying in that way.   10. You seem not to be able to hold up against sorrow.

CLVII.—§§ 369, 370

1. I happened to be present when the king appeared.   2. He was just falling asleep when I asked him that question.   3. The boy grows tired of reading the book.   4. The slave drank the wine without the master knowing it.   5. They reached the harbour before the sailors.   6. Let us not be behindhand in praising the soldiers.   7. The body is plainly not immortal.   8. The thief went off with all the gold.   9. The allies have not really done us any service.   10. It is unmanly not to be able to stop weeping.

CLVIII.—§§ 371-376

1. I showed him up for having stolen the gold. 2. I represented him as always flattering the rich. 3. The master convicted him of killing the dog. 4. He caught the slave drinking the wine. 5. I know that I shall die to-morrow. 6. I see my friend going to the city. 7. We heard that the enemy had withdrawn to the hills. 8. I forgot that you had done me any wrong. 9. We perceived the dog pursuing the hare. 10. Many men forget that they are mortal.

CLIX.—§§ 371-376

1. I am conscious that I have often spoken ill of you. 2. They were conscious of having drunk their father's wine. 3. I rejoice that I was mistaken about that matter. 4. Remember that you have been calumniated by the orator. 5. The boy did not repent of having spoken the truth. 6. We are not ashamed of loving our mother. 7. I heard the bird singing even in my house. 8. The general was vexed at seeing the soldiers. 9. He does not ·repent of having become a poet. 10. He was pleased to see the eagerness of the pupils.

CLX

1. He was delighted with the money because he had been poor. 2. They cannot sing although they have learnt many years. 3. The Athenians threatened the herald who brought the (proposals for a) truce. 4. If things go well I shall return home to-morrow. 5. All, the king among the first, went to meet the soldiers. 6. At last they ventured to call the tyranny grievous. 7. I understand that you do not fear the disease. 8. There is no hope unless men obey their generals. 9. They voted for war without fearing the immediate risk. 10. I knew that they had told you everything.

CLXI

1. A boy who says such things deserves to be flogged. 2. I will never give you money, not even if I have it. 3. The boy read the book without the master knowing it. 4. Let us attack the fort even though we shall be wounded and slain (§ 356). 5. He was delighted with the maiden because she was beautiful. 6. Hold out bravely without fearing the noise of the barbarians. 7. There is no victory for soldiers who do not obey their officers. 8. When they ought to be working they are eating or sleeping. 9. I will not abstain from this because you consider it disreputable. 10. Because he was young he hoped to be happy.

III.—THE VERBAL ADJECTIVES. §§ 377, 378

With dat. of agent, see § 158, but sometimes Accusative

Verbals in -τός. § 377

ὁ ποταμὸς διαβατός ἐστιν. ἔχεις μοι εἰπεῖν, ὦ Σώκρατες, ἆρα διδακτὸν ἡ ἀρετή; ἢ οὐ διδακτὸν ἀλλ' ἀσκητόν; ἢ οὔτε ἀσκητὸν οὔτε μαθητόν;

Verbals in -τέος. § 378

ὁ ποταμὸς διαβατέος ἐστίν. ὃ λέγω ῥητέον ἐστιν. ὠφελητέα σοι ἡ πόλις ἐστίν. ἄλλαι νῆες ἐκ τῶν συμμάχων μεταπεμπτέαι εἰσίν. οὐ γὰρ πρὸ τῆς ἀληθείας τιμητέος ἀνήρ, ἀλλ' ὃ λέγω ῥητέον. τὸν ποταμὸν διαβατέον ἐστίν. οὐχὶ ὑπεικτέον οὐδὲ ἀναχωρητέον οὐδὲ λειπτέον τὴν τάξιν. οὐ δουλευτέον τοὺς νοῦν ἔχοντας τοῖς κακῶς φρονοῦσιν. τί ἂν αὐτῷ ποιητέον εἴη; ἐψηφίσαντο πολεμητέα εἶναι. ταῦτα ἡμῖν ποιητέον ἐστίν. οἰστέον τάδε. φημὶ δὴ βοηθητέον εἶναι τούτοις. ἰτέον ἂν εἴη (ἡμᾶς) θεασομένους. οὐδενὶ τρόπῳ φαμὲν ἑκόντας ἀδικητέον εἶναι. ἐδόκει οὖν ἐπιχειρητέα εἶναι. ἐπιχειρητέα ἐδόκει εἶναι πάσῃ προθυμίᾳ καὶ καθαιρετέα ἡ τῶν Ἀθηναίων ἰσχύς.

EXERCISES

CLXII.—§ 377

1. The noise of the barbarians can be heard in the city. 2. The river may be crossed here without boats. 3. Wisdom cannot be taught to all men. 4. Self-restraint must be practised by all sensible men. 5. The slave's fetters cannot be loosed by his friend. 6. The fetters of the soul can be loosed by death alone. 7. The voice of the orator cannot be heard by the citizens. 8. The din of the battle could be heard in the city. 9. Those boys cannot be taught by any master. 10. The trench cannot be crossed by the enemy.

CLXIII.—§ 378

1. The river must be crossed by the soldiers. 2. You ought to practise virtue. 3. All men ought to imitate the good. 4. Such things ought not to be said by you. 5. The woman must be helped by us. 6. You must not yield if the enemy raise a shout. 7. There must be no retreat, no yielding ground to the enemy. 8. Brave men must not desert their posts in the hour of danger. 9. We must not enslave ourselves to men of no sense. 10. Other ships must be sent for from the harbour.

CLXIV.—§ 378

1. We must not do such deeds as this. 2. Troubles must be borne by all men. 3. Friendship must not be honoured before truth. 4. What I say to you must be said to all men. 5. We must give assistance immediately to those in the ship. 6. The citizens voted that war must be made against the savages. 7. What should we have to do if we were to promise help? 8. We ought to go immediately from the city. 9. We must send for the boy's mother to-morrow. 10. Boys ought to learn to reverence their parents.

CLXV.—RECAPITULATORY

1. I know that he acted thus from envy, not from goodwill. 2. Every one was delighted with your speech. 3. Such deeds ought never to be done by honourable men. 4. Most men fear to say all that they think. 5. He advised me to run eight furlongs every day before lunch. 6. One must try to do good to one's neighbours whilst one can. 7. If our doctors had been worth anything they would have found out the cause of this disease. 8. The farmer was robbed of all his cows in one night. 9. He said that he could never accuse the gods of injustice. 10. We must always endeavour to imitate good and honourable men.

CLXVI.—RECAPITULATORY

1. He stands there in astonishment as though he had never heard a man speak before. 2. Such an excuse would not have been made by an honourable man. 3. A liar even when he speaks the truth is not believed. 4. Men have not yet learnt to fly. 5. The stag escaped to the hills before the dogs came, so that it was not killed. 6. He is present, as it happens, and in our power: he shall not go now until he has paid the penalty of his sins. 7. Unknown to you they have done much harm to your son. 8. Do not call your enemy weak until you have overcome him. 9. Old men often love to think themselves ill, and so become a burden to their friends. 10. Life, said the philosopher, is what one makes it.

CLXVII.—RECAPITULATORY

1. He is silent although he ought now to rise and speak. 2. I am surprised that no one has discovered your wickedness before. 3. We believe that your dog killed the sheep; but he did it without any of us perceiving it. 4. When he died all his children were glad. 5. A master often acts unjustly to his pupils without knowing it. 6. May I never live to become a burden to my friends! 7. If I had wronged you, you could not have spoken worse of me. 8. I feared that you would never be able to teach my son anything. 9. I think that you would not have acted thus if you had known all the facts. 10. I was careful to find for him the best physician in the city.

CHAPTER X.—PARTICLES

§§ 379-430

EXAMPLES

I.—THE NEGATIVE PARTICLES. §§ 380-384

οὐκ ἔστιν οὐδὲν κρεῖττον ἢ νόμοι πόλει. καθεύδων οὐδεὶς οὐδένος ἄξιος οὐδὲν μᾶλλον τοῦ μὴ ζῶντος. μηδέποτε μηδεὶς γένοιτο Μεγαρέων σοφώτερος. § 381.
ἐάν τε οὐ φῆτε, ἐάν τε φῆτε. § 383.

οὐ μή with Aor. Subj., or more rarely Fut. Indic.

§ 384

ἢν ἅπαξ δύο ἢ τριῶν ἡμερῶν ὁδὸν ἀπόσχωμεν, οὐκ ἔτι μὴ δυνηθῇ βασιλεὺς ἡμᾶς καταλαβεῖν. οὐδεὶς μηκέτι μείνῃ τῶν πολεμίων. στερήσομαι τοιούτου ἐπιτηδείου οἷον ἐγὼ οὐδένα μή ποτε εὑρήσω.

EXERCISES

CLXVIII.—§§ 380-383

1. Nothing is better than courage in soldiers. 2. No one is willing to obey any one in that state. 3. No one when dead is better than any one else. 4. None of you is in any way useful to any one. 5. There is no one who does not think himself wise. 6. If you deny it you shall hear the witness. 7. Nor did you not see me; what you say is false. 8. It is not through fear at least that you deny you are his son. 9. If you had not refused to help him he would not have come to me. 10. If you do not forbid him the boy will come to me to-morrow.

CLXIX.—§ 384

1. The citizens surely will never be willing to obey such laws. 2. You never will, I am sure, suffer this from the king. 3. The dogs never will be able to catch the slave. 4. They certainly will not remain for three or four days. 5. No one shall ever catch me alive. 6. You certainly will not lose my friendship. 7. I shall never find such a friend again. 8. They never will catch the slave if he escapes to the mountains. 9. Such an orator is dead as we shall never surely hear again. 10. No one shall ever say such words to me.

II.—INTERROGATIVE ADVERBS.[1] §§ 385-392

EXAMPLES

Positive

ἐθέλοις ἂν ὑπὲρ τούτου ἀποθανεῖν ; ἢ ἐθέλοις ἂν ὑπὲρ τῆς γυναικὸς ἀποθανεῖν ; ἢ καὶ ἐθέλοι ἂν ὑπὲρ ἐμοῦ τοιαῦτα παθεῖν ; ἆρα ἐθέλοι ἂν γυνὴ ὑπὲρ τοῦ ἀνδρὸς ἀποθανεῖν ; § 386.

Negative: Answer "Yes"

οὐ συνίεις ; ἆρ᾽ οὐ συνίεις ; οὐ δεινὸν οὖν τάδε γενέσθαι ; οὐκοῦν μ᾽ ἐάσεις ἰέναι ; §§ 387, 388.

Negative: Answer "No"

μή τι ἄλλο λέγεις τὸ δίκαιον εἶναι ; ἆρα μὴ τούτῳ πιστεύεις ; μῶν τί σε ἀδικεῖ ; § 389.

ἄλλο τι ἢ ὁμολογεῖς ; ἢν τοὺς λίθους οἱ πολέμιοι ἀναλώσωσιν, ἄλλο τι ἢ οὐδὲν κωλύσει παριέναι ; § 390.

Alternative Questions

ἀποκτενεῖς τὸν ἄνδρα ἢ σώσεις ; ἆρά συ ἐγρήγορας ἢ καθεύδεις ; ἢ τοὺς πένητας φιλεῖ ἢ τοὺς πλουσίους ; § 391.

πότερα φῶμεν ἢ μὴ φῶμεν ; πότερον ἀπέκτεινε τὸν ἄνδρα ἢ ἔσωσεν ; πότερον τοὺς πένητας φιλεῖ ἢ τοὺς πλουσίους ; § 392.

[1] See also §§ 246-252.

EXERCISES[1]

CLXX.—§§ 386-390

1. Is she willing to die for her husband? 2. Would he really be willing to die for his wife? 3. Did the dog really die for his master? 4. Would you be willing to die for your brother? 5. Do you really understand all that? 6. Will you indeed allow me to go home? 7. Do you really think that this is just? 8. Would he not be willing to die for his friend? 9. Is not a friend always willing to die for a friend? 10. Surely she would not be willing to die for her husband?

CLXXI.—§§ 386-390

1. You do not understand this, do you? 2. She believes her husband, does she not? 3. He has not done you any wrong, has he? 4. He will let you go, will he not? 5. Surely nothing prevents you from passing? 6. Surely you do not agree that this is just? 7. Do you really wish to wrong your friend? 8. The enemy will use up their stock of stones, will they not? 9. Surely the enemy will prevent them from passing? 10. Do you believe the words of your wife?

CLXXII.—§§ 391, 392

1. Do you understand this or not? 2. Does she

[1] See also Exercises lxvi-lxix.

wish to kill her husband or to save him? 3. Is he asleep or awake? 4. Did the dog die for his master or no? 5. Do you really understand this or no? 6. Do you wish to become rich or poor? 7. Did he really think that this was just or no? 8. Am I to think you a friend or a foe? 9. Shall we kill the dog or give it to a friend? 10. Do you love your wife or your horse most?

CLXXIII

1. Where did you come from and where will you go to? 2. Will you go to the city or shall I? 3. Are you not ashamed when you see your father? 4. Did you or he do this? 5. Is it time for us to go or no? 6. Does this road lead to the harbour? 7. Are we to march in the night or no? 8. Am I to tell you what is pleasant or what is true? 9. Surely your father is not dead, is he? 10. Is his wife at home or in the market-place?

CLXXIV

1. Surely it is not time for you to go, is it? 2. Is your brother really a sailor? 3. Am I not to tell my wife the whole truth? 4. Does this road lead to the harbour or to the market-place? 5. Is this your house or mine? 6. Do you believe his words or your wife's? 7. Is your father a rich man or no? 8. Did you do this or no? 9. To whom did you give your father's books? 10. Why do you ask me, if you do not believe me?

III.—COPULATIVE AND DISJUNCTIVE CONJUNCTIONS

§§ 393-407

EXAMPLES

ὦ Ζεῦ καὶ θεοί. ἰατρός ἐστι καὶ μάντις. ἐν τούτῳ τῷ θορύβῳ συντριβόμεθα τὰς κεφαλὰς ἅπαντες· ... καὶ οἱ μετ' αὐτοῦ παροινήσαντες ἐδέοντό μου συγγνώμην ἔχειν. § 393.

κἂν μὲν ἀποφήνω μόνην ἀγαθῶν ἁπάντων οὖσαν αἰτίαν ἐμὲ ὑμῖν, δι' ἐμέ τε ζῶντας ὑμᾶς· εἰ δὲ μή. ... § 394.

καὶ ζῶν καὶ τελευτήσας. καὶ τῆς νυκτὸς καὶ τῆς ἡμέρας. § 395.

ἔγνωσαν τούς τε φεύγοντας καταδέξασθαι καὶ τοὺς ἀτίμους ἐπιτίμους ποιῆσαι καὶ κοινὴν τήν τε σωτηρίαν καὶ τοὺς κινδύνους ποιήσασθαι. § 396.

χαίρω τε γὰρ φειδόμενος ὡς οὐδεὶς ἀνὴρ πάλιν τ' ἀναλῶν ἡνίκ' ἂν τούτου δέῃ. § 397.

τοῦτ' ἔδρασας καὶ πονηρὸν καὶ δὴ καὶ αἴσχιστον. σφόδρα τε ἔντιμος ἐγένετο καὶ δὴ καὶ ὡς θεὸς προσεκυνήθη. § 398.

ἀναρίστητος ἦν καὶ οὐδὲν ἐβεβρώκειν. § 399.

οὐ γὰρ τοῦτο πέπονθα οὐδὲ μέλλω πάσχειν. § 400.

ὡς οὔτ' ἐκεῖν'· ἄρ' οὔτε ταῦτ' ὀρθῶς ἔδρων. καὶ μήτε θερμὴν μήθ' ὁδὸν ψυχρὰν φράσῃς. ὤμοσαν μήτε προδώσειν ἀλλήλους σύμμαχοί τε ἔσεσθαι. § 401.

σύ γ' οὐδ' ὁρῶν γιγνώσκεις οὐδ' ἀκούων μέμνησαι.
§ 402.
παραπλήσια πέπονθε καὶ ἔδρασεν. οὐχ ὅμοια σοὶ καὶ ἐκείνοις ἦν. § 403.
ἤδη ἦν ὀψὲ καὶ προσῆλθον οἱ πολέμιοι. οἱ Λακεδαιμόνιοι οὐκ ἔφθασαν πυθόμενοι τὸν περὶ τὴν Ἀττικὴν πόλεμον καὶ ἦκον ἡμῖν ἀμυνοῦντες. § 404.
τίς ἐθελήσει χαλκεύειν ἢ ναυπηγεῖν ἢ ῥάπτειν ἢ τροχοποιεῖν; τοῦτο δεῖ πυθέσθαι εἴτε τὸ πλουτεῖν εἴτε τὸ πεινῆν βέλτιον. § 405.
ῥᾷόν ἐστι λαλεῖν ἢ σιωπᾶν. ἕτερα ποιεῖς ἢ λέγεις. § 406.

EXERCISES

CLXXV

1. The god was both a prophet and a physician. 2. Your friends are wicked and indeed most unprincipled also. 3. But it happened in the daytime and not in the night. 4. For he does not take pleasure in saving, nor will he ever do so. 5. Neither in the daytime nor in the night can we escape the notice of the gods. 6. But they do not even understand when they see, nor remember when they hear. 7. He got his head broken in the same riot as I. 8. They were just beginning to break one another's heads when the guards came up. 9. Is it better to be a tailor or to starve? 10. I alone was the cause of it, and it is owing to me that you are now alive. And this I will now prove to you.

CLXXVI

1. Would you rather be a smith or a shipwright? 2. It is better to be silent than to talk foolishly. 3. It was already late in the night when they came to the city. 4. Your case is not the same as mine (§ 403). 5. We cannot trust men who act differently from what they say. 6. If only you could get as good as you give! (§ 403). 7. It is easier to spend

money than to save it. 8. Give me water, neither very hot nor yet cold. 9. We swore to be allies and not to betray one another. 10. He has not suffered as I have; I was abused by every one, and indeed banished from the city for many years.

IV.—ADVERSATIVE CONJUNCTIONS. §§ 408-420

οὐ τρεῖς ἐκεῖνοί γ' εἰσὶν ἀλλὰ τέτταρες. ἐστὶν ὄνομα κεραμέως ἀλλ' οὐ τυράννου. § 410.

πάντες ἀξιοῦσιν οὐχ ὅτι ἴσοι ἀλλὰ καὶ πρῶτος ἕκαστος εἶναι. οὐ μόνον οὐ φίλος ἦν ἀλλὰ καὶ ἐχθρός. οὐχ ὅπως τούτων χάριν ἀπέδωκας ἀλλὰ καὶ κακὰ ἀντεποίησας. οὐχ ὅπως ἔδρασεν ἀλλ' οὐδ' ἐνενόησεν. § 411.

εἰσὶ μὲν ἔνιαι τῶν ἀποκρίσεων ἀναγκαῖαι διὰ μακρῶν τοὺς λόγους ποιεῖσθαι· οὐ μὴν ἀλλὰ πειράσομαί γ' ὡς διὰ βραχυτάτων. § 412.

καὶ γὰρ οὐκ ἂν δόξειεν οὕτω γ' εἶναι ἄλογον· οὐ μέντοι ἀλλ' ἴσως ἔχει λόγον. § 413.

ἀλλ' ἴωμεν. ἀλλὰ τί οὐ βαδίζομεν πρὸς αὐτόν; ἐπὶ τὴν εἰρήνην; ἀλλ' ὑπῆρχεν ἅπασιν; ἀλλ' ἐπὶ τὸν πόλεμον; ἀλλ' αὐτοὶ περὶ τῆς εἰρήνης ἐβουλεύεσθε. § 414.

εἰ σῶμα δοῦλον, ἀλλ' ὁ νοῦς ἐλεύθερος. § 416.

πρῶτον μὲν ἐλούσατ' εἶτα δ' εἰς κουρέως ἦλθεν. ὁ μὲν τάδε εἶπεν ὁ δὲ τἀναντία. τοὺς μὲν ἔνδον ηὗρον, τοὺς δ' οὔ (see § 3). κακὸν μέν ἐστιν ἀλλ' ἀναγκαῖον κακόν. § 417.

σὺ δέ γ' εὖ πράττεις· καίτοι πρότερόν γ' ἐπτώχευες. § 418.

ἄτοπον μέντοι τί σοι ἐθέλω λέγειν.

τόδε μὴν ἄξιον ἐπίστασθαι.

λέγουσι μέν τι, οὐ μέντοι γε οἷον οἴονται. § 419.

νῦν ὅμως θαρρῶ. ἀλλ' ὅμως πειρατέον δή. § 420.

V.—THE CAUSAL CONJUNCTION γάρ. §§ 421-423

τεκμήριον δὲ τούτου· ἐνθάδε γὰρ ἀφικύμενος οὐ λάθρα ἐλακώνιζεν. § 421.

οἴκαδε ἐβαδίζομεν· ὀψὲ γὰρ ἦν τῆς ἡμέρας.

καὶ γὰρ νῦν ὁμολογῶ. καὶ γὰρ οὖν ταῦτα ἰσχυρίζοντο. § 422.

οἴει γάρ σοι μαχεῖσθαι τὸν ἀδελφόν; ταῦτα δὴ συνίεις; εὖ γὰρ δηλοῖς. § 423.

VI.—ILLATIVE CONJUNCTIONS. §§ 424-430

οὐ δεινὸν οὖν τάδε γενέσθαι; οὐκοῦν μ' ἐάσεις ἰέναι; οἴει τιν' οὖν τῶν τοιούτων ὅστις καὶ ὁπωστιοῦν δύσνους Λυσίᾳ ὀνειδίζειν αὐτῷ τοῦτο ὅτι συγγράφει; οὐκ οὖν εἰκός γε ἐξ ὧν σὺ λέγεις. οὐκ ἔγημ' ἔναγχος; πάνυ μὲν οὖν. μέγιστον ἀγαθόν. κακὸν μὲν οὖν μέγιστον. § 426. ἐπερησόμενος οὖν ᾠχόμην ὡς τὸν θεόν. ἀλλ' οὐχ οἷόν τε τὸν Παφλαγόν' οὐδὲν λαθεῖν. κράτιστον οὖν νῶν ἀποθανεῖν. § 427. πέραινε τοίνυν ὅ τι λέγεις ἀνύσας ποτέ. τοὺς μαθητὰς οἶσθ' οὓς φράζω; τούτοις τοίνυν ἄγγελλε. ... § 428. μεθύοντες ἀεὶ τὰς μάχας μάχονται. τοιγαροῦν φεύγουσ' ἀεί. οὐδένι ἀχάριστον εἴασεν εἶναι τὴν προθυμίαν· τοιγαροῦν κρατίστους δὴ ὑπηρέτας εἶχεν. § 429. πολὺ ἀμείνων ἄρα ὁ τοῦ ἀδίκου ἢ τοῦ δικαίου βίος. οὐκ ἄρ' ἦν φιλόσοφος. ἀλλ' ἐὰν ἄρα καὶ τύχῃ, Ἀθήναζε φευξόμεθα. § 430.

EXERCISES

CLXXVII.—§§ 408-420

1. We remained there not four days but three. 2. I consider you not merely not a friend but actually an enemy. 3. Not only did he not give back the money, he actually asked me for more. 4. Not only did you not show gratitude for this, but you did not even think of it. 5. I should like to be a potter but not a king. 6. He not merely did not speak well of me, he actually abused me. 7. I want not merely not to be first, but not even to be equal to you. 8. Well then, let us be off; yet I will try first to persuade you that you are not acting rightly. 9. If they kill the body, at least they cannot kill the soul. 10. But you, at any rate, were then a slave and now are free.

CLXXVIII.—§§ 408-420

1. First he said this, then the opposite. 2. He is now a beggar, yet formerly he was a king. 3. I should like however first to wash myself, and then I will come with you. 4. He used to be a barber, yet now he is a general. 5. Some went to the barber's; others remained talking in the market-place. 6. What! you will not take this? yet it will be worth

much money to you. 7. It is hard to teach a fool wisdom, but yet I must try. 8. The king knows all, nevertheless I have now no fear. 9. They know something, yet not as much as they think. 10. What! you said that with a view to peace? why, who wished for war?

CLXXIX.—§§ 421-423

1. This is indeed strange; when I first heard you I thought you a wise man. 2. And this is a proof of it; it was late in the day when he left my house. 3. Were you walking home? Yes, you saw us yourself. 4. They distrusted the general; for indeed he made no secret of his leanings to Sparta. 5. You do not say the same now as you formerly did (§ 403); for you certainly used to maintain that war was better than peace. 6. So you think you can deceive your wife, do you? 7. Well then, do you understand this now? Yes, you make it quite clear. 8. Now then, are you willing to tell us what you saw? Yes, for of course you promise to give me a reward. 9. Then be quick and say what you have to say (§ 428). I was walking home late at night when (§ 404) I heard an uproar. Yet I was not frightened, for I had just been drinking. 10. So I went back to the place and I saw the plaintiff with his head broken, and the defendant striking him and calling him a thief.

CLXXX.—§§ 424-430

1. Is it not really dreadful that he should say such things? 2. Do you think, then, that he dislikes my father? 3. Will you let me go, then? Of course I will. 4. Did you not say, then, that you had written this? 5. It is best therefore to avoid being seen by the master. 6. Did you see my friend? then run and tell him this quickly. 7. After all, wealth is better than wisdom in this life. 8. So he did not tell you the truth after all? 9. But if after all you do escape the notice of the guards, you will be able then to flee to the hills. 10. They always fight their battles with brave hearts. Then that is why they always conquer.

MISCELLANEOUS EXAMPLES

CHIEFLY ON CHAPTER VIII

CLXXXI

1. One must try to act honourably although it is not always easy or pleasant. 2. He told Cyrus that if he would give him cavalry he would easily conquer the whole district. 3. He would have been able to stop the soldiers from burning the villages if he had sent his cavalry against them. 4. Do not steal; for the laws say that any man who steals will be punished severely. 5. Whenever I come to your house I find that you have gone out. 6. He told me that if I were a wise man I should not speak so foolishly. 7. He always says that his head aches whenever he has any work to do. 8. The boy replied that if his father would send him the money he would return home as quickly as possible. 9. Every one knows that dogs ought to have black mouths. 10. When you have heard the whole matter you shall tell me what you think about it yourself.

CLXXXII

1. I knew that he spoke ill of his friends whenever they were absent. 2. The whole city is surprised that the army has done nothing. 3. The slave answered

that after he had been beaten he would still say the same. 4. When the enemy see that you destroy the villages they will wish to retreat. 5. He knew that if he had held his tongue about that he would have been rewarded by the king. 6. He came to the camp without being seen, to report those facts to the general. 7. Whenever the king came to the town all the citizens used to rejoice. 8. The poor man would have perished if I had not given him something to eat. 9. Whether you believe me or not, I have told you the whole truth. 10. The farmer said that the wolf had killed six sheep before he shot it.

CLXXXIII

1. Do not talk so much. It was a wise man who said 'Boys should be seen but not heard.' 2. I do not know what the generals intend to do. 3. He asked the natives how deep the river was. 4. Do you think that I should have said that, if it had not been true? 5. I often go to the city to see my friends. 6. How much do you think your brother would have given to the slave? 7. I hope that you will never be able to act so disgracefully. 8. I will kill you if you attempt to escape. 9. The poet used to praise all whom he saw managing the affairs of the state well. 10. This poet praises all kings and rich men who give him money.

CLXXXIV

1. He said that he would give me back the money whenever he could. 2. Does he hope to be able to deceive me also? 3. There is no one who does not think himself wiser than his neighbours. 4. He fears that he will not be elected general, as he is not an Athenian by race. 5. Foolish men think that they can do wrong without the gods knowing it. 6. Evil communication corrupts good manners. 7. The soldiers did not know whether Cyrus was marching against the great king or no. 8. I am afraid that you do not love my friends. 9. No one doubted that that man was a thief. 10. If you ask your father for all that money, will he give it to you?

CLXXXV

1. I am not afraid that the enemy will ever conquer us. 2. Do not say that, for no one will ever believe you. 3. He was so frightened that he immediately fled home. 4. We feared that you were never going to come. 5. He told me that he would not have flattered the judge if he had known that he would be found guilty of the theft. 6. The master said that he hoped the boys would be able to do it all. 7. Whenever he saw a really poor man he used to give him money. 8. Do you wish then that I should tell you all I know about your son? 9. If I

do so you will not be pleased; but I will tell you whatever you wish. 10. Do not tell me that fathers are not pleased when their sons are clever.

CLXXXVI

1. A wise general praises his soldiers whenever he sees them marching well. 2. He told me that if I went to his house he would show me the book. 3. All men, and I among the foremost, used to say that the city would never prosper if that man managed affairs. 4. He told me that if I had been really wise I should have praised the boy to his mother. 5. He said that he did not believe that I could speak the truth if I wished. 6. He sent for Cyrus that he might see him before he died. 7. Every one knew that if Cyrus had been the elder of the two sons he would have become king. 8. He told me that if he had had the money he would have gladly given it to me; but I did not believe him. 9. He said that whenever he went to the city he used to see some of his friends. 10. Let all remain in the camp lest the enemy learn that we are here.

CLXXXVII

1. He said that he would give me whatever he found. I replied that I was willing to trust him. 2. He asked why they had taken the book away from the boy. 3. The doctor said that the man would have

still been alive if he had obeyed him. 4. Whenever I went to the market-place I used to see an old man sitting there with a long staff in his hands. 5. The farmer would have sold the horse for three minae if you had not offered him more. 6. Let no one leave the city till we have found the man who slew the judge. 7. When I have talked to the general I will tell you if he is going to praise the soldiers. 8. It is a foolish man who says he will do whatever he pleases. 9. The wolf did not know which way to turn itself to escape from the dogs. 10. He would be glad to hear what men say about that book of his.

CLXXXVIII

1. You will have a headache if you read for more than eight hours a day. 2. The boy has told so many falsehoods that even if he tells the truth I cannot believe him. 3. Do you really think that I would not tell you if I knew? 4. You said that if we did that we should not prosper. 5. Did he really tell you that if I had obeyed him I should not have been punished? 6. Whenever he saw any one coming out from the city he used to ask for money. 7. I am afraid that you will never be able to cease abusing me. 8. What would *you* have done if the Athenians had prosecuted you? 9. Whenever you see any one wishing to enter the house you must persuade him to remain outside. 10. If you have the money give it to me.

CLXXXIX

1. He would never have done that had he known what I know. 2. He asked me if he would be wrong if he were to tell this to his friends. 3. He says that you are acting wisely if you are here to learn the whole matter. 4. Do not speak so fast if you wish your friends to understand and obey you. 5. He said that he did not know which way the road led. 6. If I had not seen it myself I should never have believed that you could have treated your son so ill. 7. He said that he would give me the present whenever he came to town. 8. He said that since I had killed his father he should try to kill me. 9. Though the robbers have ravaged but half the country they shall all be killed. 10. If bad citizens are ever worthy of death, that man deserves to die.

CXC

1. He said that if we had been boys we could not have talked more foolishly. 2. The sailor fell into the sea, and so he was never seen again. 3. He threw the man into the sea so as to kill him. 4. He said that he should write many letters before he went to sleep. 5. Let us hope that our soldiers will not run away till at least they see the enemy. 6. Though I might have gone to the city with him I wished to remain here. 7. He often told me that if I had been a prudent man all this would have been in my power.

8. He said that not he himself but his son had given the poor man the money. 9. Obey your rulers if you wish to be happy and prosperous. 10. Do not steal your neighbour's money lest you be found guilty of theft and banished from the country.

CXCI

1. The general himself will come to-morrow to lead us against the enemy. 2. He was chosen general with nine others that the city might be safe. 3. If you really wish to know the truth I will tell you all I can. 4. Do you think then that those men will still be your friends if you become poor? 5. They thought that if they built a large ship they would be able to make a voyage in safety to Asia. 6. The doctor advised the old man to eat and drink little, and to ride for two hours every day. 7. Call no man happy, said the philosopher, till he is dead. 8. You seem to think that when a boy has once learnt this he will remember it. That is very far from being the case. 9. Oh that I could tell you what I really think of you! 10. If our doctors were worth anything they would long ago have found out the cause of this disease.

CXCII

1. Whatever he may have suffered he kept it secret from us. 2. The gods act strangely in giving more to those who already have much. 3. Is there

no painter who can represent the beauty of that woman? 4. They were disputing about the gods existing or no. 5. To think he could say such things about his own father! 6. A wise man thinks all pleasures empty and vain. 7. The judge works hard that his wife may have more money to spend. 8. He said that he did not like the boy's mother. 9. If the dog had had a beautiful head I should not have given it to you. 10. This slave deserves to be flogged if he really stole the money.

CXCIII

1. When asked what he needed he said, I shall require two thousand cavalry and a few archers. 2. Many cavalry were there to prevent our men from crossing the river. 3. After a little toil we shall journey for the rest of the way without fighting. 4. The enemy turned aside and went off by another road. 5. I am grievously wearied with carrying my shield. 6. They were very disheartened because on one side there were lofty hills, and on the other the river twenty feet in depth. 7. While he lived all men counted him a happy man. 8. So long as thou doest well unto thyself men will speak good of thee. 9. 'Oh that I had never been born!' he cried in his grief. 10. Oh that I could pass unseen through the enemy and carry the news to our army—how we are surrounded on every side and can hold out but few days longer.

GREEK - ENGLISH VOCABULARY

FOR THE EXAMPLES ONLY

Numerals are not given in this Vocabulary.

A

ἀγαθός, adj. good.
Ἀγαμέμνων, Agamemnon.
ἀγανακτῶ (εω), I am indignant, vexed at or with, dat. 161.
ἀγγέλλω, I report, announce.
ἄγγελος ὁ, messenger.
ἀγνοῶ (εω), I am ignorant.
ἄγροικος, adj. rude, boorish.
ἀγρός ὁ, field, farm, country.
ἄγω, I lead, bring, take ; ἄγε νυν, come now ! ἄγε δή, come then !
ἀγών ὁ, struggle, contest.
ἀγωνίζομαι, I contend.
ἀδάκρυτος, adj. without weeping.
ἀδελφός ὁ, brother.
ἀδικία ἡ, injustice.
ἄδικος, adj. unjust, wicked.
ἀδικῶ (εω), I do wrong, sin ; trans. I ill - treat ; verbal, ἀδικητέος, 378.
Ἄδμητος ὁ, Admetus.
ᾄδω, I sing.
ἀεί, always.
ἀήρ ὁ, air, heaven.
ἀθάνατος, adj. deathless, everlasting.

Ἀθήναζε, adv. to or towards Athens.
Ἀθῆναι αἱ, Athens.
Ἀθηναῖος, adj. Athenian.
Ἀθήνησιν, locative, at Athens.
ἀθρόος, adj. close together, one and all.
Ἄθως ὁ, Mount Athos.
αἰδοῦμαι (εο), I feel respect for.
αἴξ ὁ ἡ, goat.
Αἰολίς, fem. adj. Aeolian, the district of Aeolia.
αἴρω, I raise.
αἱρῶ (εω), I seize, take, capture ; mid. I take for myself, choose, elect for myself.
αἰσθάνομαι, I perceive, gen. or acc. 114.
Αἰσχίνης ὁ, Aeschines.
αἰσχρός, adj. base, low.
αἰσχύνη ἡ, shame.
αἰσχύνομαι, I am ashamed, am ashamed of, feel shame before, acc.
αἰτία ἡ, cause, charge, blame ; ἐν αἰτίᾳ ἔχω, I blame ; αἰτίαν ἔχω, I am blamed.
αἴτιος, adj. causing, cause of, gen.

αἰτιῶμαι (αο), I blame, hold guilty of, *gen.* 100, 2.
αἰτοῦμαι (εο), I ask for.
Αἰτωλία ἡ, Aetolia.
Αἰτωλικός, *adj.* in *or* of Aetolia.
ἀκινάκης, (short Persian) sword.
ἀκολουθῶ (εω), I follow, *dat.* 167.
ἀκοντίζω, I throw a javelin.
ἀκόντιον τό, javelin.
ἀκοντιστής ὁ, a javelin thrower.
ἀκούω, I hear, *gen. or acc.* 114; *as pass. of* λέγω, 180; εὖ ἀκούω, I am spoken well of; κακῶς ἀκούω, I am spoken ill of.
ἄκρος, *adj.* highest, top, summit.
ἀκροῶμαι (αο), I listen to, *gen. or acc.* 114.
ἄκων, *adj.* unwilling.
ἀλγῶ (εω), I have pain; τὴν κεφαλήν, I have a headache, 76.
ἀλείφομαι, I anoint myself.
Ἀλέξανδρος ὁ, Alexander.
ἀλήθεια ἡ, truth.
ἀληθής, *adj.* true.
ἁλίσκομαι, I am taken.
Ἄλκηστις ἡ, Alcestis.
Ἀλκιβιάδης ὁ, Alcibiades.
ἀλλά, but; *in abrupt objections,* 414.
ἄλλος, *adj. pron.* other; οἱ ἄλλοι, the rest; *with gen.* different from, other than, 133.
ἄλογος, *adj.* unreasonable.
ἅμα, *adv. and prep. dat.* together with; ἅμ' ἕῳ, at dawn; ἅμ' ἡμέρᾳ, at daybreak.
ἁμαρτάνω, I err, I miss, lose, err in, *gen.* 100, 4.
Ἀμεινίας ὁ, Ameinias.
ἀμελῶ (εω), I neglect, *gen.*
ἀμελῶς, *adv.* ἀμελῶς ἔχω περί, I treat neglectingly, I slight.
ἄμοιρος, *adj.* without part *or* share in, *gen.* 131.
ἀμύνω, I help, *dat.* 153; *mid.* I defend myself against, ward off.

ἀμφισβητῶ (εω), I dispute.
ἀμφότερος, *adj.* both of two.
ἀμφοτέρωθεν, *adv.* from both sides.
ἄμφω, *adj.* both of two.
ἄν, *particle.*
ἀναβαίνω, I climb up, mount.
ἀναγιγνώσκω, I read.
ἀναγκάζω, I compel, force.
ἀναγκαῖος, *adj.* necessary.
ἀνάγκη ἡ, necessity, compulsion.
ἀνάγομαι, I stand out to sea.
ἀναγωγή ἡ, a standing out to sea; ἀναγωγὴν ποιοῦμαι, I put to sea; *pass.* ἡ ἀναγωγὴ γίγνεται, 200.
ἀναιρῶ (εω), I pick up.
ἀνακέκραγα, I cry, shout out.
ἀναλίσκω, I use up, spend.
ἀναμιμνήσκω, I remind, *acc. and gen.* 100, 3.
ἀνανδρία ἡ, unmanliness, cowardice.
ἀνάξιος, *adj.* unworthy.
ἀναρίστητος, *adj.* without lunch *or* breakfast.
ἀναχωρῶ (εω), I withdraw, retreat; *verbal,* ἀναχωρητέος, 378.
ἀνδριαντοποιός ὁ, statuary, sculptor.
ἄνειμι, I shall go up.
ἄνευ, *prep.* without, *gen.*
ἀνήκεστος, *adj.* desperate.
ἀνήρ ὁ, man.
ἀνθρώπινος, *adj.* belonging to man, human; τὰ ἀνθρώπινα, human affairs.
ἄνθρωπος ὁ, man.
ἀνίστημι, *trans. tenses,* I set up; *intrans. tenses and passive,* I stand up, rise up, leave, retire.
ἀνοίγνυμι, I open.
ἀντακούω, I listen in turn.
ἀνταμύνομαι, I resist in turn, on my side.
ἀντεῖπον, I replied, refused, gainsaid, forbade.
ἀντέχω, I hold out (against).
ἀντιλέγω, I gainsay, forbid.
ἀντίπαλος, *adj.* equal in strength to, a match for.

GREEK-ENGLISH VOCABULARY 171

ἀντιποιῶ (εω), I do in return.
ἀντιτάττω, I array against, dat. 141.
ἀνύσας, aor. part. ἀνύω, I finish off; 428, 'quickly.'
ἄξιος, adj. worthy, worthy of, guilty of, gen. 99; worth, gen. 119.
ἀξιῶ (οω), I make demands, claim.
ἀπαίρω, I march away, sail away, 177.
ἀπαλλάττω, I rid some one of something, acc. and gen. 126.
ἀπαντῶ (αω), I meet, dat.
ἅπαξ, adv. once.
ἅπας, adj. quite all, all together, one and all, whole.
ἀπειλῶ (εω), I threaten.
ἄπειμι, I am away from, absent.
ἄπειμι, I shall go away, withdraw.
ἄπειρος, adj. endless.
ἀπελαύνω, I drive away.
ἀπέρχομαι, I go away.
ἀπέχω, I am distant, distant from, gen. 126; mid. I abstain from, refrain from, gen. 126.
ἀπό, prep. from, gen.; ἀπ' ἐκείνου, from that time.
ἀποβαίνω, I go away from, I result in, turn out to be, am.
ἀποδείκνυμι, I explain, set a copy.
ἀποδημῶ (εω), I leave my country.
ἀποδιδράσκω, I run away, make off.
ἀποδίδωμι, I give away or back; mid. I sell; ἀποδίδωμι χάριν, I show gratitude.
ἀποθνῄσκω, I die, I am killed.
ἀποικία ἡ, colony.
ἄποικος ὁ, colonist.
ἀποκρίνομαι, I answer.
ἀπόκρισις ἡ, answer.
ἀποκρύπτω, I conceal, keep secret.
ἀποκτείνω, I kill.
ἀπολαύω, I enjoy, have enjoyment in, gen. 117.
ἀπολείπω, I leave behind, I fall short of, gen. 134.

ἀπόλλυμι, I destroy, ruin; pass. I perish.
ἀπολογοῦμαι (εο), I offer as a defence, defend myself, plead.
ἀπολύω, I acquit.
ἀπόμνυμι, I swear no by, acc. 63.
ἀποπέμπω, I send away.
ἀποπλέω, I sail away.
ἀπορῶ (εω), I am in doubt, I am at a loss for, gen. 130.
ἀποσπῶ (αω), I drag from; ἀπό and gen.
ἀποστερῶ (εω), I deprive of, rob of, acc. and gen. 130.
ἀποτρέπω, trans. I turn from, acc. and gen. with or without ἀπό, 129; mid. I turn aside from, desert.
ἀποφαίνω, I make plain, I prove, show, demonstrate; mid. ἀποφαίνομαι γνώμην, I give as my opinion.
ἀποφεύγω, I escape.
ἀπόχρη, it is enough.
ἅπτομαι, I fasten upon, cling to, touch, gen. 112.
ἄρα, particle, then, so, after all, 430.
ἆρα, interrog. particle, really?
ἀργύριον τό, piece of silver, money.
ἀρετή ἡ, virtue, courage, honesty.
Ἀριαῖος ὁ, Ariaeus.
ἀριθμός ὁ, number, sum.
ἄριστον τό, the morning meal, late breakfast or lunch.
ἄριστος, adj. best; superl. of ἀγαθός.
Ἀρκαδία ἡ, Arcadia.
ἅρμα τό, car.
ἁρμόττω, I make to fit, fit together; intrans. I fit.
ἀρνοῦμαι (εο), I deny.
ἀρχή ἡ, beginning, power, authority, command, office; ἀρχήν or τὴν ἀρχήν, adverbially in neg. sentences, at all, 80, 2.
ἄρχω, I begin, start, rule, rule

over, *gen.* 112; I am in command.
ἀσθενής, *adj.* weak, sick, ill.
ἀσθενῶ (εω), I am weak, sick, ill.
ἄσιτος, *adj.* without food.
ἀσκῶ (εω), I practise; *verbals*, ἀσκητέος, to be practised, ἀσκητός, may be attained by practice, 377, 378.
ἄσμενος, *adj. always used predicatively*, pleased, glad, gladly; ἐμοὶ ἀσμένῳ, 155.
ἄστυ τό, town.
ἅτε, *with participle, causal*, 355, because, inasmuch as.
ἀτέλεια ἡ, exemption from taxes.
ἀτελής, *adj.* incomplete.
ἀτιμάζω, I dishonour.
ἀτιμία ἡ, disfranchisement.
ἄτιμος, *adj.* disfranchised, deprived of, *gen.* 131.
ἄτοπος, *adj.* odd, strange.
Ἀττική ἡ, Attica.
ἀτυχῶ (εω), I am unfortunate.
αὐξάνω, I aggrandise, make to increase.
αὐτίκα, *adv.* immediately.
αὐτόν *i.e.* ἑαυτόν, himself.
αὐτός, *pron.* he, self, *reflex. in nom.*; ὁ αὐτός *or* αὑτός, the same; αὐτὸς ὁ ἀνήρ, the man himself; αὐτοῖς (τοῖς) ἀνδράσι, men and all, 166; same as, *with dat.* 139; αὐτὰ ταῦτα, for this very purpose, 80, 1.
αὐτόχθων, *adj.* indigenous, native.
ἀφαιρῶ (εω), I take away, *acc. and dat.* 153.
ἀφανής, *adj.* invisible.
ἀφίημι, I send away, let go, leave alone, leave.
ἀφικνοῦμαι (εο), I come to, arrive at, εἰς.
ἀφίστημι, *trans. tenses*, I set apart; *intrans. tenses and passive*, I leave, desert, revolt from.

ἀφομοιῶ (οω), I make to resemble. 138.
ἀχάριστος, *adj.* ungrateful, unrewarded.
Ἀχαρνεύς ὁ, inhabitant of Acharnae, an Acharnian.
ἄχθομαι, I am annoyed with, angry with, *dat.* 159.
ἀψεύδεια ἡ, sincerity

B

βαδίζω, I go, walk.
βάλλω, I throw, pelt.
βάραθρον τό, hangman's pit.
βάρβαρος, *adj.* native, barbarian.
βασίλεια ἡ, royal power.
βασιλεύς ὁ, king.
βασιλεύω, I am king, reign as king, I am king of, *with gen.* 95.
βέβαιος, *adj.* firm, certain, (of life) tranquil.
βελτίων, *comp. adj. See* ἀγαθός, better.
βία ἡ, force.
βιάζομαι, I force.
βιβρώσκω, I eat.
βίος ὁ, life.
[βιῶ (οω)], *in 2d aor.*, ἐβίων, I lived.
βλαβή ἡ, hurt, injury.
βλάπτω, I hurt, injure.
βλαστάνω, I grow.
βλέπω, I look, see; ὀξὺ β. I have keen sight.
βοή ἡ, cry, shout.
βοήθεια ἡ, aid.
βοηθῶ (εω), I go to aid of, help, *dat.* 152; *verbal*, βοηθητέον, help must be given to, 378.
Βοιωτία ἡ, Boeotia.
Βοιωτοί οἱ, men of Boeotia, Boeotians.
βόσκημα τό, a *fatted* beast.
βουκόλος ὁ, herdsman.

βουλεύω, I counsel, advise; *mid.* I deliberate upon, take counsel, make plans, determine.
βουλή ἡ, senate.
βούλομαι, I wish; ἐμοὶ βουλομένῳ, 155.
βοῦς ὁ *and* ἡ, ox, cow.
βοῶ (αω), I shout.
βραχύς, *adj.* short, small; βραχύ, for a short distance.
Βυζάντιοι οἱ, Byzantines.
βωμός ὁ, altar.

Γ

γάλα τό, milk.
γαμῶ (εω), I marry.
γάρ, *conj.* for, 421 *foll.*; καὶ γάρ, 422.
γελοῖος, *adj.* ridiculous.
γελῶ (αω), I laugh.
γενναῖος, *adj.* generous, noble.
γένος τό, race.
γεραιός, *adj.* old.
γέρας τό, privilege.
γεύω, I give to taste, *gen.* 114; *mid.* I taste, *gen.* 114.
γέφυρα ἡ, bridge.
γεωργός ὁ, farmer.
γῆ ἡ, earth, world.
γίγνομαι, I become, am, I am born of, the son of, *gen.* 125, (of numbers) I reach; τὰ γεγενημένα, what has been, the past.
γιγνώσκω, I get to know, understand, determine.
γλυκύς, *adj.* sweet.
γνῶθι, *imperat. of* ἔγνων, *aor. of* γιγνώσκω, know.
γνώμη ἡ, view, judgment, mind.
γονεύς ὁ, parent.
γραῦς ἡ, old woman.
γράφω, I write; *mid.* I prosecute.
Γύλιππος ὁ, Gylippus.
γυμναστική ἡ, gymnastics.
γυμνός, *adj.* without upper clothes, naked; *with gen.* 131, bare of, without.
γυνή ἡ, woman.

Δ

δαίμων ὁ, fate.
δάκνω, I bite.
Δαρεῖος ὁ, Darius.
δέ, *conj.* but, and; δ' οὖν, well then.
δέδια, I fear.
δέδοικα, I fear.
δεῖ, *impers. from* δέω, it behoves, is necessary, one ought; δεῖ μοι, *with gen.* I need, 140; ὀλίγου δεῖ, all but, 130; πολλοῦ δεῖ, far from, 130; ὀλίγου δεῖν, almost, 341; μικροῦ δεῖν, almost, 341, etc.
δείκνυμι, I show.
δειλία ἡ, cowardice.
δειλός, *adj.* cowardly.
δεινός, *adj.* strange, serious, terrible, awful, clever, good at; τὸ δεινόν, the risk.
δειπνῶ (εω), I dine *or* sup.
δένδρον τό, tree.
δεξιός, *adj.* right; ἐν δεξιᾷ, on the right hand.
δέρμα τό, flayed skin, hide.
δέρω, I flay, I flog.
δεσμός ὁ, fetter.
δεσμωτήριον τό, prison.
δεσπότης ὁ, master (of slave, etc.)
δεῦρο, *adv.* hither.
δέω, *and mid.* δέομαι, I lack, need, I beg for, *gen.* 130.
δή, *particle*, indeed.
δῆμος ὁ, parish; ὁ δῆμος, the people.
Δημοσθένης ὁ, Demosthenes.
δημόσια τά, public life.
διά, *prep. acc.* owing to, through, on account of; διὰ τί, why? *gen.* through, by means of; διὰ μακ-

ῥῶν, at length ; διὰ βραχυτάτων, as shortly as possible.
διαβαίνω, I go through, I cross ; verbals, διαβατέος, must be crossed, 378 ; διαβατός, may be crossed, 377.
διαβάλλω, I calumniate.
διαγίγνομαι, I last, continue.
διάγω, I lead through, (of time) I get through, pass, I live, 177.
δίαιτη ἡ, way of living, life.
διάκονος ὁ, servant.
διαλάμπω, I shine through.
διαλέγομαι, I converse with, dat.
διανέμω, I distribute.
διάνοια ἡ, mind, purpose ; διάνοιαν ἔχω, I have thoughts of, inf.
διανοοῦμαι, I intend.
διαπράττω, I do thoroughly, I finish off.
διαρπάζω, I sack, plunder.
διατελῶ (εω), I continue.
διαφέρω, I differ from, gen. 126.
διαφεύγω, I escape.
διαφθείρω, I kill, destroy, corrupt.
διάφορος, adj. differing from, gen. 128.
διδάσκαλος ὁ, master (of pupil).
διδάσκω, I teach, instruct, inform, tell ; mid. I get taught for me ; verbal, διδακτός, may be taught, 377.
δίδωμι, I give.
διέρχομαι, I go through, get across.
διέχω, I am away from, gen. 126.
δικάζομαι, I am at law with, dat. 143.
δίκαιος, adj. just, upright ; τὰ δίκαια, rights.
δικαιοσύνη ἡ, justice.
δικαστήριον τό, law court.
δίκη ἡ, right, lawsuit, trial, penalty ; δίκην δίδωμι, I am punished.
δίκτυον τό, hunting net.
Διονυσίοις, at the Dionysia, 173, 3.
διορύττω, I dig (a canal) through.
διπλάσιος, adj. double (as large, etc.)

διψῶ (αω), I am thirsty.
διώκω, I pursue, prosecute ; ὁ διώκων, the plaintiff.
δοκῶ (εω), I seem, I seem to myself, 327 ; impers. δοκεῖ, it seems ; τὸ δοκοῦν, appearances, 100, 4.
δόλος ὁ, cunning.
δόξα ἡ, reputation.
δουλεία ἡ, slavery.
δουλεύω, I am a slave to, serve ; verbal, δουλευτέος, must serve 378.
δ'οὖν, well then.
δράκων ὁ, dragon, serpent.
δρῶ (αω), I do.
δύναμαι, I am able, I can ; μέγα δ. I am very powerful, 72, 3.
δύναμις ἡ, power, force.
δυνατός, adj. able ; δυνατώτατος, strongest.
δύομαι, (of sun) I set.
δυσμενής, adj. hostile.
δύσνους, adj. hostile to.
Δωριεύς ὁ, a Dorian.
δωροδοκῶ (εω), I take bribes.

E

ἕ, pron. him.
ἐάν, conj. if.
ἑαυτόν, pron. himself.
ἐγγύς, adv. near to, gen.
ἐγείρω, I make to wake up ; mid. I wake up ; 2d perf. ἐγρήγορα, I am awake.
ἐγκύπτω, I stoop down.
ἐγκωμιάζω, I praise.
ἐγρήγορα, I am awake, 2d perf. ἐγείρω.
ἐγώ, pron. I.
ἐδέδισαν, plup. δέδοικα, they feared.
ἐθέλω, I am willing, wish.
εἰ, conj. if ; εἰ γάρ, 230-231 ; εἰ μή, 231.
εἶδον, I saw.
εἴθε, in wishes, 230-231.

εἰκάζω, I liken, compare, 138 ; I guess, *with inf.*
εἰκός, likely, probable.
εἷλον, *aor. of* αἱρῶ.
εἰμί, I am.
εἶμι, I (shall) go, come, march ; *verbal*, ἰτέος, 378.
εἴργω, I prevent, restrain from, keep (something) away from.
εἴρηκα, I have said.
εἰρήνη ἡ, peace.
εἴρηται, it has been said.
εἰς, *prep. acc.* into, to ; *with numerals*, up to, as many as.
εἰσβάλλω εἰς (*sc.* στρατιάν), I make an inroad into.
εἴσειμι, I (shall) go into, come into, enter.
εἰσέρχομαι, I go into, come into, enter.
εἰσπλέω, I sail into, *acc.*
εἶτα, *interrog. particle.*
εἴωθα, I am accustomed to ; εἰωθώς, common, customary.
ἕκαστος, *adj. pron.* each, 30.
ἑκάστοτε, *adv.* each time.
ἑκάτερος, *adj. pron.* each *of two*, 30.
ἐκβαίνω, I go out from, *gen. with* or *without* ἐκ, 129, I turn out to be.
ἐκβάλλω, I drive out.
ἐκεῖ, *adv.* there, at that point.
ἐκεῖθεν, *adv.* from there, thence.
ἐκεῖσε, *adv.* to that point, thither.
ἐκκλησία ἡ, assembly of the people.
ἐκκόπτω, I strike out.
ἐκπέμπω, I send out.
ἐκπίνω, I drink off.
ἐκπίπτω, I am driven out, 181.
ἐκπλήττομαι, I am amazed at.
ἐκτειχίζω, I thoroughly fortify.
ἐκτίθημι, I place out, expose (a child).
ἐκτίνω, I pay in full.
Ἕκτωρ ὁ, Hector.
ἑκών, willingly ; ἑκὼν εἶναι, 342.

ἔλαιον τό, olive oil.
ἐλαττοῦμαι (oo), I am at a disadvantage compared with, *gen.* 134.
ἐλαύνω, I drive, ride, march, 177. ἐλ. ἐπί, I charge.
ἐλάχιστος, least, fewest, smallest.
ἔλεος ὁ, pity.
ἐλευθερία ἡ, freedom.
ἐλεύθερος, *adj.* free, free from, *gen.* 128.
ἐλευθερῶ (οω), I set free from, *acc.* and *gen.* 126.
Ἑλλάς ἡ, Greece.
ἐλλείπω, I am wanting in.
Ἕλλην, *adj.* Greek.
Ἑλλήσποντος ἡ, Hellespont.
ἐλπίζω, I hope.
ἐλπίς ἡ, hope.
ἐμαυτόν, *pron.* myself.
ἐμβαίνω εἰς, I set foot on board, embark on.
ἐμβάλλω, I throw into.
ἐμός, *adj. pron.* my, mine.
ἔμπειρος, *adj.* acquainted with, *gen.*
ἐμποδών, *adv.* in the way ; τί ἐμπ. what prevents ? 333.
ἐμφανής, *adj.* manifest, visible, open.
ἐμφύω, I plant in, *acc. and dat.* 141.
ἐν, *prep.* in, among, *dat.*
ἔναγχος, *adv.* just now, recently.
ἐναντίος, *adj.* opposite to ; *subst.* an adversary.
ἔνδεια ἡ, want.
ἐνδέχομαι, I receive (proposals), I approve of.
ἐνδίδωμι, I give in, yield.
ἔνδοθεν, *adv.* from within.
ἔνδον, *adv.* within, indoors, at home.
ἐνδύω, I put on.
ἕνεκα, *prep. gen.* for the sake of.
ἔνθαδε, *adv.* here, there.
ἐνθένδε, *adv.* from there, thence, hence.

ἔνθεος, adj. inspired.
ἔνι for ἔνεστι, it is in, it is in the power of.
ἔνιοι, adj. some.
ἐννοῶ (εω), I have in mind, think of.
ἐνταῦθα, adv. here, there, at that branch of, gen.
ἔντιμος, adj. held in honour.
ἐντυγχάνω, I light upon, find, dat.
ἐξαγγέλλω, I bring (full) news.
ἐξαπατῶ (αω), I deceive thoroughly.
ἔξαρνος, adj. denying; ἐξ. εἰμι, I deny.
ἐξελέγχω, I convict, confute.
ἐξεργαστικός, adj. able to accomplish, gen. 98.
ἔξεστι, it is allowed, in one's power to, dat. of person and inf. 319, acc. and inf. 320.
ἐξικνοῦμαι (εο), I reach, attain to, gen.
ἔοικα, I am like, dat. 138.
ἐπαινετός, adj. praiseworthy.
ἔπαινος ὁ, praise.
ἐπαινῶ (εω), I praise.
ἐπαληθεύω, I make true, confirm.
ἐπείγομαι, I strive to, hasten to.
ἐπειδάν, conj. whenever, 301.
ἐπειδή, conj. whence, since.
ἔπειμι, I (shall) go against, attack
ἐπεκθέω, I rush out against.
ἐπεκπλέω, I sail out against.
ἐπεξάγω, I lead out against.
ἐπερήσομαι, I shall ask besides.
ἔπηλυς ὁ ἡ, a newcomer, foreigner.
ἐπί, prep. gen. upon, towards, over, in time of; dat. by, upon, on, in power of; acc. to, towards, over, against; ἐπὶ πλέον, for longer time; τὰ ἐπὶ Θράκης, the parts towards Thrace, the quarter of Thrace; ἐπὶ τούτῳ, on this condition.
ἐπιβαίνω, I mount upon, gen.
ἐπιβουλεύω, I plot against, dat.

ἐπιγίγνομαι, I fall upon, come upon, attack.
'Ἐπίδαμνος, Epidamnus.
ἐπιδείκνυμι, I exhibit.
ἐπιθυμῶ (εω), I am enamoured of, desire, gen. 100, 5.
ἐπικουρῶ (εω), I succour, dat. 152.
ἐπιλανθάνομαι, I forget, gen. 100, 3.
ἐπιμελοῦμαι (εο), I take charge of, am anxious about, take care, take precautions, make an effort to be, gen. 100, 3.
ἐπιορκῶ (εω), I commit perjury, I swear falsely by, acc.
ἐπίσταμαι, I know, understand.
ἐπιστήμων, adj. skilful in, gen. 99.
ἐπισχύω, I make strong.
ἐπιτήδεια τά, provisions, food.
ἐπιτήδειος ὁ, friend.
ἐπίτηδες, adv. intentionally.
ἐπίτιμος, adj. enfranchised.
ἐπιτρέπω, I hand over, give up, entrust to, acc. and dat.
ἐπιτρέχω, I run up against, dat.
ἐπιχειρῶ (εω), I attempt, undertake, endeavour, try; verbal, ἐπιχειρητέος, must be attempted, attacked, 378.
ἕπομαι, I follow, dat. 167.
'Ἐρασανίδης ὁ, Erasanides.
ἐργάζομαι, I work, do.
ἔργον τό, work, deed, fact, event, scene.
ἔρδω, I work at, do.
ἔρις ἡ, strife, quarrel.
ἐροίμην, opt. of ἠρόμην, I asked.
ἔρχομαι, I come, go; εἰς χεῖρας ἔρχ. come to close quarters.
ἐρῶ (εω), I shall say, as fut. of λέγω.
ἐρῶ (αω), I am enamoured of, long for, gen. 100, 5.
ἔρως ὁ, love.
ἐρώτημα τό, question.
ἐρωτῶ (αω), I ask (a question).
ἐσθίω, I eat.

ἑσπέρα ἡ, evening.
ἔσπλους ὁ, inlet.
ἔσχατος, adj. furthest, extreme, extremity of, 25, 2 ; τὰ ἔσχατα, the extreme penalties, 165.
ἕτερος, adj. pron. other, different; ἕτ. ἤ, different from, 406.
ἑτέρως, adv. differently.
ἔτι, adv. still ; οὐκ ἔτι or οὐκέτι, no longer.
ἔτος τό, year.
εὖ, adv. well.
εὐαγγέλια τά, thank-offerings for good tidings.
εὐδαιμονία ἡ, happiness, prosperity.
εὐδαιμονίζω, I congratulate, felicitate.
εὐδαιμονῶ (εω), I am happy, prosperous.
εὐδαίμων, adj. happy, prosperous.
εὐεργεσία ἡ, kindness.
εὐεργέτης ὁ, benefactor.
εὐθύς, adv. at once, immediately.
εὐκλεής, adj. famous.
εὔνοια ἡ, love, good-will, friendship.
εὐπορῶ (εω), I abound in, gen. 113.
εὐπρεπής, adj. comely.
Εὐριπίδης ὁ, Euripides.
εὑρίσκω, I find.
εὖρος τό, breadth, width.
εὐρύς, adj. broad, wide.
εὐτάκτως, adv. in good order.
εὐτυχῶ (εω), I am prosperous.
εὐφραίνω, I make happy.
εὔχομαι, I pray, vow.
ἐφέπομαι, I pursue.
ἐφίημι, I send against ; mid. with gen. I am set upon obtaining, long for, 100, 5.
ἐφίστημι, trans. tenses, I set over ; intrans. tenses and passive, I am set over ; οἱ ἐφεστηκότες, those in command, 108, 2.
ἐχθρός, adj. hostile ; subst. enemy.
ἔχω, I have ; mid. I cling to, gen. 112 ; with adverbs, I am ; with inf. I can ; ἔχει κατὰ χώραν, he keeps on the same spot, 176.
ἐῶ (αω), I allow, permit, leave.
ἕως ὁ, dawn.
ἕως, conj. until, 302-303.

Z

Ζεύς ὁ, Διός, Zeus.
ζημία ἡ, penalty, fine.
ζημιῶ (οω), I fine, punish.
ζητῶ (εω), I seek, inquire into.
ζῶ (αω), I live.
ζωγραφικός ὁ, student of painting.
ζωγράφος ὁ, painter (from life or nature).
ζῷον τό, living creature.

H

ἡγεμών ὁ, leader, commander.
ἡγοῦμαι (εο), I think, believe, consider ; I lead, guide, direct, with gen. 95, dat. 153.
ἡδέως, adv. gladly, pleasantly.
ἤδη, adv. by now, already, now.
ἥδομαι, I am pleased, I am pleased with, dat. 160 ; ἥδ. ἡδονήν, I experience pleasure, 72, 1.
ἡδονή ἡ, pleasure.
ἦθος τό, character.
ἥκω, I have come, am come, 210, 2.
ἡλικία ἡ, time of life, age, life.
ἥλιος ὁ, sun.
ἡμέρα ἡ, day.
ἡμέτερος, pron. adj. our.
ἥμισυς, adj. half, 104.
ἤν, conj. (=ἐάν), if.
ἡνίκα, conj. when ; ἡνίκ' ἄν, whenever, 301.
ἤπειρος ἡ, mainland.
ἠρόμην, I asked.

ἦσαν, 3d plur. plup. οἶδα, they knew.
ἡττῶ (αω), I worst, out-do.

Θ

θάλαττα ἡ, sea.
θάνατος ὁ, death.
θαρρῶ (εω), I have no fear, no fear of, *acc.*
θαυμάζω, I wonder, I wonder at, am surprised at, admire, *acc.*
θαυμαστός, *adj.* wonderful, surprising; θαυμαστὸν ποιῶ, I act strangely.
θεῖος, *adj.* divine.
Θεόδωρος ὁ, Theodorus.
θεός ὁ, god.
θεραπεύω, I tend, look after, nurse.
Θερμοπύλαι αἱ, Thermopylae.
θερμός, *adj.* hot.
θέρος τό, summer; θέρει, in summer, 173, 1; ὥρᾳ θέρους, in summer time, 173, 1.
Θεσπιῆς οἱ, Thespians.
θέω, I run.
θεῶμαι (αο), I see.
Θῆβαι αἱ, Thebes.
Θηβαῖοι οἱ, Thebans.
θησαυρός ὁ, treasure.
Θησεύς ὁ, Theseus.
θνῄσκω (in pres. compound ἀποθνῄσκω used), I die; τέθνηκα, I am dead; τεθνήξει, he will have passed away; οἱ τεθνεῶτες, the dead.
θνητός, *adj.* mortal.
θόρυβος ὁ, uproar, din, noise, to-do.
θορυβῶ (εω), I make an uproar, disturbance, I interrupt.
Θρᾷξ ὁ, a Thracian.
θυμοῦμαι (εο), I am provoked with, *dat.* 159.
θύρα ἡ, *generally in plural*, door.
θύραζε, *adv.* to the door, out of the door, out of doors.

θύω, I sacrifice.
θώραξ ὁ, breastplate.

Ι

ἰατρεύω, I treat medically, doctor.
ἰατρός ὁ, doctor, physician.
ἰδέα ἡ, form, make.
ἴδιος, *adj.* peculiar to, own, *gen.* 108, 2.
ἰδιώτης ὁ, private individual.
ἱερός, *adj.* sacred, sacred to, *gen.* 108, 2.
Ἰθάκη ἡ, Ithaca.
ἱκανός, *adj.* sufficient, good, able to (*with inf.*)
ἱκανῶς, *adv.* sufficiently.
ἱκέτης ὁ, suppliant.
ἱμάτιον τό, cloak.
ἵνα, *conj.* in order to, 260-262.
Ἰόνιος, *adj.* Ionian.
ἱππεύς ὁ, horseman, *plur.* cavalry.
ἱππεύω, I ride (a horse).
ἵππος ὁ, horse.
Ἰσαῖος, Isaeus.
ἴσος, *adj.* equal; ἐξ ἴσου γίγνεσθαι, to be on the same footing as, *dat.* 139.
Ἱστιαῖος ὁ, Histiaeus.
ἰσχυρίζομαι, I maintain, assert.
ἰσχύς ἡ, power, strength.
ἰσχύω, I am strong.
ἴσω (οω), I think equal, *acc. and dat.* 138.
ἴσως, *adv.* perhaps.
ἰτέον, *verbal*, εἶμι, one must go, 378.
ἰχθύς ὁ, fish.

Κ

καθαιρῶ (εω), I destroy; *verbal*, καθαιρετέος, must be destroyed, 378.
καθέζομαι, I sit down.

καθεύδω, I am asleep.
καθίζομαι, I sit down.
καθίστημι, trans. tenses, I station, set, place ; intrans. tenses and passive, I am stationed, etc.; εἰς, I bring or reduce to.
κάθοδος ἡ, going back, return (from exile).
καί, conj. and, etc. 393 foll. ; when, 404 ; as, 403 ; adv. even, very, etc.
καιρός ὁ, time of difficulty, crisis.
καίτοι, particle, strong adversative, yet, 418.
κακίζω, I call bad or cowardly, abuse.
κακός, adj. bad, evil, wretched ; τὰ κακά, misfortunes, misery.
κακῶς, adv. ill, miserably, wretchedly.
κάλλος τό, beauty.
καλός, adj. beautiful, noble, glorious ; οἱ καλοὶ κἀγαθοί, the well bred ; καλόν ἐστι, it is well.
καλῶ (εω), I call, summon.
καλῶς, adv. nobly, well, favourably ; καλῶς ἔχει, it is well ; καλῶς εὐδαίμων, really happy, 317.
Καμβύσης ὁ, Cambyses.
κάμνω, I am ill, suffer.
κἄν, for καὶ ἐάν.
κάνθαρος ὁ, beetle.
καρδία ἡ, heart.
καρτερῶ (εω), I hold up, endure.
κατά, prep. (1) acc. along, about, according to ; τὸ κατ᾽ ἐμέ, if I can help it, 79 ; κατὰ χώραν ἔχειν, to keep on the spot, 176 ; (2) gen. down from, down over, down under, against.
καταγελῶ (αω), I laugh at, gen. 121.
καταγιγνώσκω, I decide against, acc. and gen. 122.
κατάγνυμι, I break.

κατάγω, I bring back, restore.
καταδέχομαι, I receive or welcome home.
καταδικάζω, I adjudge against, acc. and gen. 122.
καταδουλῶ (οω), I enslave.
κατακάω, or κατακαίω, I burn up.
κατακλῄω, I shut up.
κατακρημνίζω, I throw headlong, precipitate.
κατακρίνω, I give sentence against, acc. and gen. 122.
καταλαμβάνω, I seize upon, surprise, occupy, find, acc.
καταλείπω, I leave behind, acc.
κατάλυσις ἡ, a breaking up, ending of, solvent of.
καταπηδῶ (αω), I jump down.
κατασιωπῶ (αω), I make silent, silence.
κατασκευάζω, I prepare, provide.
καταφεύγω, I flee.
καταφρονῶ (εω), I slight, despise, gen. 121.
καταχέω, I pour, shed over, acc. and gen. 121.
καταψεύδομαι, I tell lies against, gen. 121.
καταψηφίζομαι, I vote against, acc. and gen. 122.
κάτειμι, I (shall) go up to home, be restored from exile, 182.
κατεῖπον, I told.
κατεσθίω, I eat up, devour.
κατηγορῶ, I accuse, make a charge against, 123.
κατηχῶ (εω), I instruct, teach.
κάω or καίω, I make to burn, burn, acc.
κεῖμαι, I lie, am situated.
κείρομαι, I cut my hair.
κελεύω, I bid, request.
κενός, adj. empty, vain, groundless, empty of, gen. 131.
κένταυρος ὁ, Centaur.
κενῶ (οω), I empty of, acc. and gen. 130.

κεράμευς ὁ, potter.
κέρδος τό, gain, profit.
κεφαλή ἡ, head.
κιθαρίζω, I play the lute.
κίνδυνος ὁ, danger.
κίνησις ἡ, motion.
κλάω or κλαίω, I weep.
Κλεαρίδας ὁ, Clearidas.
Κλέαρχος ὁ, Clearchus.
Κλεινίας ὁ, Cleinias.
Κλέων ὁ, Cleon.
κλοπή ἡ, theft.
κοιμῶμαι (αο), I go to bed.
κοινός, adj. common, impartial, common to, shared in by, dat. 167; common property of, gen. 108, 2.
κολάζω, I chastise, punish.
κολακεύω, I flatter.
κόλπος ὁ, gulf.
κομίζομαι, I get back for myself, recover.
Κόνων ὁ, Conon.
κόπτομαι, I beat myself, mourn for, acc.
κόρη ἡ, maiden, pupil of eye.
Κορίνθιος, Corinthian.
Κόρκυρα ἡ, Corcyra.
κουρεύς ὁ, a barber.
κράτιστος, adj. superl. best.
κράτος τό, authority.
κρατῶ (εω), I rule over, gen. 95, I am master.
κραυγή ἡ, shouting.
κρέας τό, flesh.
κρείττων, adj. comp. better.
κρίνω, I put on trial, judge, conclude.
κρίσις ἡ, decision.
κριτής ὁ, judge.
Κροῖσος ὁ, Croesus.
κρύπτω, I conceal (from).
κτῶμαι (αο), I acquire, gain; perf. I possess.
Κύδνος, Cydnus.
κυνῆ ἡ, hat.
κύριος, adj. master of, gen.; subst. master, owner, lord.

Κῦρος ὁ, Cyrus.
κύων ὁ and ἡ, dog.
κωλύω, I hinder, prevent, acc.; hinder from, acc. and gen. 126; with inf. clause, 334.

Λ

λαγώς ὁ, hare.
λάθρα, adv. secretly.
Λακεδαιμόνιος, adj. Lacedaemonian.
λακωνίζω, I favour Sparta.
λαλῶ (εω), I talk.
λαμβάνω, I take, seize; mid. I take hold of, gen. 112.
λαμπρός, adj. famous.
λανθάνω, I escape the notice of, acc. 62; with participle, 369.
λέγω, I say, speak; εὖ λέγω, I speak well of; κακῶς λέγω, I speak ill of.
λείπω, I leave; λείπομαι, I remain; verbal, λειπτέος, must be left, 378.
Λεπτίνης ὁ, Leptines.
Λέων ὁ, Leon.
Λεωνίδης ὁ, Leonides.
λεώς ὁ, people.
λήγω, I cease from, gen. 126.
λῃστής ὁ, robber, pirate.
λῃστικόν τό, pirate navy.
λίθος ὁ, stone.
λιμήν ὁ, harbour.
λογίζομαι, I reckon, calculate.
λόγος ὁ, word, talk, speech, statement; λόγον ἔχει, it is reasonable.
λοιδορῶ (εω), I abuse, revile, dat. 153.
Λοκροί οἱ, Locrians.
λοῦμαι (ουο), I wash myself, bathe.
λόφος ὁ, knoll, hill.
Λυδός ὁ, Lydian.
Λυκοῦργος ὁ, Lycurgus.
λυποῦμαι (εο), I am sorry, in sorrow,

feel sorrow, am grieved at or with, *dat.* 160.
Λυσίας ὁ, Lysias.
λυσιτελής, *adj.* profitable.
λύω, I loosen, (of bridge) I break down, destroy.

M

μά, *in oaths*, no by, 63.
μάθημα τό, lesson.
μαθητής ὁ, pupil.
μαίνομαι, I am mad, insane; ὁ μαινόμενος, a madman, 138.
μακαρίζω, I think *or* call happy.
μακάριος, *adj.* happy, fortunate.
Μακεδονία ἡ, Macedonia.
μακρός, *adj.* long, large; μακρῷ, by far; διὰ μακρῶν, at length, fully.
Μάκρωνες οἱ, the Macrones.
μάλιστα, *adv. superl.* very much, most; *with numbers*, altogether, about.
μανθάνω, I learn; *verbal*, μαθητός, may be learnt, 377.
μανία ἡ, madness.
μάντις ὁ, prophet, seer.
Μαραθῶνι, *locative dative*, at Marathon, 172.
μαρτυρία ἡ, evidence.
μάρτυς ὁ *and* ἡ, witness.
μάταιος, *adj.* vain, unprofitable.
μάτην, *adv.* in vain.
μάχη ἡ, battle.
μάχομαι, I fight, fight against, *dat.* 141.
Μεγαρεύς ὁ, a Megarian.
Μεγαροῖ, *locative*, at Megara.
μέγας, *adj.* great; μέγα δύναμαι, I am very powerful.
μέγεθος τό, size.
μεθίστημι, *trans. tenses*, I change from; *intrans. tenses and passive*, I am changed from, *gen.* 42.
μεθύω, I am drunk (with wine).

Μειδίας ὁ, Meidias.
μείζων, *comp.* of μέγας, greater, taller.
μέλει, *impers.* it is a care to, *dat. and gen.* 100, 4; μέλει μοι, I am concerned about, 140.
μέλι τό, honey.
μέλλον τό, the future.
μέλλω, I am about to, intend; *with pres. or fut. inf.* 209, I delay.
μέμφομαι, I find fault with, censure, *acc. and dat.* 153, *cogn. acc.* 72, 1.
μέμψις ἡ, fault.
μέν, *particle, answering to* δέ; μὲν οὖν, 426.
Μένδη ἡ, Mende.
μέντοι, however, 418; οὐ μέντοι ἀλλά, 413; οὐ μέντοι, 419.
μένω, I remain.
Μένων ὁ, Menon.
μέρος τό, part, share; *adverbially*, to some extent, 79.
μεσημβρινός, *adj.* at midday.
μέσος, *adj.* middle, centre.
Μεσσήνη ἡ, Messene.
μεστός, *adj.* full of, *gen.*
μετά, *prep.* (1) *acc.* after; (2) *gen.* together with.
μεταδίδωμι, I give a share of, *gen.* 115.
μεταλαγχάνω, I have a share in, *gen.* 115, I obtain as a share.
μεταλαμβάνω, I share in, *gen.* 115.
μεταμέλει, *impers.* to repent of, *dat. and gen.* 100, 4.
μεταμέλομαι, I repent.
μεταπέμπομαι, I send for; *verbal*, μεταπεμπτέος, must be sent for, 378.
μέτειμι, I (shall) go after.
μετέχω, I have part *or* share in, *gen.* 115.
μετέωρος, *adj.* high; μετέωρόν τι, a hill.
μέτοχος, *adj.* sharing in, *gen.* 103, 2.

μέτριος, adj. moderate, abstemious.
μετρῶ (εω), I measure.
μέχρι, until ; μέχρι οὗ, until, 301-302.
μή, adv. not ; μὴ οὔ, 330.
μηδαμῇ, adv. nowhere, in no wise.
μηδείς, pron. no one.
μήν ὁ, month.
μήν, particle, truly, indeed ; οὐ μήν, 419 ; οὐ μήν . . . ἀλλά . . . 412.
μηνυντής ὁ, informer.
μηχανῶμαι (αο), I contrive.
μικρός, adj. small ; μικροῦ δεῖν, almost, 341.
μιμνήσκω, I remind ; mid. I remember, gen. 100, 3 ; with participle, 373.
μιμοῦμαι (εο), I imitate ; verbal, μιμητέος, right to imitate, 378.
Μίνως ὁ, Minos.
μισθός ὁ, pay.
μισθῶ (οω), I let ; mid. I hire.
μῖσος τό, hatred.
μνᾶ ἡ, mina.
μνημεῖον τό, memorial.
μνήμη ἡ, memory.
μνημονεύω, I remember.
μόνον, adv. only.
μόνος, adj. alone, only.
μουσική ἡ, music.
μῶν, interrog. particle, 389.
μωρία ἡ, folly.

N

ναί, yea, yes.
ναυμαχία ἡ, battle at sea.
ναυπηγῶ (εω), I am a shipwright.
ναῦς ἡ, ship.
ναύτης ὁ, sailor.
ναυτικός, adj. belonging to ships ; ναυτικόν τι, a navy.
νεανίας ὁ, young man.
νέος, adj. young.

νή, particle in oaths, yes by, 63.
νῆσος ἡ, island.
νίκη ἡ, victory.
Νικίας ὁ, Nicias.
Νικόφημος ὁ, Nicophemus.
νικῶ (αω), I conquer, am victorious over, acc. ; cogn. acc. ν. νικήν, I gain a victory ; νικῶ τοῦτο, I am victorious in this.
νομίζω, I consider, think, believe in.
νόμος ὁ, law, custom.
νόσος ἡ, disease.
νοσῶ (εω), I am ill, sick ; ὁ νοσῶν, a sick man, patient.
νουμηνίᾳ, at the new moon, 173, 3.
νοῦς ὁ, sense, mind, attention ; νοῦν ἔχω, I am a man of sense.
νῦν, adv. now ; τὸ νῦν εἶναι, for the present, 342.
νυν, then.
νύξ ἡ, night.
νῶτον τό, back.

Ξ

Ξανθίας ὁ, Xanthias.
Ξενίας ὁ, Xenias.
Ξενοφῶν ὁ, Xenophon.
Ξέρξης ὁ, Xerxes.
ξίφος τό, sword.
ξύλον τό, wood, timber.

O

ὁ, def. article, the ; οἱ μὲν . . . οἱ δέ, some . . . others, 2-3.
ὁδός ἡ, way, road, journey.
ὄζω, I smell of, gen. 117.
οἶδα, I know.
οἴκαδε, adv. to home, homewards.
οἰκεῖος, adj. proper to, gen. 108, 2.
οἰκέτης ὁ, servant.
οἰκία ἡ, house.
οἴκοι, locative, at home.

οἰκονομικός, adj. thrifty.
οἶκος ὁ, house, home.
οἰκτείρω, I pity.
οἰκῶ, I live, dwell.
οἴμαι or οἴομαι, I think.
οἴμοι, ah me! alas! alas for, gen.
Οἰνόη ἡ, Oenoë.
οἶνος ὁ, wine.
οἴομαι, I think.
οἷος, adj. such as, what sort of, of which sort, etc.; correl. of οἷα τοιοῦτος, etc., as, 257; οἷός τ' εἰμί, I can, am able; οἷον, οἷα, with participles, 355.
οἰστέος, verbal from φέρω, must be borne, 378.
οἴχομαι, I go off, I am gone, 210, 2.
ὀκνῶ (εω), I shrink from, inf.
ὀλίγος, adj. few; ὀλίγου, adv. almost; ὀλίγον δεῖν, 341.
ὀλίγωρος, adj. careless of, gen. 99.
ὅλος, adj. whole, total.
Ὀλύνθιοι οἱ, Olynthians.
ὁμιλῶ (εω), I consort, associate with, dat.
ὄμνυμι, I swear.
ὅμοιος, adj. equal to, like, dat.
ὁμολογῶ (εω), I agree, admit, agree with, dat.
ὅμορος, adj. neighbouring; subst. a neighbour.
ὅμως, adv. notwithstanding, nevertheless, 420.
ὀνειδίζω, I reproach.
ὄνομα τό, name.
ὀνομάζω, I name, call.
ὀξύς, adj. sharp, keen.
ὀπίσω, adv. backwards; τοὐπίσω, behind.
ὅπλον τό, plur. generally, arms.
ὁπόθεν, dependent interrog. and relat. whence, from which.
ὅποι, dependent interrog. and relat. whither.
ὁποῖος, of what sort.
ὁπόταν, whenever.
ὁπότε, whenever, 301.
ὁπότερος, which, whichever (of two).
ὅπως, conj. that, final, 260-262; after verbs of striving, 266-269; take care that, 269.
ὁπωστιοῦν, however, in whatever way.
ὀργίζομαι, I am angry, angry with, dat. 159.
ὀρέγομαι, I reach after, gen. 100, 5.
ὀρθῶς, adv. rightly.
ὅρκος ὁ, oath.
ὁρμῶ (αω), I move against; intrans. and mid. I hasten towards, I set out.
ὄρνις ὁ and ἡ, bird.
ὄρος τό, hill.
ὄρτυξ ὁ, quail.
ὁρῶ (αω), I see.
ὅς, rel. pron. who, which, 38-40.
ὅσος, how great; adv. ὅσον, as far as; ὅσον γ' εἰδέναι, 340.
ὅσπερ, rel. pron. the very one who or which, 38-40.
ὅστις, rel. whoever, etc.; dependent interrog. whoever; causal, since he, etc., 291.
ὀσφραίνομαι, I smell, gen. 114.
ὅταν, conj. whenever, 301.
ὅτε, conj. when.
ὅτι, conj. that.
οὐ, not; οὐ μή, 384.
οὐδέ, not even, 400 foll.
οὐδείς, no one; οὐδέν, in no way; οὐδεὶς ὅστις οὐ, every one, 40, 44.
οὐδέποτε, never.
οὐκ, not, 380 foll.
οὐκέτι, no longer.
οὖν, therefore, then, now.
οὔπω, not yet.
οὐράνιος, adj. heavenly.
οὐρανός ὁ, heaven.
οὐσία ἡ, property, money, estate.
οὔτε, neither, nor, 400 foll.
οὔτοι, certainly not.
οὗτος, pron. this, he.

οὕτω or οὕτως, adv. thus, so; οὕτως ἔχει, it is so.
οὐχ, οὐχί, not; οὐχ ὅπως, 411.
ὀφείλω, I owe.
ὀφθαλμός ὁ, eye.
ὀψέ, adv. late.

II

πάθος τό, disaster.
παιδεία ἡ, education.
παιδεύω, I teach, educate, instruct.
παῖς ὁ, child, boy, son.
πάλαι, adv. long ago, of old, once.
πάλιν, adv. again, back.
παλτόν τό, javelin.
Παναθηναίοις, at the Panathenaea, 173, 3.
παντοῖος, adj. of all sorts.
πάνυ, adv. very.
παρά, prep. (1) acc. to the presence of, past, beyond, contrary to, during; (2) gen. from the presence of, from; (3) dat. by the side of.
παραγγέλλω, I send word to, order.
παραγίγνομαι, I come up, come to.
παραδίδωμι, I hand over to, give to.
παραπλέω, I sail past.
παραπλήσιος, adj. like, equal to, as good as, 139.
παράπλους ὁ, coasting voyage.
παρασκευάζω, I prepare.
παρατάττω, I draw up, arrange.
παρατίθημι, I set before, set by the side of.
παραφρονῶ (εω), I am insane, off my head.
παραχρῆμα, adv. immediately; ἐν τῷ π. at the moment, 80, 2.
παραχωρῶ (εω), I yield from, acc. and gen. 127.
πάρειμι, I am present, come to, dat.
πάρειμι, I (shall) go past, pass.

παρέρχομαι, I go past, pass, (of time) I elapse; τὰ παρελθόντα, the past, 79.
παρέχομαι, I furnish, provide, give, 190.
παροινῶ (εω), I get drunk.
πᾶς, adj. all; ὁ πᾶς ἀριθμός, the sum total.
πάσχω, I suffer; as pass. of ποιῶ, 180.
πατήρ ὁ, father.
πάτριος, adj. belonging to one's father, ancient, native; πάτριόν ἐστι, it is the way of our fathers or in our country; τὰ πάτρια, our fathers' customs.
πατρίς ἡ, native country.
πατρῷος, adj. inherited from one's father.
πατῶ (εω), I trample under foot.
παύω, I make to cease, deprive of, acc. and gen. 126; pass. and mid. I cease, cease from, gen. 126.
Παφλαγών, adj. Paphlagonian.
πεδίον τό, plain.
πεζός ὁ, infantry.
πείθω, I persuade; mid. and pass., I obey, dat. 159.
πεινῶ (αω), I am hungry, starve.
πειρῶ (αω), act. and mid. I endeavour, try; verbal, πειρατέος, one must try.
Πελοποννήσιος, Peloponnesian.
πέμπω, I send.
πένης, adj. poor.
περαίνω, I finish.
Περδίκκας ὁ, Perdiccas.
περί, prep. (1) acc. round, about; (2) gen. about; (3) dat. round and on, on.
περί, adv. about.
περιάπτω, I fasten round; π. αἰσχύνην τινί, I shame, 141.
περιθέω, I run round.
Περικλῆς ὁ, Pericles.
περιμένω, I wait about, wait for, acc.

περιουσία ἡ, superfluity.
περιπίπτω, I fall into, become involved in, dat.
Πέρσης, a Persian.
Περσικός, adj. Persian.
πέφυκα (φύω), I have an aptitude for, am apt to.
πηδῶ (αω), I leap.
πηλός ὁ, mud, clay.
πιέζω, I crush.
πίνω, I drink.
πίπτω, I fall.
πιστεύω, I trust, dat.
πιστός, adj. faithful.
πλανῶ (αω), I wander, wander through.
Πλάταια ἡ, Plataea; locative, Πλαταιασιν, at Plataea.
Πλαταιῆς οἱ, Plataeans.
πλάττω, I mould, shape.
πλέθρον τό, a plethrum, 101 feet.
πλείων, comp. of πολύς, more.
πλεονεκτῶ (εω), I get the advantage over, gen. 134.
πλεονεξία ἡ, selfishness, covetousness.
πλέω, I sail.
πληγή ἡ, blow, flogging; πληγὰς ἔχω, I am flogged; πληγὰς ἐμβάλλω, etc. I flog, dat.
πλῆθος τό, number, numbers.
πλήρης, adj. full, full of, gen.
πληρῶ (οω), I fill, fill with, gen. 113.
πλησιάζω, I make to draw near, put near; intrans. I draw near, dat. 138.
πλοῖον τό, boat, ship.
πλούσιος, adj. rich.
πλοῦς ὁ, voyage.
Πλοῦτος ὁ, Plutus.
πλοῦτος ὁ, wealth, riches.
πλουτῶ (εω), I am rich, rich in, gen. 113.
ποθῶ (εω), I yearn for.
ποῖ, adv. whither?
ποιμήν ὁ, shepherd.

ποιῶ (εω), I make, represent; εὖ π. I do good to; κακῶς π. I do ill to, acc. 180; στρατόπεδον ποιοῦμαι, I pitch my camp; πόλεμον ποιοῦμαι, I wage war, etc. 189; verbal, ποιητέος, must be done.
πολέμιος, adj. hostile, hostile to, dat. 147; subst. an enemy.
πόλεμος ὁ, war.
πολεμῶ (οω), I fight, fight against, dat. 141; πρὸς and acc. 146; cogn. acc. πόλεμον π. I wage war.
πόλις ἡ, city, state.
πολιτεία ἡ, administration (of the state).
πολιτεύομαι, I take part in politics.
πολίτης ὁ, citizen.
πολιτικός, adj. political; τὰ πολιτικά, politics, state-craft.
πολλάκις, adv. often.
πολλαπλάσιος, adj. many times as great as, gen. 133.
πολλαχόσε, adv. towards many sides, to many places.
πολύς, adj. much, many; ἡ πολλὴ τῆς γῆς, most of the land; πολύ, much; πολλῷ, by far, 170; πολλοῦ δεῖ, far from, 317; πολλοῦ δεῖν, 318.
πονηρός, adj. unprincipled, worthless, bad.
πόνος ὁ, labour, toil.
πορεύομαι, I march, proceed, advance, set out, make my way.
πορθῶ (εω), I devastate.
πορίζω, I provide; mid. I procure, 189.
πόρρω, adv. far on in, late, gen.
πόσος, adj. how much?
ποταμός ὁ, river.
πότε, adv. ever.
πότερα, interrog. whether, if, 392.
πότερον, interrog. whether, if, 392.
ποτήριον τό, cup.
Ποτίδαια ἡ, Potidaea.
πού, anywhere, somewhere, perhaps, surely.

ποῦ, where?
πούς ὁ, foot.
πρᾶγμα τό, affair, matter, action, deed.
πρακτικός, verbal adj. active in, gen. 98.
πράττω, I do, manage, transact; π. τὰ δημόσια, I take part in public life, 323; π. ὅπως, I exert myself to, 266; intrans. εὖ, κακῶς π. I fare well, ill.
πρέπει, it beseems, dat. 140, dat. and inf. 319, acc. and inf. 320.
πρεσβεῖς οἱ, ambassadors.
πρέσβυς, adj. old.
πρίν, adv. before; conj. before, until; πρὶν ἄν, 304, 305.
πρό, prep. gen. before, in preference to.
προαπόλλυμαι, I perish before.
πρόγονος ὁ, ancestor.
προδοσία ἡ, treachery.
προδότης ὁ, traitor.
πρόειμι, I (shall) go forward, proceed on.
προεῖπον, I proclaimed.
προέχω, I am superior to, gen.
προθυμία ἡ, zeal, eagerness.
πρόθυμος, adj. eager, active.
προΐσταμαι, I stand forward in defence of, gen.
προκαταλαμβάνω, I seize beforehand.
πρόκειμαι, I lie in front of, gen.; προκείμενος, appointed.
πρόνοια ἡ, premeditation.
Πρόξενος ὁ, Proxenus.
προορῶ (αω), I see beforehand, foresee.
προσβάλλω, I make an attack upon, dat.
προσδέχομαι, I admit.
προσδοκῶ (αω), I expect.
πρόσειμι, I (shall) go to, approach.
προσέρχομαι, I go to, approach.
προσέχω, I turn, bring to; with νοῦν expressed or understood, I devote attention to, attend to, dat. 178, 156.
προσήκει, it behoves, it is right, dat. 140, dat. and inf. 319.
πρόσθημα τό, addition, appendage, 341.
προσκυνῶ (εω), I do obeisance to, worship.
πρόσοδος ἡ, revenue.
προσπολεμῶ (εω), I fight against.
προστάτης ὁ, champion.
προστάττω, I order, enjoin upon, acc. and dat. 201.
προτεραῖος, adj. on the day before; τῇ προτεραίᾳ, on the day before, gen. 133.
πρότερον, adv. sooner, before.
πρότερος, comp. adj. former.
πρόφασις ἡ, excuse.
πρυτάνεις οἱ, presidents.
πρῴ, adv. early in the day.
πρῶτος, superl. adj. and ordinal, first.
πτωχεύω, I am a beggar.
πυγμή ἡ, boxing.
Πυθοῖ, locative, at Delphi.
πύλαι αἱ, gates.
Πύλος, Pylus.
πυνθάνομαι, I am informed, am told of.
πῦρ τό, fire.
πωλῶ (εω), I sell.
πώποτε, adv. ever yet.
πως, adv. somehow.
πῶς, how?

P

ῥᾴδιος, adj. easy.
ῥάπτω, I stitch together, I am a tailor.
ῥέω, I flow.
ῥητέος, verbal, must be said, 378.
ῥήτωρ ὁ, orator.

GREEK-ENGLISH VOCABULARY

Σ

Σαλαμίς ἡ, Salamis.
σάλπιγξ ἡ, trumpet.
σαυτόν, thyself, yourself.
σεαυτόν, thyself, yourself.
σημεῖον τό, sign, indication.
σιγῶ (αω), I am silent.
Σικελία ἡ, Sicily.
σιτία τά, provisions.
σῖτος ὁ, plur. τὰ σῖτα, food, corn.
σιωπή ἡ, silence.
σκαιός adj. stupid.
σκοπός ὁ, watcher.
σκοπῶ (εω), I see, examine, consider.
σκοταῖος, adj. in the dark, 25, 4.
Σόλων ὁ, Solon.
σός, pron. adj. thy, your.
σοφία ἡ, wisdom.
σοφιστής ὁ, wise man.
σπανίζω, I lack, gen.
Σπάρτη ἡ, Sparta.
σπένδομαι, I make a truce with, dat. 145, πρός and acc. 146.
σπεύδω, I hasten.
σπονδαί αἱ, truce.
στάδιον τό, plur. στάδιοι, rarely στάδια, stade, furlong.
σταθμός ὁ, plur. σταθμοί or σταθμά, halting-place, stage, station.
στάσις ἡ, disunion, sedition.
στεροῦμαι (εο), I am deprived of, gen.
στέφανος ὁ, crown.
στήλη ἡ, slab.
στολή ἡ, dress.
στόμα τό, mouth.
στοχάζομαι, I guess at, gen. 100, 4.
στρατεία ἡ, expedition.
στράτευμα τό, army, force.
στρατεύομαι, I serve as a soldier, go on an expedition.
στρατηγός ὁ, general.
στρατηγῶ (εω), I am general, command an army.
στρατιά ἡ, army.

στρατιώτης ὁ, soldier.
στρατόπεδον τό, camp.
στρατός ὁ, army.
στυγῶ (εω), I loathe.
σύ, pron. thou, you.
συγγιγνώσκω, I pardon, dat.
συγγνώμη ἡ, pardon ; συγ. ἔχω, I am pardoned.
συγγράφω, I codify, I write history.
συκοφάντης ὁ, malicious accuser.
συλλαμβάνω, I arrest, apprehend.
συλῶ (αω), I rob.
συμβαίνω, I come to terms with, dat. ; impers. happen, dat. 319.
συμβουλεύω, I give advice, recommend.
σύμμαχος ὁ, ally.
συμμαχῶ (εω), I am allied with, dat.
συμμίγνυμι, I mix together, I come to blows with.
σύμπας, adj. all together.
συμπλέκω, I clasp together.
σύμπτωμα τό, position, plight.
συμφορά ἡ, misfortune, disaster.
συμφωνῶ (εω), I agree, am in harmony with, dat. 141.
σύνειμι, I am with, keep company with, dat.
συνεργός, adj. working together ; as subst. fellow-worker, helpmate.
συνέρχομαι, I come, meet, flock together.
συνίημι, I understand.
σύνοιδα, I am conscious of, 374.
συντρίβομαι τὴν κεφαλήν, I get my head broken.
Συρακόσιοι οἱ, Syracusans.
συστρατεύω, I take the field with, dat.
σφάλλομαι, I am foiled in, gen. 100, 4.
σφενδονητής ὁ, slinger.
σχολή ἡ, leisure ; σχολῇ, scarcely, 168.
σώζω, I save.

GREEK-ENGLISH VOCABULARY

Σωκράτης ὁ, Socrates.
σῶμα τό, body.
σῶς, adj. safe.
σωτηρία ἡ, safety, salvation.
σωφρονῶ (εω), I show sense.
σώφρων, adj. sensible, prudent.

T

τάλαντον τό, talent (60 minae, 6000 drachmae, about £245).
τάξις ἡ, rank, post, arrangement.
ταράττω, I throw into confusion.
ταραχή ἡ, confusion, trouble.
τάττω, I arrange, I fix (a price).
τάφος ὁ, burial, tomb.
τάφρος ἡ, trench.
τάχος τό, swiftness; ὡς εἶχε τάχους, as fast as he could, 97.
ταχύ, adv. swiftly, quickly, soon; ὡς τάχιστα, as quickly as possible.
ταχύς, adj. swift; τὴν ταχίστην, the quickest way, 80, 2.
τε, and, 396 foll.
τειχίζω, I fortify.
τείχισμα τό, fort.
τεῖχος τό, wall (especially of a city), fort.
τεκμαίρομαι, I judge, conjecture.
τεκμήριον τό, proof.
τέκνον τό, child.
τελευτῶ (αω), I end, I die, 177.
τέμνω, I ravage.
τέχνη ἡ, art, craft.
τηλικουτοσί, of such a size.
τηλοῦ, far off.
τίθημι, I place; ὅπλα τίθεμαι, I ground arms; νόμους τίθημι, I make laws; νόμους τίθεμαι, I pass laws.
τιμή ἡ, privilege, honour, price.
τιμῶ (αω), I honour, I value, assess; verbal, τιμητέος, must be honoured, 378.
τιμωρῶ (εω), I take vengeance on.

τίς; interrog. pron. who?
τις, indef. pron. any one, some one.
Τισσαφέρνης ὁ, Tissaphernes.
τιτρώσκω, I wound.
τοίνυν, therefore.
τοιόσδε, adj. such, of this sort, so many, 28 note.
τοιοῦτος, adj. of such a sort, of this sort, such, etc., 28 note.
τολμῶ (αω), I dare.
τόξευμα τό, arrow.
τοσοῦτος, adj. so great, so high, so much, etc., 28 note; εἰς τοσοῦτον τῶν μανιῶν, to such a pitch of madness, 90.
τότε, adv. at that time, then.
τρέπω, I make to turn, I put to flight; mid. and pass. I turn, rout.
τρέφω, I feed, nourish, rear, bring up.
τρόπος ὁ, way, manner, character.
τροφή ἡ, food.
τροχοποιῶ (εω), I am a wheelwright.
τυγχάνω, I happen, I find, meet with, gen. 100, 4; with participle, I am just.
τύπτω, I strike.
τυραννίς ἡ, kingdom, crown.
τύραννος ὁ, tyrant, despot, king.
τυρός ὁ, cheese.
τυφλός, adj. blind.
τύχη ἡ, fortune, lot.

Υ

ὑβρίζω, I insult.
ὕβρις ἡ, wanton insolence or violence.
ὑγιαίνω, I am healthy.
ὑγίεια ἡ, health.
ὑγιής, adj. healthy.
υἱός or ὑός ὁ, son.
ὕλη ἡ, wood.
ὑμέτερος, adj. your.

υός or υἱός ὁ, son.
ὑπάγω τῆς ὁδοῦ, I proceed on the journey, 91.
ὑπάρχω, I am to begin with, I belong to, fall to the lot of, *dat.* 150.
ὑπείκω, I yield, *acc. and gen.* 127; *verbal*, ὑπεικτέον, one must yield, 378.
ὑπέρ, *prep. gen.* on behalf of.
ὑπεραλγῶ (εω), I grieve for, *gen.*
ὑπερβαίνω, I pass over.
ὑπερέχω, I am beyond, outflank, *gen.*
ὑπερφαίνομαι, I appear over, *gen.*
ὑπηρετῶ (εω), I serve, *dat.*
ὑπισχνοῦμαι (εο), I promise.
ὕπνος ὁ, sleep.
ὑπό, *prep.* (1) *acc.* under (motion); (2) *gen.* under (rest), by (agent), ὑπὸ σάλπιγγος, at the sound of the trumpet; (3) *dat.* under (rest), subject to.
ὑπομιμνήσκω, I remind.
ὑπονοῶ (εω), I think in my heart.
ὑποπτεύω, I suspect.
ὑπουργῶ (εω), I serve, help, *dat.*
ὑποφαίνω, I appear slightly, (of day) I break.
ὑποχωρῶ (εω), I give way to, yield to, *dat.*
ὑστεραῖος, *adj.* late; ἡ ὑστεραία, the day after, the morrow, next day.
ὕστερον, *adv.* later, afterwards.
ὕστερος, *adj.* later.
ὑστερῶ (εω), I come too late for, *gen.* 134.
ὑφίστημι, I place under; *mid. and 2d aor. and perf. act.* I undertake, engage, promise.
ὑψηλός, *adj.* high.

Φ

φαίνομαι, I appear, am visible.
Φαληρόθεν, *adv.* from Phalerum.
φανερός, *adj.* evident, clear, plain.
φανερῶς, *adv.* openly.
φάσκω, I assert, say.
φείδομαι, I spare, save, *gen.*
φέρω, I bring; φέρε νυν, φέρε δή, come then!
φεῦ, alas! *gen.* 100.
φεύγω, I flee, am exiled, am prosecuted.
φημί, I say.
φθάνω, I am beforehand with, forestall, anticipate, 62 *foll.*; *participle*, 369; οὐκ ἔφθασαν πυθόμενοι καὶ ἦκον, they had no sooner heard than they came, 404.
φθόνος ὁ, envy.
φθονῶ (εω), I envy, am jealous of, *gen.* 100, 1, *dat.* 153.
Φίλιππος ὁ, Philip.
Φιλοκράτης ὁ, Philocrates.
φίλος ὁ, friend.
φιλοσοφῶ (εω), I act as a philosopher.
φιλῶ (εω), I love.
φοβερός, *adj.* formidable.
φόβος ὁ, panic, fear.
φοβοῦμαι (εο), I am afraid of, fear, *cogn. acc.* 72, 1.
φόνος ὁ, murder.
φόρημα τό, burden, encumbrance.
φόρος ὁ, tribute.
φράζω, I point out, indicate, tell, show, mean.
φροντίζω, I am anxious about, take thought for, have regard for, *gen.* 100, 3.
φρονῶ (εω), I think, am minded; κακῶς φρονῶ, I am a fool.
φυγάς ὁ, exile.
φυλακή ἡ, guard.
φύλαξ ὁ, guard, sentinel.
φυλάττω, I guard, watch, am on the watch.
φύσις ἡ, nature.
φυτόν τό, plant.

φύω, I produce ; τὰ φυόμενα ἐκ, the produce of.
φωνή ἡ, dialect.
φώρ ὁ, thief.
φωρῶ (αω), I detect (a thief).
φῶς τό, light.

Χ

Χαιρεφῶν, Chaerephon.
χαίρω, I am glad, I rejoice at, *dat.* 161, *participle,* 375.
χαλεπαίνω, I am angry with, *dat.* 161.
χαλεπός, *adj.* difficult, harsh.
χαλεπῶς, *adv.* with difficulty.
χαλκεύω, I am a smith.
χαμαί, *locative adv.* on the ground.
χαρίζω, I gratify, do a favour for, *acc. and dat.*
χάρις ἡ, favour, gratitude.
χάσκω, I yawn ; *perf.* κέχηνα, I am yawning, 214.
χειμών ὁ, winter ; χειμῶνι, in winter, 173.
χείρ ἡ, hand ; εἰς χεῖρας ἐλθεῖν, come to close quarters.
χελώνη ἡ, tortoise.
χέω, I pour.
χιτών ὁ, tunic.
χοή ἡ, drink offering.
χορηγία ἡ, expense of chorēgus.
χρή, it is necessary, one must.
χρῆμα τό, what one uses or needs, hence *plur.* χρήματα, riches, money ; ζημιοῦν χρήμασι, to fine, 165.
χρήσιμος, *adj.* useful.
χρηστός, *adj.* honest, virtuous.
χρόνος ὁ, time.

χρυσίον τό, a piece of gold, gold coin.
χρυσός ὁ, gold.
χρῶμαι (αο), I use, make use of, (*of life*) I lead, *dat.*
χώρα ἡ, country.
χωρίζω, I separate, *acc. and gen.* 126.

Ψ

ψεύδομαι, I am deceived in, *gen.* 100, 4.
ψεῦδος τό, lie, falsehood.
ψηφίζομαι, I vote for.
ψήφισμα τό, decree, ordinance.
ψῆφος ἡ, vote.
ψιλός, *adj.* bare of, *gen.* 131.
ψυχή ἡ, soul, mind.
ψυχρός, *adj.* cold.

Ω

ὤμοι, alas ! ah me !
ὠνητός, *verbal adj.* to be bought.
ὥρα ἡ, time, season.
ὡς, *prep.* to.
ὡς, *conj.* as ; *with participles, causal* 355, *final* 356 ; ὡς εἰπεῖν, so to speak, 340 ; ὡς εἶχε τάχους ἕκαστος, each as fast as he could, 97.
ὥστε, *conj. consec.* so that, and so, 255-259 ; on condition that, 258.
ὠφελεία ἡ, assistance.
ὠφελητέος, *verbal adj.* must be helped, 378.
ὤφελον, *in wishes,* would that, 232.
ὠφελῶ (εω), I help.

ENGLISH - GREEK VOCABULARY

For tenses of irregular verbs see *Grammar*, pp. 170 *foll.*
Numerals are not given in this Vocabulary; see *Grammar*, pp. 143-145.
References are to the sections of the *Syntax*, unless otherwise stated.

A

abandon, I, προ·δίδωμι, προ·ίημι (generally middle).
able, I am, *see* can.
able, *adj.* ἱκανός, ή, όν, *with inf.* 338.
abound in, I, εὐπορῶ (εω), *gen.* 113.
about, *prep.* (=near), περί, *gen.*
about, *with numbers,* ὡς.
about to, I am, μέλλω, *with pres. or fut. inf.*
absent, I am, ἄπ·ειμι.
absolutely necessary, it is, ἅπασα ἀνάγκη ἐστίν, 316.
abstain from, I, ἀπ·έχομαι, *gen.*
abuse, I, κακῶς λέγω, κακίζω; *pass.* κακῶς ἀκούω.
accept, I, λαμβάνω.
accuse, I, κατα·γιγνώσκω, *acc. of person, gen. of charge,* 122; κατηγορῶ (εω), *gen. of person, acc. of charge,* 123.
ache, I have a head-ache, ἀλγῶ (εω) τὴν κεφαλήν.
aches, his heart aches, δάκνει τὴν καρδίαν, 335.
acquainted with, ἔμπειρος, ον, *gen.*
acquire, I, κτῶμαι (αο).

acquit, I, ἀπο·λύω, *acc. and gen.* 100, 2.
act, πρᾶγμα, -ατος, τό.
act, I, πράττω, ποιῶ (εω); I act thus, πράττω ταῦτα *or* τοιαῦτα; I act like, πράττω τὰ αὐτά, *with dat.* 139.
action, πρᾶγμα, -ατος, τό; τὸ πράττειν.
actually, καί; but actually, ἀλλὰ καί.
addition to, in, πρός, *dat.*
admire, I, θαυμάζω.
advance, I, πορεύομαι, εἶμι (*fut.*)
advantage over, I get the, πλεονεκτῶ (εω), *gen.* 134.
advice, λόγος, βουλή, συμβούλευμα, γνώμη.
advice, I give, συμ·βουλεύω, *acc. of thing, dat. of person.*
advise, I, συμ·βουλεύω.
affair, πρᾶγμα, -ατος, τό.
afraid, I am, φοβοῦμαι (εο).
after, after this, μετὰ τοῦτο, ἐκ τούτου; the day after, ἡ ὑστεραία, *gen.*; after all, ἄρα, 430.
again, αὖθις, αὖ, πάλιν.
against, ἐπί, *acc.*; εἰς, *acc.*; πρός, *acc.*

agree, I, συμ·φωνῶ (εω), dat.; ὁμολογῶ (εω), dat.; I agree that, ὁμολογῶ, with inf.
aid, I, βοηθῶ (εω), dat. ; my aid has been given to, βεβοήθηταί μοι, with dat. 202.
alas, φεῦ.
Alexander, Ἀλέξανδρος.
alive, ζῶν; part. of ζῶ (αω).
all, πᾶς, πᾶσα, πᾶν, ἄπας; all sorts or kinds of, παντοῖος; men and all, αὐτοῖς (τοῖς) ἀνδράσι, 166.
allow, I, ἐῶ (αω).
ally, σύμμαχος.
almost, ὀλίγου δεῖν, μικροῦ δεῖν, 341.
alone, μόνος, η, ον.
already, ἤδη.
also, καί.
although, καὶ εἰ or καὶ ἐάν, written κεἰ, κἄν, 289; with participle, καί, καίπερ, or καὶ ταῦτα, 358.
always, ἀεί; I always, δια·τελῶ (εω), δια·γίγνομαι, δι·άγω, with participle, 369.
am, I, εἰμί; ἔχω with adverbs.
amazed at, I am, θαυμάζω, acc.
ambassador, πρεσβευτής; in plural πρέσβεις.
among, ἐν, dat.
among the first, you, ἀρξάμενος ἀπὸ σοῦ.
ancestor, πρόγονος ὁ.
ancient, παλαιός, ά, όν; πάλαι, with article.
and, καί, δέ, τε (connecting propositions, never words); and indeed also, καὶ δὴ καί, 393.
angry, I am, ὀργίζομαι, dat.
announce, I, ἀγγέλλω.
anoint myself, I, ἀλείφομαι.
another, ἄλλος, ἄλλος τις; one another, ἀλλήλω.
answer, I, ἀπο·κρίνομαι.
anxious, I am or grow, φροντίζω.
any, τις: partitive genitive, 111; anybody, anyone, τις, ὅστις

after negatives, 40; as good as anybody, οὐδένος ἥττων, 328; anything, τι, (=everything) πᾶν, πάντα, οὐδὲν ὅτι οὔ, 44; not anything, οὐδέν; any longer, ἔτι.
appear, I, φαίνομαι; I appear above, ὑπερ·φαίνομαι, gen. 121.
appearance, εἶδος τό.
appoint, I, αἱροῦμαι (εο), see Grammar, p. 182.
appointed (day, etc.), προκείμενος.
arms, ὅπλα τά.
army, στράτευμα τό, στρατιά ἡ.
arrive at, I, ἀφικνοῦμαι (εο) εἰς.
arrow, τόξευμα τό.
Artemis, Ἄρτεμις ἡ.
artist, τεχνίτης ὁ.
as, ὡς, ὥσπερ; καί, 403; as anybody, see anybody.
ashamed, I am, αἰσχύνομαι, acc.; with participle, 375.
Asia, Ἀσία ἡ, 9.
ask, I, αἰτοῦμαι (εο).
ask (a question), I, ἐρωτῶ (αω).
asleep, I am, καθ·εύδω.
assert, I, φάσκω.
assistance, give, βοηθῶ (εω), dat.; verbal, βοηθητέος, 378.
associate with, I, ὁμιλῶ (εω), dat.
Athena, Ἀθήνη ἡ.
Athenian, Ἀθηναῖος.
Athens, Ἀθῆναι αἱ; at Athens, locative, Ἀθήνῃσιν, 172.
attack, I, προσ·βάλλω, dat.
attack, I make an, upon, προσ·βάλλω, dat.
attention, I pay, προσ·έχω (νοῦν), dat. 177, 178.
Attica, Ἀττική ἡ.
authority, κράτος τό, ἀρχή ἡ.
avoid, I, φεύγω.
avoid being seen by, I, λανθάνω, acc.
awake, I, trans. ἐγείρω; I am or lie awake, ἐγρήγορα.

away, he has sailed, *etc.*, οἴχεται πλέων, *etc.* 369.

B

back, νῶτον τό.
back, *adv.* πάλιν.
bad, κακός, ή, όν.
banish, I, ἐλαύνω.
banished, I am, φεύγω, ἐκ·πίπτω.
barber, κουρεύς, έως, ὁ.
bare of, ψιλός, ή, όν, *gen.* 125.
baseness, κακία ἡ.
bathe, I, λοῦμαι (ούο), 188.
battle, μάχη ἡ.
battle at sea, ναυμαχία ἡ.
be, to, εἶναι; be off, let us, ἴωμεν, ἀπ·ίωμεν.
bear, I, φέρω (see Grammar, p. 185); *verbal*, οἰστέος, 378.
beautiful, καλός, ή, όν.
beauty, κάλλος, ους, τό.
because, ὅτι, 253-254; διὰ τό *with inf.*
become, I, γίγνομαι.
bed, I go to, κοιμῶμαι (ao).
beetle, κάνθαρος ὁ.
befalls, it, συμβαίνει, 319.
befitting, it is, πρέπει, 319; προσ-ήκει, 319.
before, πρό, *gen.* (*of time or in preference to*), πρίν, *gen.*; I do this before, φθάνω *with part.* 369; *expressed by fut. participle*, 218; *adv.* πρίν, πάλαι; *conj.* πρίν... 304, 305; day before, ἡ προτεραία, *gen.*
beg, I (=entreat), αἰτοῦμαι (εο), δέομαι, *gen.*
beg off, I, ἐξ·αιτοῦμαι.
beg, I (=ask alms), πτωχεύω.
beggar, πτωχός; I am a beggar, πτωχεύω.
begin, I, ἄρχω, ἄρχομαι, *gen.* 112.
beginning, ἀρχή ἡ.

beginning with..., ἀρξάμενος ἀπό...
behind, ὀπίσω, εἰς τοὐπίσω.
behindhand, I am, ἡττῶμαι (αο), *with part.* 370.
believe, I, πιστεύω, *dat.*; *pass.* 200; *see* I think.
belong to, I, εἶναι, *with gen.* 106, 2.
beneath, ὑπό, *gen.* (*rare*), *dat.* Grammar, p. 106.
benefactor, εὐεργέτης ὁ.
benefit, I, εὖ ποιῶ (εω), *acc.*
beseech, I, δέομαι, *gen.*; *see* I beg.
best, *adj.* ἄριστος, κράτιστος; *adv.* ἄριστα, κράτιστα.
betray, I, προ·δίδωμι.
better, κρείττων, ἀμείνων.
better-bred, οἱ καλοί τε κἀγαθοί, 102.
between ourselves, ὡς πρὸς ὑμᾶς εἰρῆσθαι, 340.
bid, I, κελεύω.
bird, ὄρνις, ὄρνιθος, ὁ, ἡ.
birth, γένος τό; by birth, τὸ γένος.
bite, I, δάκνω.
blame, αἰτία ἡ.
blame, I, αἰτιῶμαι (αο), ἐν αἰτίᾳ ἔχω, μέμφομαι, *dat.*; *pass.* αἰτίαν ἔχω.
blind, τυφλός, ή, όν.
blow, πληγή ἡ.
boat, πλοῖον τό.
body, σῶμα τό.
Boeotia, Βοιωτία ἡ.
bone, ὀστοῦν τό.
book, βίβλος, ου, ἡ.
born from, I am, γίγνομαι, *gen.* 125.
borrow, I, δανείζομαι, *acc.* 191 *note.*
both... and..., καί... καί, 395; τε... καί, 396.
bought, to be, ὠνητός, *gen.* 119.
bow, τόξον τό.
boxing, πυγμή ἡ.
boy, παῖς, παιδός, ὁ.

O

brave, ἀγαθός, ή, όν; ἀνδρεῖος, a, ον.
breadth, εὖρος τό.
break, I (of day), δια·λάμπω; a head, συν·τρίβω τὴν κεφαλήν, 393; I get my head broken, συν·τρίβομαι τὴν κεφαλήν
breakfast, ἄριστον τό.
bribe, μισθός ὁ.
bring, I, φέρω (see I bear); news, ἀγγέλλω, ἐξ·αγγέλλω
broad, εὐρύς, εῖα, ύ.
brother, ἀδελφός ὁ.
build, I (houses, etc.), οἰκοδομῶ (εω); ships, ναυπηγῶ (εω).
burden (=burdensome), adj. βαρύς, εῖα, ύ.
burn, I, καίω, κάω.
bury, I, θάπτω.
business, πρᾶγμα τό; bad business, κακὸν πρᾶγμα.
but, ἀλλά, 408 seq.; δέ, 417 seq.
buy, I, ὠνοῦμαι. For tenses see Syntax, p. 48 note.
by, agent ὑπό gen.; dat. of agent, 158.
by Zeus, νὴ Δία, 63; no by Zeus, μὰ τὸν Δία, 63.

C

call, I; καλῶ (εω), λέγω; I call by name, ὀνομάζω; I call a coward, κακίζω.
calumniate, I; see abuse.
camp, στρατόπεδον τό.
can, I, δύναμαι, οἷός τ' εἰμι.
canals through, I dig, δι·ορύττω, acc. 175.
capture, I, συλ·λαμβάνω, αἱρῶ.
care, I take, φροντίζω, ἐπι·μελοῦμαι, σκοπῶ (εω), εὐλαβοῦμαι, all with ὅπως, 266-269; I take care to keep dark, ἀπο·κρύπτομαι, 190; I care not for, οὐ φροντίζω, 100.
careful, I am; see care, I take.

careless about, ὀλίγωρος, gen. 99.
carry, I, ἄγω, φέρω.
carry off, ἀφ·αιρῶ (εω).
case, in, εἰ (πως), ἐάν (πως), 288; your case is the same as mine, 403.
cast out of, I am, ἐκ·πίπτω, 181.
catch, λαμβάνω, κατα·λαμβάνω, εὑρίσκω, (of animals or fish) θηρῶ (αω); in act of doing something, φωρῶ (αω).
cause, αἰτία ἡ; αἴτιος, α, ον.
cavalry, ἱππεύς, έως, ὁ.
cease from, I, παύομαι, λήγω, gen. 126.
certainly, δή, οὖν, 422.
champion of, I am, ἐπι·κουρῶ (εω), dat. 152.
champion, προστάτης ὁ.
chance, I have a, ἔξ·εστί μοι.
change, I (intrans.), μεθ·ίσταμαι.
character, ἦθος τό, τρόπος ὁ.
charge, αἰτία ἡ.
charge, I (attack), ἐλαύνω εἰς.
chariot, ἅρμα τό.
chase, I, διώκω.
cheese, τυρόν τό.
child, τέκνον τό.
choose, I, αἱροῦμαι.
circumstances, the, τὸ πρᾶγμα.
citizen, πολίτης ὁ.
city, πόλις, εως, ἡ.
clasp (hands), συμ·πλέκω.
clear, δῆλος, η, ον; φανερός, ά, όν; σαφής, ές.
clear, I make quite, εὖ δηλῶ (οω).
clearly, σαφῶς.
clever, δεινός, ή, όν.
climb, I, ἀνα·βαίνω.
cling to, I, ἔχομαι, gen. 112.
cloak, χλαῖνα ἡ, ἱμάτιον τό.
clothing, ἐσθής, ῆτος, ἡ.
cold, ψυχρός, ά, όν.
collect, I, συλ·λέγω.
colony, ἀποικία ἡ.
column, κέρας, ἄτος and (military) κέρως τό (Grammar, p. 14).

come, I, ἔρχομαι, εἶμι (fut.), ἐπι·γίγνομαι, ἀφ·ικνοῦμαι, ἥκω (perf. meaning), πάρ·ειμι (I am present). For tenses see Grammar, p. 183.
—— down, κατ·έρχομαι, etc.
—— into, εἰσ·έρχομαι, etc.
—— out of, ἐξ·έρχομαι ἐκ, etc.
—— too late for, ὑστερῶ (εω), 134,
come now, ἄγε δή, ἄγε νυν.
comely to the eye, εὐπρεπὴς ἰδεῖν, 339.
command (=office), ἀρχή ἡ.
cómmand, I (army), στρατηγῶ (εω).
common, κοινός, ή, όν; property or lot, κοινός, gen. 108.
company, ὁμιλία ἡ.
compose (poems), I, ποιῶ (εω).
conceal, I, κρύπτω; conceal from, κρύπτω, double acc.
condemn, I, κατα·δικάζω, κατα·κρίνω, κατα·ψηφίζομαι, 122.
condition that, on, ἐφ' ᾧ, ἐφ' ᾧτε, ὥστε, 258.
confusion, θόρυβος ὁ.
confusion, I throw into, ταράττω; I am in confusion, ταράττομαι.
congratulate, I, εὐδαιμονίζω, μακαρίζω, acc. of person, gen. of thing, 100.
conquer, I, νικῶ (αω), acc. (with cogn. acc. 72, 2); περι·γίγνομαι, gen.
conscious that, I am, σύν·οιδα ἐμαυτῷ, 374.
consider, I, νομίζω, ἡγοῦμαι.
constitution, πολιτεία ἡ.
contend in, I, ἀγωνίζομαι, acc. 72, 2.
continue, I, δια·τελῶ (εω), with part. 369.
contrive, I, μηχανῶμαι (αο), τεχνῶμαι (αο), 193; cunning schemes, μηχανῶμαι μηχανάς, τεχνῶμαι τέχνας.

convict of, I, ἐλέγχω, ἐξ·ελέγχω, acc. of person, gen. of charge, 100, 2; with part. 371.
convicted of, I am, ἁλίσκομαι, gen.
corn, σῖτος ὁ, plur. σῖτα τά (Grammar, p. 9).
corrupt, I, δια·φθείρω; corrupt, διεφθαρμένος; he is corrupt, διέφθαρται.
counsel, I, βουλεύω, συμ·βουλεύω; I take counsel, βουλεύομαι.
country, πόλις ἡ, γῆ ἡ, χώρα ἡ, (native) πατρίς, ίδος, ἡ.
courage, ἀρετή ἡ.
course, of course, πάνυ μὲν οὖν, 426.
course of, in the, μεταξὺ with part. 354.
court (of law), δικαστήριον τό.
cow, βοῦς ἡ.
coward, cowardly, δειλός, ή, όν; I call a coward, κακίζω.
cowardice, δειλία ἡ.
creature, ζῷον τό.
crew, ναῦται οἱ, ἄνδρες οἱ; crew and all, αὐτοῖς (τοῖς) ἀνδράσι, 166.
cross, I, δια·βαίνω; verbal, δια·βατός, may be crossed, 377; δια·βατέος, must be crossed, 378.
crown, στέφανος ὁ.
crush, I, πιέζω.
cry, βοή ἡ.
cry, I, κλαίω, κλάω.
cry aloud, I, ἀνα·κέκρᾱγα, 214.
cunning, δόλος ὁ.
cup, ποτήριον τό.
cut down, I, κόπτω, κατα·κόπτω.
cut my hair, I, or have my hair cut, κείρομαι, 188.
Cyrus, Κῦρος ὁ.

D

dance, ὀρχοῦμαι (εο), 194.
danger, κίνδυνος ὁ.
dare, I, τολμῶ (αω).
Darius, Δαρεῖος ὁ.

dark, in the, σκοταῖος, α, ον.
dark, I take care to keep, ἀπο·κρύπτομαι, 190.
daughter, θῠγάτηρ, θυγατρός, ἡ.
day, ἡμέρα ἡ; at daybreak, ἅμ' ἡμέρᾳ; in the day-time, τῆς ἡμέρας; day before, τῇ προτεραίᾳ, with gen. 133; day after, τῇ ὑστεραίᾳ, with gen. 133; to-day, τήμερον (adv.); thrice a day, τρὶς τῆς ἡμέρας.
dead, τεθνηκώς; he is dead, τέθν. ἐστι.
death, θάνατος ὁ.
death, I put to, ἀπο·κτείνω; pass. ἀπο·θνῄσκω.
deceive, I, ἀπατῶ (αω).
deceived in, I am, ψεύδομαι, gen. 100.
deed, ἔργον τό, πρᾶγμα τό.
defeat, I, νικῶ (αω), ἡττῶ (αω), acc.; περι·γίγνομαι, gen.
defence, I offer as (legal), ἀπο·λογοῦμαι (εο).
defend myself against, I, ἀμύνομαι, acc. 189; (legal) ἀπο·λογοῦμαι (εο).
defendant, ὁ φεύγων.
delay, I, μέλλω.
deliberate, I, βουλεύομαι.
delighted with, I am, ἥδομαι, dat.
demand, I, or make demands, ἀξιῶ (οω).
Demosthenes, Δημοσθένης, ους, ὁ.
deny, I, ἀρνοῦμαι (εο), ἔξαρνός εἰμι, 330.
depart, ἀπ·έρχομαι, etc.; see I go away.
deprive of, I, παύω, acc. of person, gen. of thing, 126; ἀφαιρῶ (εω), double acc.
deprived of privileges, ἄτιμος γερῶν, 131.
descend from, I, κατα·βαίνω, κατ·έρχομαι, κάτ·ειμι. For tenses see Grammar, p. 183.

desert, λείπω; verbal, λειπτέος, 378; see leave.
deserve to, I, ἄξιός εἰμι, gen. 119, inf. 339.
desire, I, ποθῶ (εω), (=wish) βούλομαι.
despise, I, κατα·φρονῶ (εω), gen. 121.
destroy, I, καθ·αιρῶ (εω), ἀπ·όλλυμι, δια·φθείρω.
determine, I, βουλεύομαι.
devote myself to, I, προσ·έχω (νοῦν), dat. 178.
die, I, ἀπο·θνῄσκω, τελευτῶ (αω), 177.
differ from, I, δια·φέρω, gen. 126.
differently from, ἕτερα ... ἤ ... 406.
difficult, χαλεπός, ή, όν.
dig canals through, I, δι·ορύττω, acc. 175.
din, θόρυβος ὁ.
dinner, δεῖπνον τό.
Dionysia, at the, Διονυσίοις, 173, 3.
discover, I, εὑρίσκω.
disease, νόσος ἡ.
disgraceful, αἰσχρός, ά, όν.
disgracefully, αἰσχρῶς.
disheartened, I am, ἀθυμῶ (εω).
dishonour, I, ἀτιμάζω.
dislike, I, οὐ φιλῶ (εω), acc.; χαλεπῶς or βαρέως φέρω, acc.; μισῶ (εω), acc.
dispute, I, ἀμφισβητῶ (εω), 330, dat. 143; ἐρίζω, dat. 143.
disreputable, αἰσχρός, ά, όν.
distant from, I am, ἀπ·έχω, gen. with or without ἀπό, 126; δι·έχω, gen. 126.
distinguished, ἐπίσημος, ον; τίμιος, α, ον; δόκιμος, ον; λαμπρός, ά, όν.
distribute, I, διανέμω.
distrust, I, οὐ πιστεύω, dat.
ditch, τάφρος ἡ.
divine, θεῖος, α, ον.
do, I, πράττω, δρῶ (αω), ἐργάζομαι,

ENGLISH-GREEK VOCABULARY

ποιῶ (εω); verbal, must do, ποιητέος, 378; I do well to, εὖ ποιῶ, acc.; do ill to, κακῶς ποιῶ, acc.; I do a favour to, χαρίζομαι, dat.
doctor, ἰατρός ὁ.
dog, κύων, κυνός, ὁ and ἡ.
doomed to, I am, fut. part. or μέλλω with inf. (pres. or fut.)
doors, θύραι al.
double (as large, etc.), διπλάσιος, α, ον, gen.
down, κατά, gen.; see Grammar, p. 102.
drag from, I, ἀπο·σπῶ (αω), gen. with or without ἀπό, 129.
draw near to, I, πλησιάζω, dat.
draw up, I, παρα·τάττω, acc.
dreadful, δεινός, ή, όν.
drink, I, πίνω.
drinking, I have been, I am drunk, μεθύω.
drink offering, χοά ἡ.
drive from, I, ἀπ·ελαύνω.
drive out, I, ἐκ·βάλλω; pass. ἐκπίπτω, 181.
drunk, I am, μεθύω.
during my whole life, παρὰ ὅλον τὸν βίον.

E

each, ἑκάτερος, α, ον (article, 30); ἕκαστος, η, ον (article, 30).
each time, ἑκάστοτε.
eager to, I am, ἐπιθυμῶ (εω), gen. 100, 5.
eagerness, προθυμία ἡ, ἐπιθυμία ἡ.
eagle, ἀετός ὁ.
ear, οὖς, ὠτός, τό.
early, πρῴ; early in life, πρῴ τῆς ἡλικίας, 94; early in the day, in the early morning, πρῴ τῆς ἡμέρας.
earth, γῆ ἡ.
easily, ῥᾳδίως.
easy, ῥᾴδιος, α, ον.

eat, I, ἐσθίω, for tenses see Grammar, p. 183; I eat or get my lunch (or breakfast), ἀριστο·ποιοῦμαι.
educate, I, παιδεύω.
elapse, I (of time), παρ·έρχομαι.
elder, πρεσβύτερος.
elect, I, αἱροῦμαι (εο).
empire, ἀρχή ἡ.
empty of, I, κενῶ (οω), acc. and gen. 130.
encourage one another, to, παρα·κελεύεσθαι.
end, ἔσχατος, η, ον, 25, 2.
endeavour, I (= try), πειρῶμαι (αο); ἐπι·χειρῶ (εω), dat.
enemy, πολέμιος, α, ον; ἐχθρός, ά, όν; δυσμενής, ές.
enjoy, ἀπο·λαύω, gen. 117.
enquire into, I, ζητῶ (εω).
enslave, I, δουλῶ (οω), κατα·δουλῶ (οω); one must enslave, δουλευτέος, 378 (lit. serve as a slave, from δουλεύω, I am a slave).
enter, I (= sail into), εἰσπλέω.
entirely, πάνυ.
entrust to, I, ἐπι·τρέπω, acc. and dat. 201.
envy, φθόνος ὁ.
envy, I, φθονῶ (εω), dat. 100.
equal to, ἴσος, η, ον, dat.
equal in strength, ἀντίπαλος, dat.
err, I, ἁμαρτάνω; I err in, gen. 100.
escape, I, φεύγω; escape from, ἐκ·φεύγω ἐκ.
escape notice of, I, λανθάνω, acc.
even, καί, etc.
even if, καί, οὐδέ, or μηδέ, immediately preceding εἰ or .ἐάν, 289.
ever, πότε; better etc. than ever, αὐτὸς αὑτοῦ.
every, πᾶς, ἅπας, see all; everyone, πᾶς, πᾶς τις; everything, πᾶν.
everywhere, πανταχοῦ, πανταχῇ.
evidence, αἱ μαρτυρίαι.
evil, κακός, ή, όν.

evils, τὰ κακά.
exact vengeance, I, see vengeance.
exactly what, ὅσπερ, § 38.
excuse, I make an, or plead as excuse, προφασίζομαι, πρόφασιν ποιοῦμαι, 199; pass. ἡ πρόφασις γίγνεται, 199.
exert myself to, I, πράττω ὅπως, 266, 7.
exile, φυγάς, άδος, ὁ.
exiled, I am, φεύγω ἐκ.
expect, I, προσ·δοκῶ (αω).
experience pleasure, I, ἥδομαι ἡδονήν, 72, 1.
explain, I, ἀπο·δείκνυμι, δηλῶ (οω).
expose, I, ἐκ·τίθημι.
eye, ὀφθαλμός ὁ.

F

faithful, πιστός, ή, όν.
fall asleep, I, κατα·δαρθάνω, generally in 2 aor. κατέδαρθον.
fall short of, I, ἀπο·λείπομαι, gen. 134.
false, ψευδής, ές.
falsehood, ψεῦδος, ους, τό; τὸ ψευδές.
falsehoods against, I tell, κατα·ψεύδομαι, gen. 121.
famous, see distinguished.
far (=by much), πολύ, πολλῷ, 170.
far advanced in years, πόρρω τῆς ἡλικίας, τοῦ βίου.
far from, I am, πολλοῦ δέω, 318.
far from it indeed, πολλοῦ γε δεῖ, 130; as far as I know, ὅσον γ' ἔμ' εἰδέναι, 340.
fare well, I, εὖ πράττω; fare ill, κακῶς πράττω.
farm, ἀγρός ὁ.
farmer, γεωργός ὁ.
fast, ταχύς, εῖα, ύ.
fasten on, I, περι·άπτω, acc. and dat. 141.

fate, I suffer the same as, τὸ αὐτὸ πάσχω, dat.
father, πατήρ, πατρός, ὁ.
fault with, I find, μέμψιν μέμφομαι, dat. 72, 1.
favour, I do a, χαρίζομαι, dat.
fear, φόβος ὁ; fear of me, ὁ ἐμὸς φόβος; my fear, ὁ φόβος μου, 106, 4.
fear, I, φοβοῦμαι (εο), δέδοικα, δέδια : I feel fear, φόβον φοβοῦμαι; I have no fear of, θαρρῶ (εω), acc.
feel inspiration, I, ἔνθεος γίγνομαι.
fetter, δεσμός ὁ, plur. δεσμοί and δεσμά; Grammar, p. 9.
few, ὀλίγος, η, ον.
field with, I take the, συ·στρατεύω, dat.
fight with, I, μάχομαι, dat.
find, I, εὑρίσκω, acc.; τυγχάνω, gen. 100; I find guilty of, κατα·γιγνώσκω, κατα·ψηφίζομαι, acc. penalty, gen. person, 122; pass. ἁλίσκομαι, gen.; find (money) for, πορίζω, πορίζομαι.
fire, πῦρ, πυρός, τό.
first, πρῶτος; you among the first, ἀρξάμενος ἀπὸ σοῦ, 359.
fish, ἰχθύς, ύος, ὁ.
fix the penalty at, I, τιμῶ (αω), gen. 119.
flatter, I, κολακεύω.
flee, I, φεύγω; I flee from, φεύγω ἐκ.
flesh, κρέας, κρέως, τό.
flock together, I, συν·έρχομαι.
flog, I, πληγὰς ἐμβάλλω, dat.; δέρειν, acc.; pass. πληγὰς ἔχω, πληγῶν τυγχάνω.
flogging, a, πληγαί al (=blows).
fly, I, πέτομαι, 194.
foe, see enemy.
follow, I, ἕπομαι, dat. 167; ἀκολουθῶ (εω), dat. 167.
folly, μωρία ἡ.
food, σῖτος ὁ, plur. σῖτα, σιτία τά, τροφή ἡ.
fool, μωρός, σκαιός.

foolish, μωρός, ά, όν; σκαιός, ά, όν.
foot, πούς, ποδός, ό; on foot, πεζῇ, 168.
for, conj. γάρ; for indeed, καὶ γάρ, 422.
for, prep. ὑπέρ, gen. (on behalf of); for food, εἰς τροφήν, 53.
forbid, ἀπ᾽ἀγορεύω, ἀντι᾽λέγω; ἀντ᾽εἶπον, οὐ φημί, followed by μή and inf. 332; God forbid, μὴ γένοιτο, 290.
force, βία ἡ: (=army) δύναμις, εως, ἡ, στράτευμα τό.
force, I, βιάζομαι, ἀναγκάζω, double acc. 74; I am forced to this, τοῦτο ἀναγκάζομαι, 75.
foreigner, ξένος ὁ.
foresee, I, προ᾽ορῶ (αω).
forestall, I, φθάνω, acc., with participle.
forget, λανθάνομαι, ἐπι᾽λανθάνομαι, gen. 100; with part. 372.
form the plan of, I, ἐπι᾽βουλεύω, with inf.
former, πρότερος, ὁ πρίν, ὁ πάλαι.
formerly, in former days, adv. πρότερον, τὸ πρότερον, πρίν, τὸ πρίν, πάλαι, τὸ πάλαι, πρόσθεν.
fort, τείχισμα, ατος, τό.
fortify, I, τειχίζω, ἐκ᾽τειχίζω.
fortune (good), τύχη ἡ.
free, ἐλεύθερος, α, ον.
free, I, ἐλευθερῶ (οω).
free from, I, ἀπ᾽ἀλλάττω, λύω, ἐλευθερῶ (οω); acc. and gen. 126.
friend, φίλος ὁ.
friendly, φίλος, η, ον; φίλιος, α, ον.
friendship, φιλία ἡ, εὔνοια ἡ.
frighten, φοβῶ (εω), acc.; φόβον ἐμ᾽βάλλω, dat.; ταράττω, acc.; ἐκ᾽πλήττω, acc.; pass. φοβοῦμαι, φόβον ἔχω, ἐκ᾽πλήττομαι, etc.
from, ἀπό, gen.; ἐκ, gen.; (=owing to) διά, acc.
full speed at, ἀνὰ κράτος, τάχιστα, ὡς τάχιστα.
full of, πλήρης, gen. 108.

furlong, στάδιον, plur. στάδιοι.
future, τὸ μέλλον, τὰ μέλλοντα; for the future, ἀπὸ τοῦδε, τὸ ἀπὸ τοῦδε.

G

gain for myself, I, κτῶμαι (αο).
gain a victory, νικῶ (αω) νίκην, 72, 1.
general, στρατηγός ὁ.
general, I am, στρατηγῶ (εω).
gentle, πρᾶος, πραεῖα, πρᾶον, Grammar, p. 139.
geometer, γεωμέτρης ὁ.
get, I, λαμβάνω, κτῶμαι (αο); I have got, possess, κέκτημαι.
get as good as I give, I, παραπλήσια πέπονθα καὶ ἔδρασα, 403.
gift, δῶρον τό.
girl, κόρη ἡ.
give, I, δίδωμι: (=entrust) ἐπι᾽-τρέπω, acc. and dat. 336.
—— back, ἀπο᾽δίδωμι.
—— advice, συμ᾽βουλεύω.
—— up to, ἐπι᾽τρέπω, inf. 336.
—— way to, ὑπο᾽χωρῶ (εω), dat.
glad, I am, ἥδομαι; ἡδέως, with verb, § 25, 5.
gladly, ἡδέως, ἄσμενος, 25, 5.
glorious, καλός, ή, όν.
glory, κάλλος, ους, τό.
go, I, ἔρχομαι, εἶμι, βαίνω; see Grammar, p. 183, for tenses.
—— after, μέτ᾽ειμι (-ιέναι), acc. 64.
—— away, ἀπ᾽ἔρχομαι, ἄπ᾽ειμι, ἀπο᾽βαίνω.
—— off with, οἴχομαι λαβών or ἔχων, 369.
—— out, ἐξ᾽ἔρχομαι, ἔξ᾽ειμι, ἐκ᾽-βαίνω.
—— to bed, κοιμῶμαι (αο).
—— to law with, δικαιολογοῦμαι (εο), 196.
—— to meet, ἀπ᾽αντῶ (αω), dat.
—— to war, πολεμῶ (εω), dat. or

ἐπί and acc., πρός and acc. etc.; πόλεμον ποιοῦμαι.
goat, αἴξ, αἰγός, ὁ and ἡ.
god, θεός ὁ; God forbid, see forbid.
goddess, θεός ἡ.
gold, χρυσός ὁ, χρυσίον τό (piece of gold or something made of gold).
good, ἀγαθός, ή, όν; good at, δεινός with inf. 338.
good fortune, τύχη ἡ.
good will, εὔνοια ἡ.
grant, I, δίδωμι; see allow.
gratitude, I show, χάριν ἀπο‍-δίδωμι.
great, μέγας, μεγάλη, μέγα; great deal, πολύς, πολλή, πολύ; greatly, μέγα, πολύ.
Great King, βασιλεύς (έως), without article.
Greece, Ἑλλάς, άδος, ἡ.
Greek, Ἕλλην, ηνος.
grieve, I (intr.), λυποῦμαι (εο), λύπην ἔχω.
grieved at, I am, λυποῦμαι (εο), dat.
grievous, χαλεπός, ή, όν; βαρύς, εῖα, ύ.
ground arms, I, τίθεμαι ὅπλα; see 190 note.
ground, on the, χαμαί, locative, 172.
grove, ἄλσος τό.
guard, φύλαξ, ἄκος, ὁ, φυλάκή ἡ.
guard, I, φυλάττω; I am on my guard against, φυλάττομαι, acc. 189.
guide, ἡγεμών, όνος, ὁ.
guilty of, ἄξιος, gen. 99.
gymnastics, γυμναστική ἡ.

H

habit of performing, in the, πρακτικός, gen. 98.
half, ἥμισυς, εια, υ; generally agrees in gender with the word depending on it, e.g. ἡ ἡμίσεια τῆς νήσου, half of the island, 104.
halt, I, ὅπλα τίθεμαι, 190 note.
hand, χείρ, χειρός, ἡ.
hand over, I, παραδίδωμι.
happen, I, τυγχάνω with part. 369; γίγνομαι.
happily, ἡδέως.
happiness, εὐδαιμονία ἡ.
happy, μακάριος, α, ον; εὐδαίμων, ον; ἡδύς, εῖα, ύ.
happy in, I am, ἐν εὐδαιμονῶ (εω), 336.
happy, I make, εὐφραίνω.
harbour, λιμήν, ένος, ὁ.
hard, χαλεπός, ή, όν.
hare, λαγώς, ώ, ὁ.
harm to, I do, see I injure.
hasten, I, σπεύδω.
hate, στυγῶ (εω), μισῶ (εω).
hateful, ἐχθρός, ά, όν; ἔχθιστος; λυπηρός, ά, όν.
hatred, μῖσος τό, ἔχθρα ἡ.
have, I, ἔχω.
have, I have the same views as you, δοκεῖ μοι ὅπερ σοί, 355.
have keen sight, I, ὀξύ βλέπω.
head, κεφαλή ἡ.
headache, I have a, ἀλγῶ (εω) τήν κεφαλήν.
health, ὑγίεια ἡ.
healthy, ὑγιής, ές.
hear, ἀκούω, with part. 372.
heard, can be, ἀκουστός, 377.
heart, I take. θαρρῶ (εω).
heaven, οὐρανός ὁ.
heavy injury on, I inflict, μέγα βλάπτω.
helmet, κόρυς, -υθος, ἡ.
help, βοήθεια ἡ, ὠφέλεια ἡ.
help, I, ὠφελῶ (εω), dat.; βοηθῶ (εω), dat.; verbal, βοηθητέος, 378; pass. I am helped, ὠφελείας τυγχάνω, 184; if I can help it, τό κατ' ἐμέ, 79.
helpmate, συνεργός ὁ.
herald, κῆρυξ, υκος, ὁ.

herdsman, βουκόλος ὁ.
here, ἐνταῦθα, ἐνθάδε, τῇδε ; here
... there, τῇ μέν ... τῇ δέ;
I am here; πάρ·ειμι.
hero, ἥρως, ωος, ὁ.
high, ὑψηλός, ή, όν ; (honour) μέγας;
I leap high, ὑψηλὰ πηδῶ (αω),
72, 3.
hill, ὄρος τό, λόφος ὁ.
himself, ἑαυτόν.
hinder, I, κωλύω ; special construction, 334.
hire, I, μισθῶ (οω) and μισθοῦμαι ;
with gen. of price, 119.
his, ἑαυτοῦ, etc., 32-35.
hold out, I, ἀντ·έχω ; ... against, dat.
hold up against sorrow, I, καρτερῶ (εω) λυπούμενος, 370.
home, οἰκία ἡ, οἶκος ὁ; homewards, to home, οἴκαδε ; at home, οἴκοι, ἔνδον.
honest, χρηστός, ή, όν.
honey, μέλι, -ιτος, τό.
honour, I, τιμῶ (αω).
honour, τιμή ἡ.
honour of, in, expressed by dat.
honourable, καλός, ή, όν.
honourably, καλῶς.
honoured, must be, τιμητέος, 378.
hope, ἐλπίζω, fut. inf., or aor. inf. with ἄν, 326 ; in the hope of, εἰ or ἐάν πως, 288.
hope, ἐλπίς, ίδος, ἡ ; I am in hope of, ἐν ἐλπίδι εἰμί, 316.
horse, ἵππος ὁ ; horses and all, αὐτοῖς (τοῖς) ἵπποις, 166.
hot, θερμός, ή, όν.
hour, ὥρα ἡ.
house, οἶκος ὁ, οἰκία ἡ.
how (interrogative), πῶς; (indirect) ὅπως ; τίνι τρόπῳ ;
how large, πόσος; (indirect) ὁπόσος.
hungry, I am, πεινῶ (αω).

I
I, ἐγώ.
if, conditional, εἰ, ἐάν, 275-289 ;
interrogative, εἰ, εἴτε, πότερον, 246-249.
ignorant, I am, ἀγνοῶ (εω).
ill, I am, νοσῶ (εω) ; I do ill to, κακῶς ποιῶ (εω), acc. ; I fare ill, κακῶς πράττω.
ill treat, I, κακῶς ποιῶ, acc.
imitate, I, μῑμοῦμαι (εο) ; verbal, μιμητέος, 378.
immediately, αὐτίκα, εὐθύς, with part. 354.
immortal, ἀθάνατος, ον.
impeach, I, γράφομαι.
impiety, ἀσέβεια ἡ.
importance, of great, μεγάλου ἀξιώματος.
impossible, ἀδύνᾰτος, ον ; οὐ δυνατός, ή, όν ; though it is impossible, ἀδύνατον ὄν, acc. absol. 366.
impudence, ἀναίδεια ἡ.
in, ἐν, dat.
in order to, ἵνα, 260-264 ; τοῦ with inf. 315.
inasmuch as he, ὅστις, 39.
indeed, τοίνυν.
independence, ἐλευθερία ἡ.
indoors, from, ἔνδοθεν.
infantry, πεζός ὁ.
infirm, ἀσθενής, ές.
inflict injury on, I, βλάπτω, acc.
informed, I am, πυνθάνομαι.
informer, μηνυτής ὁ.
inherited from, καταλειφθεὶς ὑπό, gen.
injure, I, βλάπτω, acc.; κακῶς ποιῶ (εω), acc.
injustice, ἀδικία ἡ.
inlet, ἔσπλους ὁ.
insolence, ὕβρις, εως, ἡ.
intend, I, μέλλω, with pres. or fut. inf. 209.
interrupt, I (intr.), θορυβῶ (εω).

interval, χρόνος ὁ, ὁ μεταξὺ χρόνος.
invite, καλῶ (εω).
involved in, I am, or I have involved myself in, περιπεπτωκώς εἰμι, *with dat.*
island, νῆσος ἡ.
islander, νησιώτης ὁ.

J

javelin, παλτόν τό, ἀκόντιον τό.
journey, I, πορεύομαι.
judge, κριτής ὁ.
judge, I, κρίνω, τεκμαίρομαι.
judgment, γνώμη ἡ.
just, δίκαιος, α, ον.
just what, ὅπερ.
just, I have just . . ., τυγχάνω, *with part.* 369.
justice, δικαιοσύνη ἡ.
justly, δικαίως.

K

keen, ὀξύς, εῖα, ύ; I have keen sight, ὀξὺ βλέπω, 72, 3.
keep, I, ἔχω; keep (laws, *etc.*), φυλάττω.
keep on the spot, I, ἔχω κατὰ χώραν, 176.
keep silent, I (intr.), σιγῶ (αω).
kept, I am (=remain), μένω.
kill, I, ἀπο·κτείνω; *pass.* ἀπο·θνῄσκω.
king, βασιλεύς, έως, ὁ; τύραννος ὁ.
knock out, I, ἐκ·κόπτω.
know, I, οἶδα, γιγνώσκω, ἐπίσταμαι; I know how to, ἐπίσταμαι *with inf.*; I know that, *part.* 372.

L

labour, πόνος ὁ.
lady, γυνή, γυναικός, ἡ.

land, χώρα ἡ, γῆ ἡ; mainland, ἤπειρος ἡ.
land at, I, κατ·άγομαι εἰς.
large, μέγας, μεγάλη,·μέγα; πολύς, πολλή, πολύ.
last, I, δια·τελῶ (εω), μένω.
last, at, τέλος.
last year, ἐν τῷ πρόσθεν ἔτει.
late, ὀψέ; late in, ὀψέ *with gen.*;
   late in the night, πόρρω τῆς νυκτός.
late for, I am, *or* I come too late for, ὑστερῶ (εω), *gen.* 134.
laugh, I, γελῶ (αω); laugh at, κατα·γελῶ (αω), *gen.* 121; *for pass. see* 200.
law, νόμος ὁ.
law, to go to law with one another, δικαιολογεῖσθαι, 196.
lead, I, ἄγω; lead life, δι·άγω (βίον), 177.
leap, I, πηδῶ (αω); leap down, κατα·πηδῶ (αω).
learn, I, μανθάνω; *verbal*, μαθητέος, 378; πυνθάνομαι.
leave, I, λείπω; leave behind, κατα·λείπω; let go, ἀφ·ίημι, 336; (=go away) ἔξ·ειμι ἐξ, *etc.*, *see* I go.
left (hand), ἀριστερός, ά, όν; on the left, ἐν ἀριστερᾷ.
leisure, σχολή ἡ.
lend to, I, ἐπι·τρέπω.
lest, ἵνα μή, *final*, 260-265; after verbs of fearing, μή, μὴ οὐ, 270-274.
let go, I, ἀφ·ίημι.
liar, ψευδής ὁ.
liberty, ἐλευθερία ἡ.
lie, I (tell falsehoods), ψεύδομαι, ψευδῆ λέγω.
lie, I (recline), κεῖμαι.
—— before, πρό·κειμαι, *gen.* 121.
—— awake, ἐγρήγορα (ἐγείρω).
life, βίος ὁ, ἡλικία ἡ.
light, φῶς, φωτός, τό.
like, I, φιλῶ (εω), ἀγαπῶ (αω).

like to, I should, ήδέως άν with
 opt. 224.
like, I am, έοικα, dat. 138.
like, very, adj. παραπλήσιος, α,
 ον, dat. 139.
likely to, I am, μέλλω, with pres.
 or fut. inf., or expressed by fut.
 part.
line (of battle), τάξις, εως, ή.
listen, I, ἀκούω, ἀκροῶμαι (ao), acc.
 or gen.
live, ζῶ (αω); διάγω, 177.
long, μακρός, ά, όν; πολύς, πολλή,
 πολύ.
long run, in the, τελευτῶν (pres.
 part.), 359.
long for, I, ποθῶ (εω), ἐρῶ (αω),
 ἐπιθυμῶ (εω), ἐφίεμαι, all with
 gen. 100.
longer, ἐπὶ πλείω, ἔτι; no longer,
 οὐκέτι, μηκέτι.
look after, I (=tend), θεραπεύω.
loosen, I, λύω; verbal, can be
 loosed, λυτός, 377; λυτέος, 378.
lose, I, ἀπόλλυμι, acc.; ἁμαρτάνω,
 gen.
loss, I am at a, ἀπορῶ (εω).
lost to reason, I become so, εἰς
 τοσοῦτον ὕβρεως ἔρχομαι, 255.
lost, we are, οὐκ ἔστι σωτηρία, 346.
loud (shouting), πολύς, πολλή,
 πολύ.
love, I, φιλῶ (εω), ἀγαπῶ (αω).
love, ἔρως, ωτος, ὁ.
luck, I have the good luck to be,
 συμβαίνει μοι εἶναι.
lunch, ἄριστον τό.

M

mad, I am, μαίνομαι.
madness, μανία ή.
maiden, κόρη ἡ.
mainland, ἤπειρος, ου, ή.
maintain, I, ἰσχυρίζομαι.
make, I, ποιῶ (εω), πράττω.

make afraid, I, φοβῶ (εω), see I
 frighten.
—— an effort to, ἐπιμελοῦμαι (εο),
 gen.
—— laws, νόμους τίθημι.
—— poems, ποιῶ (εω).
—— ready, παρασκευάζω.
—— terms with, συμβαίνω, dat.
—— use of, χρῶμαι (αο), dat.
—— voyage, πλοῦν ποιοῦμαι.
man, ἄνθρωπος ὁ; ἀνήρ, ἀνδρός, ὁ.
manage (affairs), I, πράττω.
mankind, οἱ ἄνθρωποι.
manner, τρόπος ὁ; in this manner,
 τούτῳ τῷ τρόπῳ; good manners,
 τὸ κόσμιον.
many, πολύς, πολλή, πολύ; in many
 points, πολλά, 72, 4; so many,
 τοσοῦτος.
Marathon, Μαραθών; at Marathon,
 (locative) Μαραθῶνι, 172.
march, I, (of army) πορεύομαι, εἶμι,
 fut.; (of general) ἐλαύνω, 177.
market-place, ἀγορά ἡ.
master (of slave), δεσπότης ὁ;
 (teacher) διδάσκαλος ὁ.
master of, κύριος, α, ον, gen.
matter, πρᾶγμα τό.
may, I, ἔξεστί μοι, with inf.
me, see I.
mean to, I, μέλλω, with pres. or
 fut. inf.
meet, I, ἀπαντῶ (αω), dat.
Megara, at, Μεγαροῖ, locative, 172.
memorial, μνημεῖον τό.
merely, not, οὐ μόνον ... ἀλλὰ
 καί, 411.
message, ἀγγελία ἡ, ἄγγελμα τό.
messenger, ἄγγελος ὁ.
mid-day, μεσημβρινός, ή, όν, 25, 4.
middle, μέσος, η, ον; in the middle
 of the country, ἐν μέσῃ τῇ χώρᾳ,
 25, 2.
might, I, ἔξεστί μοι, with inf.;
 when one might, ἐξόν, acc. absol.
 306.
milk, γάλα, γάλακτος, τό.

Miltiades, Μιλτιάδης ὁ.
mina, μνᾶ ἡ.
mind, ψυχή ἡ, νοῦς ὁ.
miserable, see unhappy.
misery, κακά τά.
misfortune, συμφορά ἡ, κακὴ τύχη.
miss, ἁμαρτάνω, gen.
mistake, ἁμαρτία ἡ.
mistaken, I am, ἁμαρτάνω.
model, I, πλάττω.
modesty, αἰδώς, οῦς, ἡ.
money, χρήματα τά, ἀργύριον τό, οὐσία ἡ, πλοῦτος ὁ.
month, μήν, μηνός, ὁ.
moon, new, νουμηνία ἡ; at the new moon, νουμηνίᾳ, 173, 3.
more, πλείων, etc., see much; adv. μᾶλλον.
morrow, to-, αὔριον, ὁ, ἡ, τό.
mortal, θνητός, ή, όν.
most, πλεῖστος, etc., see many; most men, οἱ πολλοί.
mother, μήτηρ, μητρός, ἡ.
mould, I, πλάττω.
mount, I (horse), ἀνα·βαίνω ἐπί, acc.; ἐπι·βαίνω, gen.
mountain, ὄρος τό.
mourn for, κόπτομαι, 188.
move against, I, ὁρμῶ (αω) ἐπί, acc.
much, πολύς, πολλή, πολύ; adv. πολύ, πολλά, μάλα; very much, μάλιστα.
mud, πηλός ὁ.
murder, φόνος ὁ, σφαγή ἡ.
music, μουσική ἡ.
must, χρή, δεῖ; also verbal, e.g. we must advance, πορευτέον ἐστι, 378.
my, ἐμός, ή, όν.

N

name, ὄνομα, ατος, τό.
name, I (call by name), ὀνομάζω.

nation, γένος τό.
native land, πατρίς, ίδος, ἡ.
natives, οἱ βάρβαροι, αὐτόχθονες.
nature, φύσις, εως, ἡ.
necessary, ἀναγκαῖος, α, ον.
—— it is, δεῖ, ἀνάγκη (ἐστι); absolutely necessary, see absolutely.
need, I, δέομαι, gen. 130; σπανίζω, gen. 130; I need this, δεῖ μοι τούτου, 140; there is need of, δεῖ, gen.; why need we? τί δεῖ;
neglect, I, ἀμελῶ (εω), gen.
neighbour, ὅμορος, ον; πλησίος, α, ον; one's neighbour, ὁ πλησίον.
neither ... nor, οὔτε ... οὔτε.
never, οὔποτε, μήποτε; never yet, οὐδεπώποτε.
new moon, νουμηνία ἡ; at the new moon, νουμηνίᾳ, 173, 3.
news, the, τὰ ἀγγελθέντα.
—— thank-offering for good, εὐαγγέλια τά.
next day, ἡμέρα ἡ ἐπιοῦσα, ἐπιγιγνομένη, δευτεραία.
night, νύξ, νυκτός, ἡ; to-night, ταύτῃ τῇ νυκτί.
no, οὔ, οὐκ.
—— longer, οὐκέτι, μηκέτι.
—— man, οὐδείς.
—— one, οὐδείς.
—— one in the world, οὐδεὶς τῶν ἀνθρώπων, 102.
no by Zeus, μὰ τὸν Δία, 63.
noble, καλός, ή, όν; γενναῖος, α, ον.
noise, θόρυβος ὁ.
nor, οὐδέ, οὔτε, 401, 402.
not, οὔ, οὐκ, οὐχ, οὐχί, μή.
nothing, οὐδέν.
notice of, I escape the, λανθάνω, acc.
now, νῦν, ἤδη; come now, ἄγε δή, ἄγε νυν.
number, πλῆθος τό.
numbers, in, πολλοί, αἱ, ά.
numerous, see many.
nurse, I, θεραπεύω.

O

O or oh, ὤ.
oath, ὅρκος ὁ.
obey, I, πείθομαι, dat.
obtain, I, see I get; where he obtains this from, ὅθεν τοῦτο γίγνεται αὐτῷ, 150.
offer, I, δίδωμι.
offer thank-offerings for good news, I, εὐαγγέλια θύω, 72, 3.
officer, ἄρχων, οντος, ὁ.
often, πολλάκις.
old, γεραιός, ά, όν; πρεσβύτης; παλαιός, ά, όν; thirty years old, τριάκοντα ἔτη (acc.) γεγονώς; of old days, οἱ πάλαι; old age, in one's, γεραιὸς ὤν.
on, ἐν, ἐπί, dat.; on earth, ἐπὶ τῆς γῆς.
once (=formerly), πρότερον; once a day, ἅπαξ τῆς ἡμέρας; at once, ἅμα, ἤδη (go away at once).
one, εἷς, μία, ἕν, indef. τις.
one another, ἀλλήλω.
only, μόνος, η, ον; adv. μόνον.
open, I, ἀν·οίγνυμι.
open, ἐμφανής, ές; φανερός, ά, όν.
openly, φανερῶς.
opinion, in my, ἐμοὶ δοκεῖν, 340.
oppose, I, ἐναντιοῦμαι (οο), dat. 197.
opposite, ἐναντίος, α, ον.
—— principles, τὰ ἐναντία.
orator, ῥήτωρ, ορος, ὁ.
order, I, κελεύω, acc. 331; προσ·τάττω, dat.
—— to supply, προσ·τάττω, 201; when he was ordered, προσταχθέν, acc. absol. 366.
order to, in, ἵνα, final, 260-264.
other, ἕτερος, α, ον; ἄλλος, η, ο; see some.
ought, δεῖ, χρή, προσ·ήκει; when one ought, δέον, προσῆκον, acc. absol. 366; also verbal, e.g. ought to help, ὠφελητέος, etc., 378.
our, ἡμέτερος, α, ον, 32-35.

out, ἐκ, ἐξ, gen.; out of doors, ἔξω; (drive) out of the house, θύραζε, 181.
out of (=owing to), διά, acc.
out-flank, I, ὑπερ·έχω, gen.
overcome, I, see I conquer.
owe, I, ὀφείλω.
owing to, διά, acc.; διὰ τὸ with inf.

P

pain in my head, I have, ἀλγῶ τὴν κεφαλήν.
painter, ζωγράφος ὁ.
pardon, I, συγ·γιγνώσκω, dat.; pass. συγγνώμην ἔχω, συγγνώμης τυγχάνω.
parent, γονεύς, έως, ὁ.
parish, δῆμος ὁ.
part, to what (interrog.), ποῖ; (indirect) ὅποι.
partly, τὰ μὲν . . . τὰ δέ.
pass, I (=go past), παρ·έρχομαι, πάρ·ειμι (fut.), etc.; see go.
—— a law, τίθημι νόμον.
pass away, I, see I die.
pass sentence on, κατα·κρίνω, κατα·δικάζω, acc. of penalty, gen. of person, 122.
past, in things, τὰ παρελθόντα, 79.
past, the, τὰ γεγενημένα, τὰ παρελθόντα, 164.
pay, μισθός ὁ.
pay attention to, προσ·έχω (νοῦν), 177-178.
pay fine, ἐκ·τίνω.
—— penalty, δίκην δίδωμι.
peace, εἰρήνη ἡ.
peculiar to, ἴδιος, α, ον, gen. 108.
penalty, ζημία ἡ; δίκη ἡ.
perceive, I, αἰσθάνομαι, ὁρῶ (αω).
perform, I, πράττω.
performing, in the habit of, πρακτικός, gen. 98.
perish, I, ἀπ·όλλυμαι, ἀπο·θνήσκω.
Persian, Πέρσης, Περσικός.

persuade, I, πείθω, acc.
Philip, Φίλιππος ὁ.
philosopher, φιλόσοφος ὁ.
physician, ἰατρός ὁ.
pious, εὐσεβής, ές; towards, εἰς or πρός with acc.
piracy, λῃστεία ἡ.
pirate, λῃστής ὁ.
—— navy, τὸ λῃστικόν.
pity, I, οἰκτείρω, acc.; pass. ἐλέου τυγχάνω, 184.
place, in one ... in another, τῇ μὲν ... τῇ δέ.
plain, subst. πεδίον, τό.
plain, δῆλος, η, ον; φανερός, ά, όν; plainly, φανερῶς.
plain, I make, δηλῶ (οω), acc.
plainly, I am, φαίνομαι, with part. 369.
plaintiff, ὁ διώκων.
Plataea, Πλάταια ἡ; at Plataea, (locative) Πλαταίασιν, 172.
Plataeans, Πλαταιῆς, οἱ.
pleasant, ἡδύς, εῖα, ύ.
pleasantly, ἡδέως; as pleasantly as possible, ὡς ἥδιστα.
please, I (=wish), θέλω, ἐθέλω.
please, I (=make pleased), ἀρέσκω, dat.
please, ethic dat. 156.
pleased at, I am, ἥδομαι, etc., with part. 375.
pleasing to me, this is, τοῦτό ἐστιν ἐμοὶ βουλομένῳ, etc., 155; what pleases me, ἅ μοι δοκεῖ.
pleasure, ἡδονή; I experience pleasure, ἡδονὴν ἥδομαι; I take pleasure in, ἥδομαι with part.
plenty, in, πολύς, πολλή, πολύ, 25, 1.
plot against, I, ἐπιβουλεύω, dat.
plunder, I, ἁρπάζω, συλῶ (αω), ἄγω καὶ φέρω.
poet, ποιητής ὁ.
point, at one ... at another, τῇ μὲν ... τῇ δέ.
points, in many, πολλά, 72, 4.

poor man, πένης, ητος, ὁ.
possess, I, ἔχω, κέκτημαι (perf. of κτῶμαι).
possession, κτῆμα τό, or neut. of adj., e.g. τὰ ἐμά.
possible, δυνατός, η, ον; it is possible, ἔν'εστι, πάρ'εστι, 319; οἷός τ'εἰμί, see I can.
potter, κεραμεύς, έως, ὁ.
pour, χέω.
power, δύναμις, εως, ἡ; in the power of, ἐπί, dat.; it is in my power, ἔξ'εστι, πάρ'εστι, ἔν'εστί μοι, 319.
powerful, I am, μέγα δύναμαι; a powerful man, ὁ μέγα δυνάμενος.
practise, I, ἀσκῶ (εω); verbal, ἀσκητέος, 378; ἀσκητός, 377.
praise, ἔπαινος ὁ.
praise, I, αἰνῶ (εω), ἐπ'αινῶ, ἐγ'κωμιάζω; pass. ἔπαινον ἔχω, ἐπαίνου τυγχάνω.
praiseworthy, ἐπαινετός, ή, όν.
pray, I, εὔχομαι, dat.
pray (interjection), δή.
prayer, εὐχή ἡ.
precious, τίμιος, α, ον; πολλοῦ ἄξιος, α, ον.
prefer, I, with subst. αἱροῦμαι (εο), προ'τιμῶ (αω); with inf. βούλομαι, ἐθέλω.
premeditation, πρόνοια ἡ; without premeditation, οὐκ ἐκ προνοίας, ἄνευ προνοίας, 285.
preparation, παρασκευή ἡ, τὸ παρασκευάζειν.
prepare, I, παρα·σκευάζω; all is prepared, παρεσκεύασται, impersonal, 202.
present, δῶρον τό.
present, I am, πάρ'ειμι.
present, ὁ νῦν; for the present, τὸ νῦν εἶναι, 342.
prevent, I, κωλύω, 334; εἴργω, 332.
price, at what, πόσου, gen. of price, 120.
priest, ἱερεύς, έως, ὁ.

prison, δεσμωτήριον τό.
privilege, τιμή ή, γεράς τό.
proclaim, I, κηρύττω, προ·εῖπον (aorist).
procure for myself, I, πορίζομαι, 189.
profit, κέρδος τό.
profitable, λυσιτελής, ές; χρήσιμος, [η], ον.
promise, I, ὑπ·ισχνοῦμαι (εο); (engage to), ὑφ·ίσταμαι.
proof, τεκμήριον τό.
prophet, μάντις, εως, ὁ.
prosecute, I, διώκω; pass. φεύγω, 100.
prosecutor, ὁ διώκων, ὁ γραφόμενος.
prosper, I, εὖ πράττω.
prosperity, εὐδαιμονία ή; in his prosperity, εὐδαίμων.
prosperous, εὐδαίμων, ον; a prosperous man, ὁ εὖ πράττων.
prove, I, ἀπο·φαίνω.
provisions, σιτία τά, ἐπιτήδεια τά.
prudence, σωφροσύνη ή, φρόνησις, εως, ή.
prudent, σώφρων, ον; φρόνιμος, ον.
public life, I am in, πράττω τά δημόσια.
public men, οἱ πολιτευόμενοι.
punish, κολάζω, acc.
punished, I am, δίκην δίδωμι.
punishment, δίκη ή; I escape punishment, δίκην οὐ δίδωμι.
pupil, μαθητής ὁ.
pursue, I, διώκω.
put on, I, ἐν·δύω, double acc.
put on an equal footing with, I am, ἐξ ἴσου γίγνομαι, dat. 139.
put to death, I, ἀπο·κτείνω; pass. ἀπο·θνῄσκω.

Q

quarrel, ἔρις, -ιδος, ή.
quick, ταχύς, εῖα, ύ; be quick and . . ., ἀνύσας . . ., 428; the

quickest way, τήν ταχίστην, 80, 2; as quickly as possible, ὡς τάχιστα.

R

race, (family) γένος τό; (contest) ἀγών, ῶνος, ὁ.
rage, I am put in a, ὤργισμαι (ὀργίζω).
ransom, I, λύω.
rather, I would rather, see I prefer, ἐθέλοιμι ἄν, βουλοίμην ἄν; rather than, ἀντί gen., μᾶλλον ἤ.
ravage, I, τέμνω.
reach, I, ἐξ·ικνοῦμαι (εο), gen.; (come to) ἀφ·ικνοῦμαι (εο) εἰς.
read, I, ἀνα·γιγνώσκω.
really, καί, emphasising word; οὖν, 425; τῷ ὄντι; perf. part. with εἰμί, 369.
reason, αἰτία ή; for this reason, διά τοῦτο, τοῦδ' ἕνεκα; for this very reason, τοῦτ' αὐτό, etc., 80, 1.
recalled from banishment, I am, κατ·έρχομαι.
refuse (to help), I, οὔ φημί, οὐ λέγω, οὐκ ἐθέλω, ἀντ·εῖπον (aorist).
reign (over), I, βασιλεύω, gen.; ἄρχω, gen. 95.
rejoice, I, ἥδομαι, χαίρω, with part. 375.
remain, I, μένω.
remember, I, μέμνημαι, with part. 372, 3 (μιμνήσκω).
remind, I, ἀνα·μιμνήσκω, double acc.
repay, I, ἀπο·δίδωμι.
repent of, I, μετα·μέλομαι, with part. 375.
reply, I, ἀπο·κρίνομαι.
report, I, ἀγγέλλω.
represent, I, ἀπο·δείκνυμι, with part. 371; (of artist) πλάττω.

reputation, δόξα ἡ.
repute, I am in bad, among or with, κακῶς ἀκούω ὑπό, 180.
resist, I, ἀντ·έχω.
respect, I, αἰδοῦμαι (εο).
respects, in all, τά πάντα.
rest, ἄλλος, η, ο; οἱ ἄλλοι.
restore, I (bring back, *especially* exiles), κατ·άγω; *pass.* κατ·έρχομαι, 182.
retreat, I, ἀνα·χωρῶ (εω); *verbal*, ἀναχωρητέος, 378; πάλιν ἔρχομαι, φεύγω.
return, I, πάλιν ἔρχομαι, *etc.*; *see* I go.
revolt from, I, ἀφ·ίσταμαι ἀπό.
rich in, I am, πλουτῶ (εω), *gen.* 113.
rich, πλούσιος, α, ον; *with gen.*, rich in, 108.
riches, τά χρήματα.
ride, I, ἐλαύνω, ἱππεύω.
—— forth from, ἐξ·ελαύνω ἐκ, *gen.*
ridiculous, γελοῖος, α, ον.
right, ὀρθός, ἡ, όν; (right hand), δεξιός, ά, όν; on the right hand, ἐν δεξιᾷ; it is right, ὀρθῶς ἔχει; πρέπει (beseems); προσ·ήκει (behoves), 319; rightly, ὀρθῶς.
riot, θόρυβος ὁ.
rise, I, ἀν·ίσταμαι.
risk, κίνδυνος ὁ.
river, ποταμός ὁ.
road, ὁδός ἡ.
rob, I, συλῶ (αω), *double acc.*; rob of, ἀπο·στερῶ (εω), *acc. person, gen. thing*, 130.
robber, *see* thief *or* pirate.
rout, I, τρέπω, 189.
rude, ἄγροικος, ον.
rule over, I, ἄρχω, *gen.* 95.
run, I, τρέχω, θέω.
—— away, ἀπο·τρέχω, φεύγω.
—— round, περι·τρέχω, *acc.*; περι·θέω, *acc.*

S

sack, I (town), δι·αρπάζω.
sacred to, ἱερός, ά, όν, *gen.* 108.
safe, ἀσφαλής, ές; σῶς, σῶα, σῶν; (trustworthy) πιστός, ή, όν.
sail I, πλέω.
—— away, ἀπο·πλέω, ἀπ·αίρω (ναῦν), 177.
—— into, εἰσ·πλέω, *acc.*; as one sails in, εἰσπλέοντι, 154.
—— out against, ἐπ·εκ·πλέω.
—— past, παρα·πλέω; set sail, ἀναγωγὴν πειῶμαι, 199; *pass.* sail is made, ἡ ἀναγωγὴ γίγνεται, 199.
sailor, ναύτης ὁ.
salvation, σωτηρία ἡ.
same, self-same, ὁ αὐτός (αὐτός), ἡ αὐτή (αὐτή), τὸ αὐτό (ταὐτό).
Sardis, Σάρδεις, εων, αἱ.
savages, βάρβαροι, οἱ.
save, I, σῴζω; (money) φείδομαι; what saves us from, τί ἐμποδὼν μὴ οὔ, 333.
say, λέγω, φημί, φάσκω, ἀγορεύω; *for tenses see Grammar*, 182; must be said, *verbal*, ῥητέος, *etc.* 378.
scarcely, σχολῇ.
sculptor, ἀνδριαντοποιός ὁ.
sea, θάλαττα ἡ.
sea-fight, ναυμαχία ἡ.
seamanship, θάλαττα ἡ, 99.
season, ὥρα ἡ.
secret, I make no, οὐ λάθρα, *with verb*, 421.
see, I, ὁρῶ (αω).
see that, I, σκοπῶ (εω) ὅπως, 267; ὅπως (alone), 269.
seek, I, ζητῶ (εω).
seem, I, δοκῶ (εω); I seem like, ἔοικα; it seems good to me, δοκεῖ μοι.
seize, I, λαμβάνω, συλ·λαμβάνω; hold of, λαμβάνομαι, *gen.* 112.
self, αὐτός, ή, ό.

self-restraint, σωφροσύνη ή.
sell, I, πωλῶ (εω), gen. of price, 119; ἀπο·δίδωμι.
send, I, πέμπω.
—— for, μετα·πέμπω; verbal, μεταπεμπτέος, 378.
—— out, ἐκ·πέμπω.
sense, a man of no, ὁ κακῶς φρονῶν.
sensible, νοῦν ἔχων, φρόνιμος; people of sense, οἱ φρόνιμοι τῶν ἀνθρώπων.
—— I am, νοῦν ἔχω, σωφρονῶ (εω).
sentry, φύλαξ, -ακος, ὁ.
separate, I, χωρίζω, 126.
serious, μέγας, μεγάλη, μέγα.
servant, οἰκέτης ὁ, διάκονος ὁ.
serve, I (benefit), εὖ ποιῶ (εω), acc.; ὑπουργῶ (εω), dat.
set free, I, καθ·ίστημι ἐλεύθερον, 69.
set out, I, πορεύομαι.
set up, I, ἵστημι, ἀν·ίστημι.
severe (penalty), μέγας, μεγάλη, μέγα.
shame before, I feel, αἰσχύνομαι, acc. 60.
share in, I have a, μετ·έχω, gen.; μετα·λαγχάνω, gen. 115.
share, I (=give a share of), μετα·δίδωμι, gen. 115; (=have a share in) μέτοχός εἰμι, gen. 108, 2.
shared in by all, κοινόν ἐστιν ἅπασι, 167.
sharer in, μέτοχος, gen. 108.
sheep, πρόβατα τά.
shepherd, ποιμήν, ένος, ὁ.
ship, ναῦς, νεώς, ἡ.
shipwright, I am a, ναυπηγῶ (εω).
shoot, I (arrows), τοξεύω; (=kill) κατα·τοξεύω.
short, in, ὡς συνελόντι εἰπεῖν, 340.
shout, I, βοῶ (αω).
shouting, κραυγή ἡ.
show, I, δείκνυμι, δηλῶ (οω).
show gratitude, I, ἀπο·δίδωμι χάριν.

show up for, I, ἐπι·δείκνυμι, with part. 371.
shrink from, I, ὀκνῶ (εω), with inf.
shrink from, if we shrink from defending ourselves, μὴ τολμῶντες ἀμύνεσθαι, 346.
sick, I am, νοσῶ (εω), ἀσθενῶ (εω); a sick man, ὁ νοσῶν, ὁ ἀσθενῶν; the sick, οἱ νοσοῦντες.
sight, I have keen, ὀξὺ βλέπω.
silence, σιγή ἡ, τὸ σιγᾶν.
silence, I (=make silent), κατα·σιωπῶ (αω).
silent, I am, σιγῶ (αω); σεσίγηκα, 214.
silver, ἄργυρος ὁ, ἀργύριον τό (= piece of silver, money).
simply because I wish, τοῦδ' ἕνεκα or διὰ τοῦτο βουλόμενος, 355.
sin, ἁμαρτία ἡ.
since, ἐπεί, ἐπειδή.
sit down, I, καθ·ἕζομαι, 192.
size, μέγεθος τό.
skilful in, ἐπιστήμων, ον, gen.
slave, δοῦλος ὁ.
slay, I, ἀπο·κτείνω; see I kill.
sleep, I, καθ·εύδω, aorist κατ·έδαρθον.
small, μικρός (or σμικρός), ά, όν; ὀλίγος, η, ον; βραχύς, εῖα, ύ; at small wages, ὀλίγου.
smell of, I have a bad, κάκιστον ὄζω, gen. 117.
smell, I, trans. ὀσφραίνομαι, gen. 114.
smith, I am a, χαλκεύω.
so (=as it seems), particle, ἄρα.
so, οὕτως; it is so, οὕτως ἔχει, 176;
so much, so many, τοσοῦτος; and so, ὥστε, consec.
so as to (final), ὅπως, ὡς, 260-264.
Socrates, Σωκράτης, ους, ὁ.
soldier, στρατιώτης ὁ.
solvent, κατάλυσις ἡ.
some, indef. τις; some ... others, οἱ μέν ... οἱ δέ; to some extent, τρόπον τινά, τί, 80, 2.

son, υἱός, υἱός, οὗ or ἑος, ὁ; παῖς, παιδός, ὁ.
soon, ταχύ.
sooner, πρότερον.
sort, the sort to, τοιοῦτος, -αύτη, -οῦτο, 257; of the sort, τοιοῦτος.
sorts, of all, παντοῖος, α, ον.
soul, ψυχή ἡ.
spare, I, φείδομαι, gen. 126.
Sparta, I lean to, favour, λακωνίζω.
speak, I, λέγω, δια·λέγω, etc.; see I say; I speak well of, εὖ λέγω, acc.; I speak ill of, κακῶς λέγω, acc.; pass. εὖ and κακῶς ἀκούω; 'speak the word,' φράζε.
speech, λόγος ὁ, τὸ λαλεῖν.
spend time, I, δι·άγω, 177.
spend, I (money), ἀν·αλίσκω.
spot, at that, ἐνταῦθα, with gen. 88; I keep on the spot, ἔχω κατὰ χώραν.
stable, σταθμός ὁ, plur. σταθμοί and σταθμά; Grammar, p. 9.
stag, ἔλαφος ἡ and ὁ (as name of class always fem. in Attic).
stand, I, ἵσταμαι, and intrans. tenses of ἵστημι; ἕστηκα, 214.
stand out to sea, I, ἀν·άγομαι.
star, ἀστήρ, ἐρος, ὁ; ἄστρον τό (generally plural).
start, I, πορεύομαι.
starve, I (intrans.), πεινῶ (αω).
state, πόλις, εως, ἡ.
statecraft, τὰ πολιτικά; good at statecraft, ἀγαθὸς τὰ πολιτικά, 82.
station, I, τάττω, καθ·ίστημι.
stay, I, μένω.
steal, I, κλέπτω.
still (= yet), ἔτι.
stock of, I use up my, ἀν·αλίσκω, acc.
stone, λίθος ὁ; (made) of stone, gen. λίθου.
stoop down, I, ἐγ·κύπτω.
stop, I, trans. παύω, acc.; intrans. παύομαι, λήγω, with part. 370.

straightway, εὐθύς.
strange, δεινός, ἡ, όν; θαυμαστός, ἡ, όν.
strangely, δεινῶς; I act strangely, θαυμαστὸν ποιῶ (εω).
stranger, ξένος ὁ.
strength, ἰσχύς, ύος, ἡ; κράτος τό; δύναμις, εως, ἡ.
strengthen, I ἐπ·ισχύω.
strife, ἔρις, ιδος, ἡ; στάσις, εως, ἡ.
strike, I, τύπτω; strike a blow, τύπτω πληγήν, 74, double acc. 74; πληγὰς ἐμ·βάλλω, πατάσσω. For tenses see Grammar, p. 185.
strong, ἰσχυρός, ά, όν.
stupid, σκαιός, ά, όν.
such (a sort), τοιοῦτος, -αύτη, -οῦτο; (a size, etc.) τοσοῦτος, -αύτη, -οῦτο.
suddenly, ἐξαίφνης, αὐτίκα.
suffer, I, ἀλγῶ (εω), 76; πάσχω.
sum total, ὁ πᾶς ἀριθμός.
summer, θέρος τό.
summon, I, καλῶ (εω).
sun, ἥλιος ὁ.
suppliant, ἱκέτης ὁ.
supply, I order to, προσ·τάττω, 201.
suppose, οἶμαι or οἴομαι.
surprised, I am, θαυμάζω (... that, ὅτι, or more commonly εἰ ...)
surround, I, κυκλοῦμαι (οο), κύκλῳ ἀπο·τειχίζω.
suspect, I, ὑπ·οπτεύω, constr. 270-274.
swear, I, ὄμνυμι; swear by, ὄμνυμι, acc.; no by, ἀπ·όμνυμι; I swear no by Zeus, ἀπ·όμνυμι τὸν Δία; swear to do, ὄμνυμι, with inf. often preceded by ἦ μήν; not to do, ἀπ·όμνυμι, 63; falsely by, ἐπι·ορκῶ (εω), 63.
swift, ταχύς, εῖα, ύ.
sword, ξίφος τό.
sympathise with, I, συν·αλγῶ (εω), dat.

ENGLISH-GREEK VOCABULARY

T

tailor, to be a, ῥάπτω.
take, I, λαμβάνω, αἱρῶ (εω).
—— away, ἀφ'αιρῶ.
—— care, σκοπῶ (εω) ὅπως, or ὅπως alone, 267-269.
—— counsel, βουλεύομαι ὅπως.
—— heart, θαρρῶ (εω).
—— place, γίγνομαι.
—— thought, φροντίζω ὅπως.
—— up, αἴρω.
talent (money), τάλαντον τό.
talk, I, δια·λέγομαι; talk with, dat.
taller, μείζων, ον.
task, ἔργον τό.
taste, I, γεύομαι, gen. 114; give to taste, γεύω, gen. 114.
teach, I, διδάσκω, double acc.; in passive sometimes μανθάνω; I have or get taught, διδάσκομαι, mid.; verbal, can be taught, διδακτός, 377.
tear, δάκρυον τό.
tell, I, λέγω, φημί, κατ·αγορεύω, κατ·εῖπον; for tenses see Grammar, p. 182; I tell falsehoods against, κατα·ψεύδομαι, gen. with or without κατά, 121; I am told, μανθάνω.
temple, νεώς, ώ, ὁ; ἱερόν τό.
terrible, δεινός, ή, όν.
test, I, κρίνω.
than, ἤ.
that, pron. ἐκεῖνος, η, ο.
that, conj. ὅτι, after verbs of saying, etc., 235-244; μή, μὴ οὐ, after verbs of fearing, 270-274.
Thebes, Θῆβαι αἱ.
theft, κλοπή ἡ.
their, §§ 32-35.
Themistocles, Θεμιστοκλῆς, οῦς, ὁ.
then, τότε, εἶτα (417), ἔπειτα, ἐνταῦθα; illative, οὖν, 425 foll.; then and there, ἐνταῦθα δή.
there, ἐκεῖ, ἐνταῦθα, ἐνθάδε, τῇδε.
therefore, οὖν.

Thermopylae, Θερμοπύλαι, ῶν, αἱ.
thief, φώρ, φωρός, ὁ.
thing, πρᾶγμα, ατος, τό.
think, I, οἶμαι, οἴομαι, νομίζω; in my heart, ὑπο·νοοῦμαι (εο); I think (myself) as good as (or equal to), ἴσῶ (οω), acc. and dat. 138.
thirsty, I am, διψῶ (αω).
this, οὗτος, αὕτη, τοῦτο.
though, see although.
thoughts of, I have, διάνοιαν ἔχω, 316.
threaten, I, ἀπειλῶ (εω), dat.
three times, or thrice to-day, τρὶς ταύτης τῆς ἡμέρας, 93.
thrifty, οἰκονομικός, ή, όν.
through, διά, acc.
throughout, ὅλος, 28.
throw, I, βάλλω; passive, πίπτω.
—— into confusion, ταράττω.
—— out, ἐκ·βάλλω; passive, ἐκ·πίπτω.
—— overboard, ἐκ·βάλλω.
thus much, τοσαῦτα.
till, μέχρι, gen., see until; till late in the night, μέχρι πόρρω τῆς νυκτός.
time, χρόνος ὁ; in the time of, ἐπί, gen.; in my time, ἐπ' ἐμοῦ; at one time, at another time, τότε μέν, τότε δέ; summer time, ὥρα θέρους; I am at the time, τυγχάνω with part. 369; it is time to, ὥρα ἐστίν, with inf.
tired, I grow, ἀπ·αγορεύω, part. 370.
to, εἰς, acc.; πρός, acc.; παρά, acc. (to the side of); ἐπί, acc.
to-day, τήμερον; see day.
to-morrow, αὔριον; see morrow.
to-night, τήμερον καθ' ἑσπέραν, ταύτῃ τῇ νυκτί, τῇ ἐπιούσῃ νυκτί.
toil, πόνος ὁ.
top, ἄκρος, α, ον.
tortoise, χελώνη ἡ.
touch, I, ἅπτομαι, gen. 112.
towards, εἰς, ἐπί, πρός, παρά, acc.

town, ἄστυ, εως, τό.
traitor, προδότης ὁ.
tranquil (life), βέβαιος, [a], ον.
treasure, θησαυρός ὁ.
treat ill, I, κακῶς ποιῶ (εω); treat well, εὖ ποιῶ; pass. κακῶς or εὖ πάσχω.
tree, δένδρον τό (dat. pl. δένδρεσι).
trench, τάφρος ἡ.
trial (judicial), δίκη ἡ; κρίσις, εως, ἡ; ἀγών, ῶνος, ὁ.
tried for, I am (legal), φεύγω, gen.
trophy, τρόπαιον τό.
troubles, τὰ κακά, αἱ συμφοραί.
truce, σπονδαί αἱ.
truce, I make a, σπένδομαι, dat. or πρὸς and acc. 146.
true, ἀληθής, ές.
true (a true philosopher), see really.
trust, I, πιστεύω, dat.
truth, ἀλήθεια ἡ; τὸ ἀληθές, τὰ ἀληθῆ.
try, I, πειρῶμαι (αο); verbal, one must try, πειρατέον, 378.
turn, I, trans. τρέπω; intrans. τρέπομαι.
tyrant, τύραννος ὁ.

U

understand, I, ἐπίσταμαι, with part. 372; γιγνώσκω, συνίημι.
understanding that, on the, see condition that.
undertake, I (to do a thing), ἐπιχειρῶ (εω), (an office) ὑφίσταμαι.
unhappy, κακοδαίμων, ον; τάλας, αινα, αν; δυστυχής, ές; σχέτλιος, α, ον.
unjustly, I act, ἀδικῶ (εω), acc.
unknown to, λανθάνω, with participle.
unless, εἰ μή.
unmanly, it is, ἀνανδρία ἐστί.
unprincipled, πονηρός, ά, όν.
—— creature, πονηρόν.

until, ἕως, μέχρι οὗ, 302-303; πρίν, 304.
unworthy, ἀνάξιος, a, ον, gen.
uproar, θόρυβος ὁ.
use, I make use of, χρῶμαι (αο), dat.
use up a stock of, ἀναλίσκω.
useful, χρήσιμος, η, ον.

V

value at, τιμῶμαι (αο), gen. 119.
vengeance, I exact, τιμωρῶ (εω), dat.; vengeance has been exacted, τετιμώρηται (impers.), dat. 202.
venture, I, see dare.
very (= same), ὁ αὐτός.
very, superl. degree or μάλα, etc.
very much, μάλα, μάλιστα.
vexed at, I am, ἀγανακτῶ (εω), with part. 375; χαλεπῶς or βαρέως φέρω, part. 375.
vice, κακία ἡ, πονηρία ἡ.
victory, νίκη ἡ; I gain a victory, νικῶ (αω) νίκην.
view to, with a, ἐπί, acc. 414.
violate, I, (agreement, etc.), παραβαίνω, λύω.
violence, βία ἡ.
virtue, ἀρετή ἡ.
voice, φωνή ἡ.
vote, I, ψηφίζομαι.
—— against (legal), καταψηφίζομαι, acc. penalty, gen. person, 122.
—— for, ψηφίζομαι, acc.
voyage, πλοῦς ὁ; I make a voyage, πλοῦν ποιοῦμαι (εο).

W

wage, μισθός ὁ.
wait, I, μένω, περιμένω.
—— for, περιμένω, acc.

walk, I, βαδίζω.
wall, τεῖχος τό.
want (to be), I, ἀξιῶ (οω).
want of, I am in, σπανίζω, gen.
war, πόλεμος ὁ.
war, I make, πολεμῶ (εω), πόλεμον ποιοῦμαι (εο) ἐπί; war must be made, πολεμητέος, 378.
wash myself, I, λοῦμαι (ονο).
watch for, I am on the, φυλάττω, acc.; I watch that, σκοπῶ (εω) ὅπως, 267.
water, ὕδωρ, ὕδατος, τό.
way, ὁδός ἡ; (manner) τρόπος ὁ; in this way, τοῦτον τὸν τρόπον, τούτῳ τῷ τρόπῳ; in one way, in another way, τὰ μέν... τὰ δέ.
way, I give, ὑπο·χωρῶ (εω), dat.
weak, ἀσθενής, ές.
wealth, πλοῦτος ὁ, χρήματα τά, οὐσία ἡ.
wealthy, πλούσιος, α, ον.
weep, I, κλαίω, κλάω, δακρύω.
well, adv. εὖ, καλῶς; it is well, καλῶς ἔχει.
what, rel. ὅς, ἥ, ὅ; just what, ὅσπερ; interrog. τίς, τί;
when, interrog. πότε; (indirect) ὁπότε; temp. conj. ὅτε, ὁπότε, ἡνίκα, ἐπεί, ἐπειδή, simply or compounded with ἄν, 301.
whence, rel. ὅθεν; interrog. πόθεν; (indirect) ὁπόθεν.
whenever, ὅταν, etc. 302.
where, rel. οὗ, ὅπου; interrog. ποῦ; (indirect) ὅπου.
where from, see whence.
where to, see whither.
wherever, ὅπου ποτέ.
whether, εἰ, πότερον, 247-249.
which, rel. ὅς, ὅσπερ; interrog. τίς; (indirect) ὅστις.
which way = whither, τίνα ὁδόν.
whither, ποῖ; (indirect) ὅποι.
who, rel. ὅς; interrog. τίς; (indirect) ὅστις.

whoever, ὅστις.
whole, ὅλος, η, ον; πᾶς, πᾶσα, πᾶν, ἅπας.
why, τί; διὰ τί;
wicked, κακός, ή, όν.
wickedness, κακία ἡ, πονηρία ἡ, τὰ κακά.
wife, γυνή, -αικός, ἡ.
willing, I am, ἐθέλω.
willingly, ἑκών, οὖσα, όν.
win, I, νικῶ (αω).
wine, οἶνος ὁ.
wing, (bird) πτέρυξ, υγος, ἡ; (military) κέρας, -ως, τό.
winter, χειμών, ῶνος, ὁ.
—— time or season, ὥρα χειμῶνος.
wisdom, σοφία ἡ.
wise, σοφός, ή, όν.
wisely, σοφῶς.
wish, βούλομαι; (=am willing), ἐθέλω.
with, μετά, gen.; ἔχων, acc.
withdraw, I, ἀνα·χωρῶ (εω).
without, ἄνευ, χωρίς gen.; without the enemy seeing, λαθὼν τοὺς πολεμίους; without food, ἄσιτος, ον; without knowing, λανθάνω, etc.
witness, μάρτυς, υρος, ὁ and ἡ.
woe is me! οἴμοι, 41.
wolf, λύκος ὁ.
woman, γυνή, γυναικός, ἡ.
word, λόγος ὁ; in a word, ὡς συνελόντι εἰπεῖν, 340.
work, ἔργον τό.
work at, I, ἐργάζομαι, πονῶ (εω).
world, no man in the, οὐδεὶς τῶν ἀνθρώπων, 102.
worth, ἄξιος, α, ον, gen. 119.
worthless, πονηρός, ά, όν; worthless possession, πονηρόν.
worthy of, ἄξιος, α, ον, gen. 99.
write, I, γράφω.
wrong, I, ἀδικῶ (εω), acc.
wrong, I am, ἁμαρτάνω.

X

Xenophon, Ξενοφῶν, ῶντος, ὁ.

Y

yawn, κέχηνα, 214.
year, ἔτος τό.
yes, καὶ γάρ, 422; γάρ, 423.
yet, καίτοι, 418; ἀλλά, 408 *foll.*;
but yet, ἀλλ' ὅμως, οὐ μὴν ἀλλά, 412.

yield, I, *or* yield ground, παρα'-χωρῶ (εω), ὑπ'είκω, *dat. and gen.* 127; *verbal,* ὑπεικτέος, 378.
young, νέος, [a], ον.
—— man, νεανίας, ου, ὁ.
your, σός, σή, σόν; ὑμέτερος, α, ον.
yourself, σεαυτόν, ήν, *or more commonly* σαυτόν, ήν.

Z

Zeus, Ζεύς, Διός, ὁ.

THE END

Printed by R. & R. CLARK, *Edinburgh.*

MESSRS. MACMILLAN AND CO.'S GREEK CLASS BOOKS.

MACMILLAN'S GREEK COURSE.

Edited by Rev. W. G. RUTHERFORD, M.A., LL.D., Headmaster of Westminster. Globe 8vo.

FIRST GREEK GRAMMAR—ACCIDENCE. By the Editor. 2s.
FIRST GREEK GRAMMAR—SYNTAX. By the same. 2s.
ACCIDENCE AND SYNTAX. In one volume. 3s. 6d.
EASY EXERCISES IN GREEK ACCIDENCE. By H. G. UNDERHILL, M.A., Assistant Master at St. Paul's Preparatory School. 2s.
A SECOND GREEK EXERCISE BOOK. By Rev. W. A. HEARD, M.A., Headmaster of Fettes College, Edinburgh. 2s. 6d.
EASY EXERCISES IN GREEK SYNTAX. By Rev. G. H. NALL, M.A., Assistant Master at Westminster School.
MANUAL OF GREEK ACCIDENCE. By the Editor. [*In preparation.*
MANUAL OF GREEK SYNTAX. By the Editor. [*In preparation.*
ELEMENTARY GREEK COMPOSITION. By the Editor. [*In preparation.*
MACMILLAN'S GREEK READER.—STORIES AND LEGENDS. A First Greek Reader, with Notes, Vocabulary, and Exerc es. By F. H. COLSON, M.A., Headmaster of Plymouth College. Gl. 8vo.
A TABLE OF IRREGULAR GREEK VERBS, classified according to the arrangement of Curtius's Greek Grammar. By J. M. MARSHALL, M.A., Headmaster of the Grammar School, Durham. 8vo. 1s.
FIRST GREEK READER. By Prof. JOHN E. B. MAYOR, M.A., Fellow of St. John's College, Cambridge. Fcap. 8vo. 4s. 6d.
GREEK FOR BEGINNERS. By Rev. J. B. MAYOR, M.A., late Professor of Classical Literature in King's College, London. Part I., with Vocabulary, 1s. 6d. Parts II. and III., with Vocabulary and Index. Fcap. 8vo. 3s. 6d. Complete in one Vol. 4s. 6d.
FIRST LESSONS IN GREEK. Adapted to GOODWIN'S GREEK GRAMMAR, and designed as an Introduction to the ANABASIS OF XENOPHON. By JOHN WILLIAMS WHITE, Assistant Professor of Greek in Harvard University, U.S.A. Cr. 8vo. 3s. 6d.
ATTIC PRIMER. Arranged for the use of beginners. By J. WRIGHT, M.A. Ex. fcap. 8vo. 2s. 6d.
GREEK AND ENGLISH DIALOGUES FOR USE IN SCHOOLS AND COLLEGES. By JOHN STUART BLACKIE, Emeritus Professor of Greek in the University of Edinburgh. New Edition. Fcap. 8vo. 2s. 6d.
A GREEK PRIMER, COLLOQUIAL AND CONSTRUCTIVE. By the same. Cr. 8vo. 2s. 6d.
GREEK PROSE EXERCISES based upon Thucydides. By C. BRYANS, M.A. [*In preparation.*
FIRST STEPS TO GREEK PROSE COMPOSITION. By BLOMFIELD JACKSON, M.A. 18mo. 1s. 6d. KEY, for Teachers only. 18mo. 3s. 6d.
SECOND STEPS TO GREEK PROSE COMPOSITION, with Examination Papers. By the same. 18mo. 2s. 6d. KEY, for Teachers only. 18mo. 3s. 6d.
EXERCISES IN THE COMPOSITION OF GREEK IAMBIC VERSE. By Rev. H. KYNASTON, D.D., Professor of Classics in the University of Durham. With Vocabulary. Ex. fcap. 8vo. 5s. KEY, for Teachers only. Ex. fcap. 8vo. 4s. 6d.
PARALLEL PASSAGES FOR TRANSLATION INTO GREEK AND ENGLISH. With Indexes. By Rev. E. C. MACKIE, M.A., Classical Master at Heversham Grammar School. Gl. 8vo. 4s. 6d.

WORKS BY W. W. GOODWIN, LL.D., D.C.L.
Professor of Greek in Harvard University.

SYNTAX OF THE MOODS AND TENSES OF THE GREEK VERB. New Ed. revised and enlarged. 8vo. 14s.
A GREEK GRAMMAR. Cr. 8vo. 6s.
A GREEK GRAMMAR FOR SCHOOLS. Cr. 8vo. 3s. 6d.

MACMILLAN AND CO., LONDON

MESSRS. MACMILLAN AND CO.'S LATIN CLASS BOOKS.

SHORT EXERCISES IN LATIN PROSE COMPOSITION AND EXAMINATION PAPERS IN LATIN GRAMMAR. Part I. By Rev. H. BELCHER, LL.D., Rector of the High School, Dunedin, N.Z. 18mo. 1s. 6d. KEY, for Teachers only. 18mo. 3s. 6d.
Part II., On the Syntax of Sentences, with an Appendix, including EXERCISES IN LATIN IDIOMS, etc. 18mo. 2s. KEY, for Teachers only. 18mo. 3s.

LATIN PROSE EXERCISES BASED UPON CÆSAR'S GALLIC WAR. With a Classification of Cæsar's Chief Phrases and Grammatical Notes on Cæsar's Usages. By CLEMENT BRYANS, M.A., Assistant Master at Dulwich College. Ex. fcap. 8vo. 2s. 6d. KEY, for Teachers only. 4s. 6d.

FIRST LESSONS IN LATIN. By K. M. EICKE, B.A., Assistant Master at Oundle School. Gl. 8vo. 2s. 6d.

EXERCISES ON LATIN SYNTAX AND IDIOM. ARRANGED WITH REFERENCE TO ROBY'S SCHOOL LATIN GRAMMAR. By E. B. ENGLAND, Assistant Lecturer at the Owens College, Manchester. Cr. 8vo. 2s. 6d. KEY, for Teachers only. 2s. 6d.

MYTHOLOGY FOR LATIN VERSIFICATION. Fables for rendering into Latin Verse. By F. HODGSON, B.D., late Provost of Eton. New Ed., revised by F. C. HODGSON, M.A. 18mo. 3s.

AN INTRODUCTION TO LATIN ELEGIAC VERSE COMPOSITION. By J. H. LUPTON, Sur-Master of St. Paul's School. Gl. 8vo. 2s. 6d. KEY TO PART II. (XXV.-C.) Gl. 8vo. 3s. 6d.

AN INTRODUCTION TO LATIN LYRIC VERSE COMPOSITION. By the same. Gl. 8vo. 3s. KEY, for Teachers only. Gl. 8vo. 4s. 6d.

FIRST LATIN GRAMMAR. By M. C. MACMILLAN, M.A. Fcap. 8vo. 1s. 6d.

MACMILLAN'S LATIN COURSE.—By A. M. COOK, M.A., Assistant Master at St Paul's School.
FIRST PART. Gl. 8vo. 3s. 6d.
SECOND PART. 2s. 6d. [Third Part in preparation.

MACMILLAN'S SHORTER LATIN COURSE.—By A. M. COOK, M.A. Abridgment of "Macmillan's Latin Course," First Part. Gl. 8vo. 1s. 6d. KEY, for Teachers only. 4s. 6d. [In the Press.

MACMILLAN'S LATIN READER.—A LATIN READER FOR THE LOWER FORMS IN SCHOOLS. By H. J. HARDY, M.A., Assistant Master at Winchester. Gl. 8vo. 2s. 6d.

SYNTHETIC LATIN DELECTUS. With Notes and Vocabulary. By E. RUSH, B.A. Ex. fcap. 8vo. 2s. 6d.

FIRST STEPS TO LATIN PROSE COMPOSITION. By Rev. G. RUST, M.A. 18mo. 1s. 6d. KEY, for Teachers only. By W. M. YATES. 18mo. 3s. 6d.

PASSAGES FROM LATIN AUTHORS FOR TRANSLATION INTO ENGLISH. Selected with a view to the needs of Candidates for the Cambridge Local, and Public Schools' Examinations. By E. S. SHUCKBURGH, M.A. Cr. 8vo. 2s.

LATIN PROSE AFTER THE BEST AUTHORS: Cæsarian Prose. By F. P. SIMPSON, B.A. Ex. fcap. 8vo. 2s. 6d. KEY, for Teachers only. 5s.

A LATIN GRADUAL. By the Rev. E. THRING, M.A., late Headmaster of Uppingham. A First Latin Construing Book. Fcap. 8vo. 2s. 6d.

A MANUAL OF MOOD CONSTRUCTIONS. By the same. Fcap. 8vo. 1s. 6d.

LATIN ACCIDENCE AND EXERCISES ARRANGED FOR BEGINNERS. By W. WELCH and C. G. DUFFIELD. 18mo. 1s 6d.

Works by J. WRIGHT, M.A., late Headmaster of Sutton Coldfield School.

A HELP TO LATIN GRAMMAR; or, the Form and Use of Words in Latin, with Progressive Exercises. Cr. 8vo. 4s. 6d.

THE SEVEN KINGS OF ROME. An Easy Narrative, abridged from the First Book of Livy by the omission of Difficult Passages; being a first Latin Reading Book, with Grammatical Notes and Vocabulary. Fcap. 8vo. 3s. 6d.

MACMILLAN AND CO., LONDON.

www.ingramcontent.com/pod-product-compliance
Lightning Source LLC
Chambersburg PA
CBHW021828230426
43669CB00008B/905